NELSON MANDELA

THE AUTHORISED COMIC BOOK

NELSON MANDELA FOUNDATION

WITH

UMLANDO WEZITHOMBE

JONATHAN BALL PUBLISHERS
JOHANNESBURG & CAPE TOWN

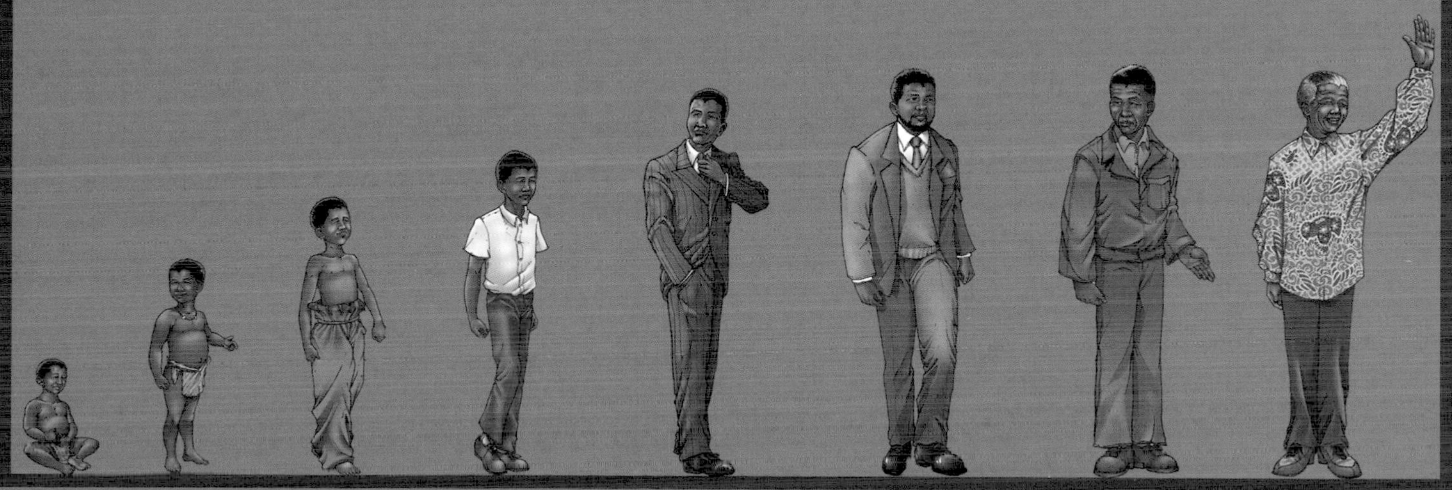

CONTENTS

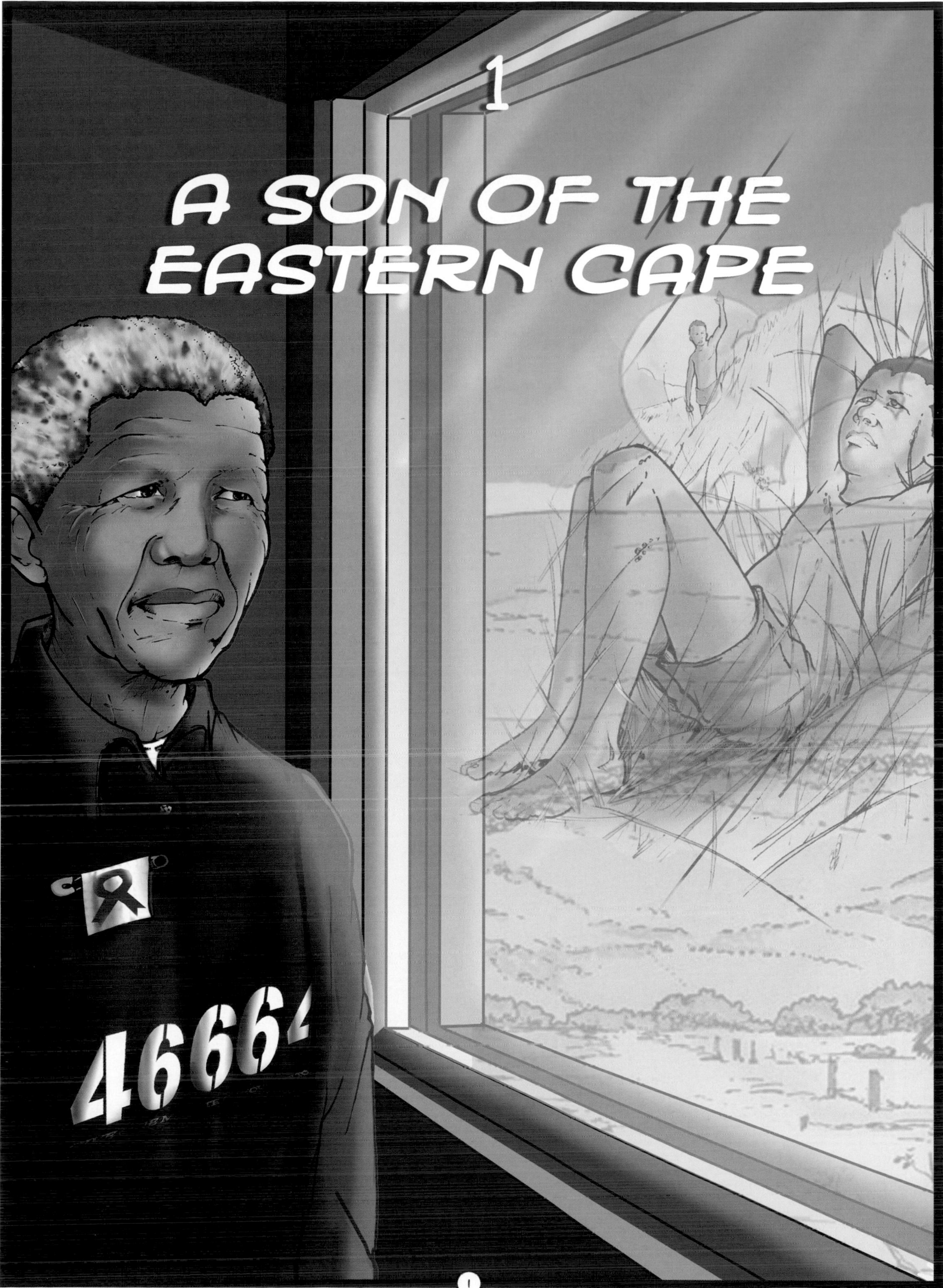
1
A SON OF THE
EASTERN CAPE
46664

ONCE UPON A TIME, LONG AGO, IN A SMALL VILLAGE CALLED MVEZO, OUR STORY BEGINS...
WAAAAAAHHHHH!
YOUR SON.
WE WILL CALL HIM ROLIHLAHLA.
THE NAME ROLIHLAHLA MEANS 'TROUBLE MAKER'.

IN PRESENT-DAY SOUTH AFRICA, A TOUR GUIDE IS LEADING A GROUP OF CHILDREN AROUND MVEZO, NOW A NELSON MANDELA MUSEUM SITE.
BOYS AND GIRLS, THIS IS MVEZO WHERE MADIBA WAS BORN, ON 18 JULY 1918.
WHY IS HE CALLED MADIBA?

MADIBA IS NELSON ROLIHLAHLA MANDELA'S CLAN NAME.
NELSON'S FATHER, MPHAKANYISWA GADLA MANDELA, WAS THE CHIEF OF MVEZO. IT IS PART OF THE THEMBU KINGDOM...
...WHICH FORMED PART OF THE GREATER XHOSA NATION.

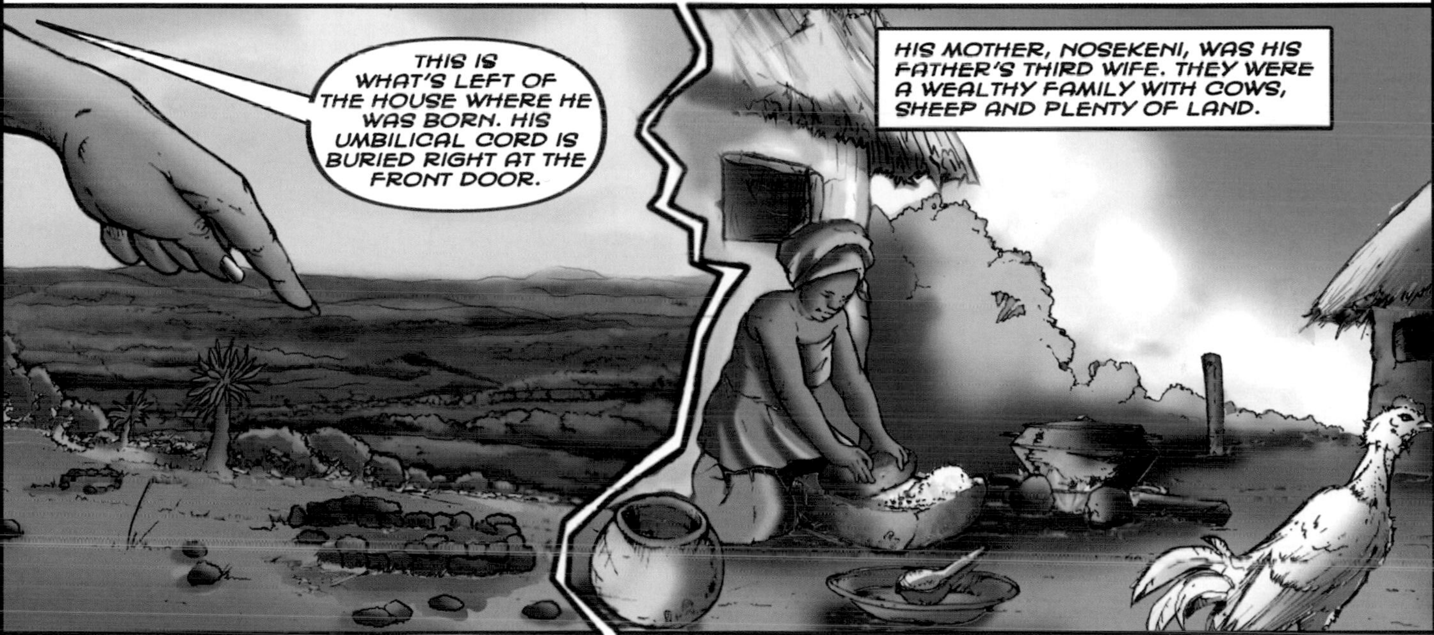
THIS IS WHAT'S LEFT OF THE HOUSE WHERE HE WAS BORN. HIS UMBILICAL CORD IS BURIED RIGHT AT THE FRONT DOOR.
HIS MOTHER, NOSEKENI, WAS HIS FATHER'S THIRD WIFE. THEY WERE A WEALTHY FAMILY WITH COWS, SHEEP AND PLENTY OF LAND.

THE SOUTH AFRICAN GOVERNMENT CONTROLLED TRADITIONAL CHIEFS. THE GOVERNMENT APPOINTED, DISMISSED AND ADMINISTERED CHIEFS THROUGH LOCAL MAGISTRATES.

...AND THE YOUNG ROLIHLAHLA'S FATHER WAS IN BIG TROUBLE...
BRING ME MPHAKANYISWA NOW!!
YES SIR !
CHIEF MPHAKANYISWA HAD NOT REPORTED A TRIBAL MATTER TO THE MAGISTRATE AS WAS REQUIRED.

YOU MAY LOSE EVERYTHING. HAVE YOU THOUGHT ABOUT IT?
OUR CUSTOMS ARE BEING IGNORED. IT IS MY RIGHT AS CHIEF TO MAKE THE MAN PAY A FINE IN CATTLE. THE MAGISTRATE SHOULD NOT INTERFERE.
THE MAGISTRATE WANTS TO SEE YOU RIGHT AWAY. HE SENT ME TO GET YOU.
...YOU TELL THE MAGISTRATE THAT THIS MATTER IS MY BUSINESS, NOT HIS!
SLAM!
TAKE ALL HIS ANIMALS AND LAND, GET THEM OUT OF THERE!
MVEZO IS NO LONGER HOME.
SO THE MANDELA FAMILY PACKED THEIR BELONGINGS AND WALKED MANY MILES TO A NEW HOME IN QUNU.

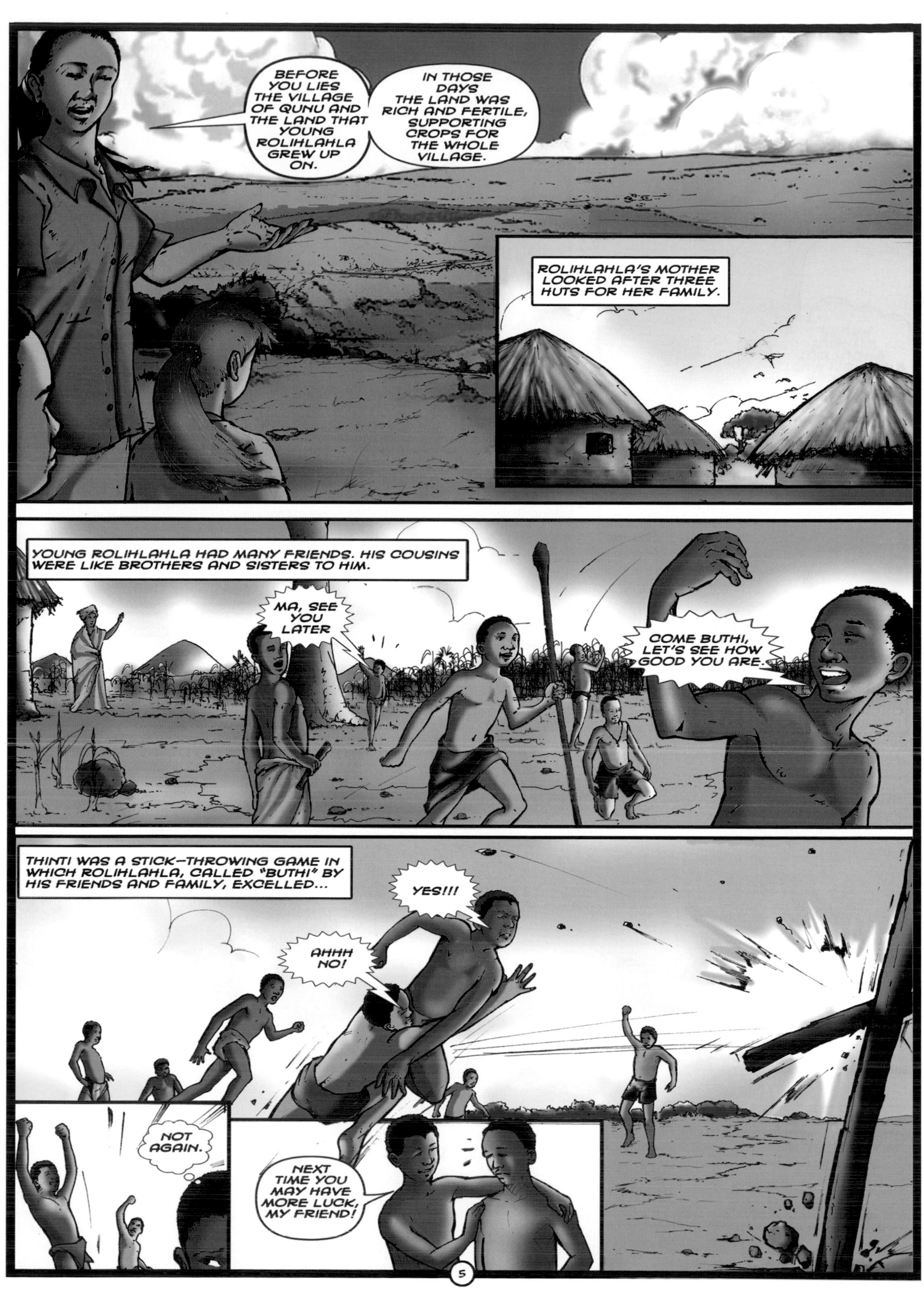
BEFORE YOU LIES THE VILLAGE OF QUNU AND THE LAND THAT YOUNG ROLIHLAHLA GREW UP ON.
IN THOSE DAYS THE LAND WAS RICH AND FERTILE, SUPPORTING CROPS FOR THE WHOLE VILLAGE.
ROLIHLAHLA'S MOTHER LOOKED AFTER THREE HUTS FOR HER FAMILY.
YOUNG ROLIHLAHLA HAD MANY FRIENDS. HIS COUSINS WERE LIKE BROTHERS AND SISTERS TO HIM.
MA, SEE YOU LATER
COME BUTHI, LET'S SEE HOW GOOD YOU ARE.
THINTI WAS A STICK-THROWING GAME IN WHICH ROLIHLAHLA, CALLED "BUTHI" BY HIS FRIENDS AND FAMILY, EXCELLED...
YES!!!
AHHH NO!
NOT AGAIN.
NEXT TIME YOU MAY HAVE MORE LUCK, MY FRIEND!

THINTI WASN'T THE ONLY GAME BEING PLAYED IN QUNU. IN BETWEEN WORKING IN THE LANDS AND HERDING CATTLE, THERE WERE MANY OTHER ACTIVITIES.
COME ON BUTHI, ALL THE WAY!!!
SLIDING DOWN ROCKS WAS A BIG FAVOURITE!
WHOOOO!!
...AND HUNTING.
YES YOU GOT IT!
WOOF WOOF!
...ALSO FISHING.
THE MOTHER OF YOUR FOREFATHER WHO WAS NAMED MANDELA, LED THE THEMBU IN THE FIGHT AGAINST THE INVADING WHITES.
AT NIGHT, THE CHILDREN WOULD HUDDLE AROUND THE COOKING FIRE AND LISTEN TO STORIES.
SSSHHH

I WISH TO RAISE THE MATTER OF ROLIHLAHLA'S SCHOOLING.

VERY FEW RURAL CHILDREN ATTENDED SCHOOL.
YOUR SON IS A CLEVER YOUNGSTER, HE SHOULD GO TO SCHOOL.

YOU ARE GOING TO PROPER SCHOOL NOW...YOU HAVE TO LOOK SMART.
MY FIRST REAL PANTS.
...AND TODAY WE WELCOME ROLIHLAHLA MANDELA TO OUR CLASS.

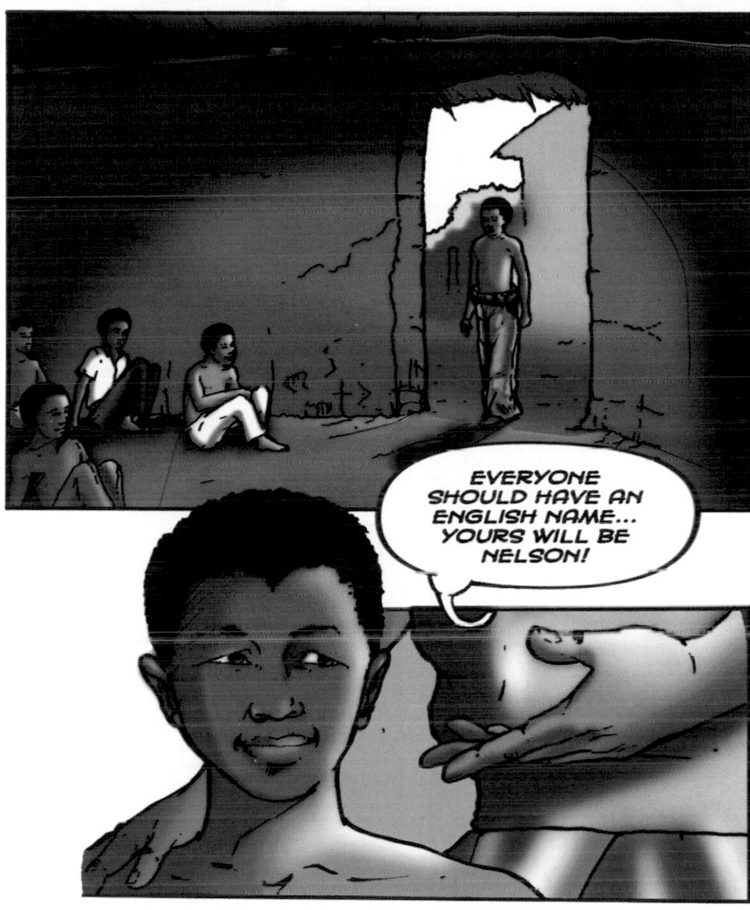
EVERYONE SHOULD HAVE AN ENGLISH NAME... YOURS WILL BE NELSON!

IN THE END, JESUS GAVE UP HIS LIFE FOR HIS PEOPLE...

...AND BEING A GOOD CHRISTIAN IS VERY IMPORTANT.

AT HIS FATHER'S HUT...
COUGH, COUGH!
ROLIHLAHLA, YOUR FATHER ISN'T WELL...
THE REGENT, JONGINTABA, CAME TO VISIT.
IT'S THE REGENT!
THE DEAD KING'S SON, SABATA, WAS TOO YOUNG TO TAKE OFFICE. THE REGENT ACTED AS KING UNTIL SABATA WAS OLD ENOUGH.
THE TIME IS NEAR.
DO NOT WORRY ABOUT ROLIHLAHLA, I WILL LOOK AFTER HIM AS ONE OF MY OWN.
I THANK YOU!
GOODBYE MY FRIEND.
GO WELL, CHIEF.
ROLIHLAHLA'S FATHER TOOK HIS PIPE FOR THE LAST TIME.
HE WAS LAID TO REST, WHILE ROLIHLAHLA AND HIS THREE SISTERS MOURNED FOR HIM.
PACK YOUR THINGS. IT'S TIME TO GO.
MOTHER AND SON SET OFF...

THAT EVENING THEY ARRIVED AT MQHEKEZWENI, ALSO KNOWN AS THE GREAT PLACE. IT WAS THE HOME OF JONGINTABA.
HERE WE ARE, MY SON...
WOW!
THE REGENT WAS ADDRESSING THE VILLAGE ELDERS.
I AM GRATEFUL TO YOU FOR TAKING IN ROLIHLAHLA. HE NOW HAS A BRIGHTER FUTURE.
I AM REPAYING HIS FATHER, WHO GAVE ME MUCH WISE COUNSEL.
YOU WILL HAVE TO BE STRONG, MY SON.
IN LATER YEARS NELSON MANDELA RECALLED THAT THE SHOWING OF EMOTION WAS DISCOURAGED IN THE FAMILIES OF ROYALTY.

YOUNG ROLIHLAHLA TOOK NO TIME TO SETTLE IN.
MEET MY SON... JUSTICE.
MOLO ROLIHLAHLA.
THE BOYS WORKED ON THE LANDS...
HERDED CATTLE...
AND SOMETIMES THE REGENT WOULD LET THEM RIDE THE HORSES.
COME ON ROLIHLAHLA, YOU'RE TOO SLOW!!
DOOF DOOF
DOOF DOOF
THERE WERE MANY GATHERINGS AT THE GREAT PLACE, AND PLENTY OF DANCING.
... CHURCH WAS A BIG PART OF THEIR LIVES. IT ALSO GAVE THEM A MODERN EDUCATION.
WE ARE ALL GOD'S CHILDREN AND MUST LOVE ONE ANOTHER.
AMEN... PRAISE THE LORD.
ROLIHLAHLA SOON BECAME A MEMBER OF THE METHODIST CHURCH...
MANY YEARS LATER, HE STILL HAD HIS CHURCH MEMBERSHIP CARDS FROM THE 1930'S.

WHEN BIG DECISIONS HAD TO BE MADE, THE CLANS GATHERED AT THE GREAT PLACE.
MY PEOPLE ARE WORRIED...

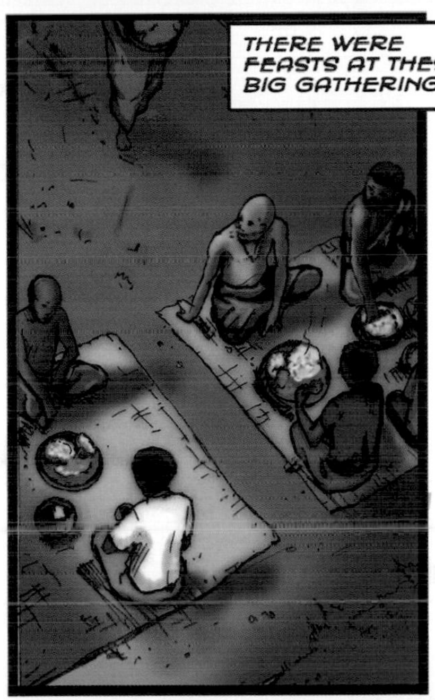
THERE WERE FEASTS AT THESE BIG GATHERINGS.

ALL THAT LISTENING HAS MADE YOU HUNGRY, ROLIHLAHLA!
GRR GR

AT THE GATHERINGS, EVERY VOICE WAS HEARD, AND NO OPINION DISCOUNTED. WOMEN, HOWEVER, COULD ONLY BE OBSERVERS.

IT WAS THE REGENT'S DUTY TO SUM UP ALL THE POINTS OF VIEW AND TO FIND ANSWERS TO PROBLEMS.
LET US RETURN TOMORROW. WE MUST FIND A LASTING SOLUTION.

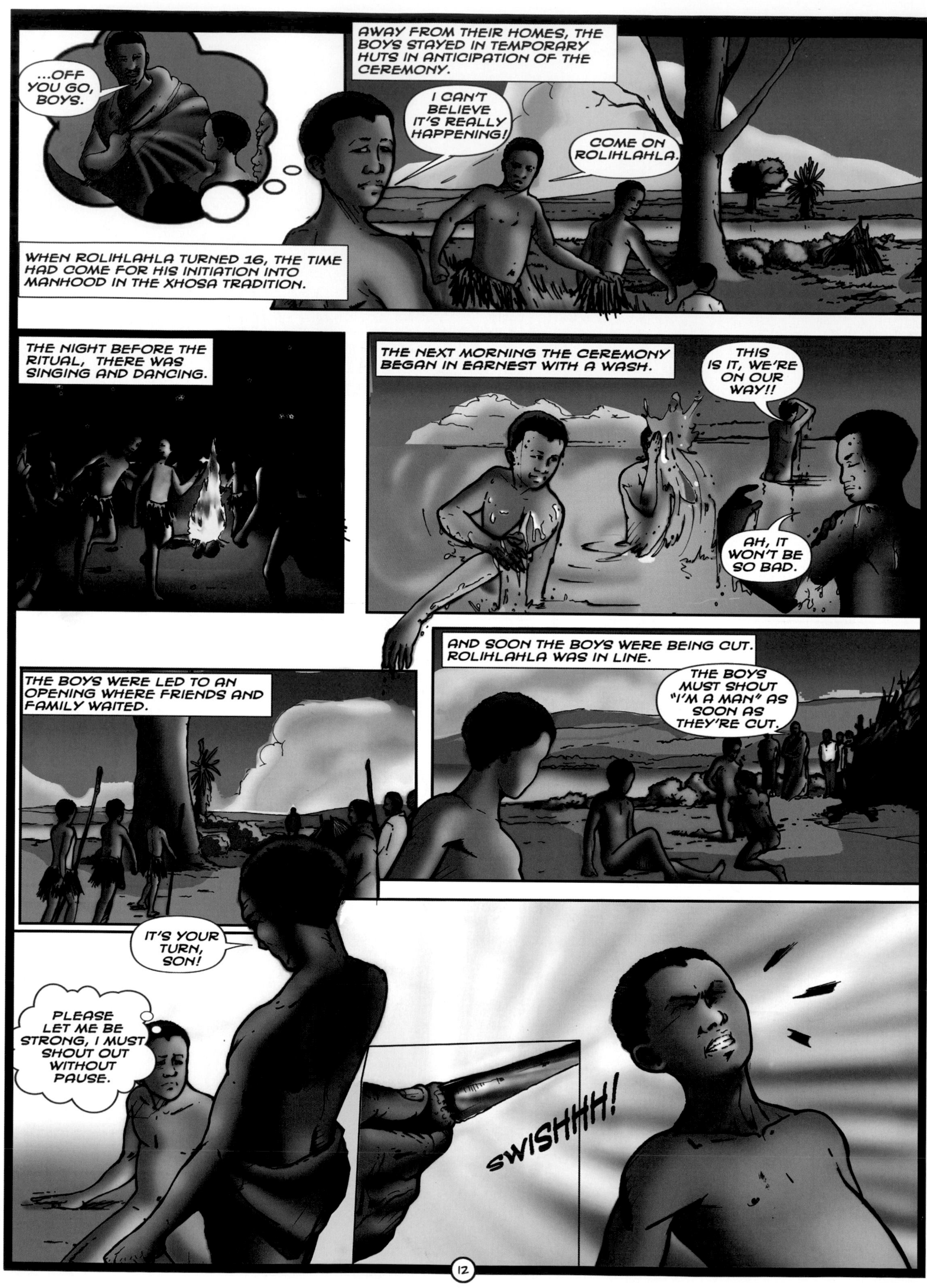
...OFF YOU GO, BOYS.
AWAY FROM THEIR HOMES, THE BOYS STAYED IN TEMPORARY HUTS IN ANTICIPATION OF THE CEREMONY.
I CAN'T BELIEVE IT'S REALLY HAPPENING!
COME ON ROLIHLAHLA.
WHEN ROLIHLAHLA TURNED 16, THE TIME HAD COME FOR HIS INITIATION INTO MANHOOD IN THE XHOSA TRADITION.
THE NIGHT BEFORE THE RITUAL, THERE WAS SINGING AND DANCING.
THE NEXT MORNING THE CEREMONY BEGAN IN EARNEST WITH A WASH.
THIS IS IT, WE'RE ON OUR WAY!!
AH, IT WON'T BE SO BAD.
THE BOYS WERE LED TO AN OPENING WHERE FRIENDS AND FAMILY WAITED.
AND SOON THE BOYS WERE BEING CUT. ROLIHLAHLA WAS IN LINE.
THE BOYS MUST SHOUT "I'M A MAN" AS SOON AS THEY'RE CUT.
IT'S YOUR TURN, SON!
PLEASE LET ME BE STRONG, I MUST SHOUT OUT WITHOUT PAUSE.
SWISHHH!

I AM A MAN!
ALL PARTICIPANTS WERE GIVEN A CEREMONIAL NAME. ROLIHLAHLA'S WAS DALIBHUNGA...
AH – DALIBHUNGA, YOU ARE A MAN NOW.
AFTER THE CEREMONY, THE YOUNG MEN RESTED IN THE SMOKE-FILLED HUTS.
AFTER THEY HAD HEALED, THEY WENT FOR A WASH IN THE RIVER...
...THEN THEY BURNT THEIR HUTS AND WALKED AWAY FROM THEIR CHILDHOOD FOR EVER.

IN THE MEANTIME ROLIHLAHLA HAD BEEN DOING WELL AT SCHOOL...
HE PASSED GRADE EIGHT.
I KNEW YOU WOULD MANAGE HERE. I'M PROUD OF YOU.
YOU KNOW, NOBODY SHOULD SETTLE FOR DIGGING OUT THE WHITE MAN'S GOLD. I WANT A REAL EDUCATION FOR YOU, AND CLARKEBURY IS THE PLACE TO GO.
REALLY!
A GREAT FEAST WAS HELD IN HIS HONOUR – A CELEBRATION OF HIS ACHIEVEMENTS AND HIS FUTURE.
GO WELL ROLIHLAHLA, A GREAT FUTURE AWAITS YOU ...DO US PROUD.
BEFORE WE GO TOMORROW, I HAVE A SURPRISE FOR YOU.
SHOES! I'VE NEVER HAD A PAIR.
I'M NEVER GOING TO LET THESE GET DIRTY!

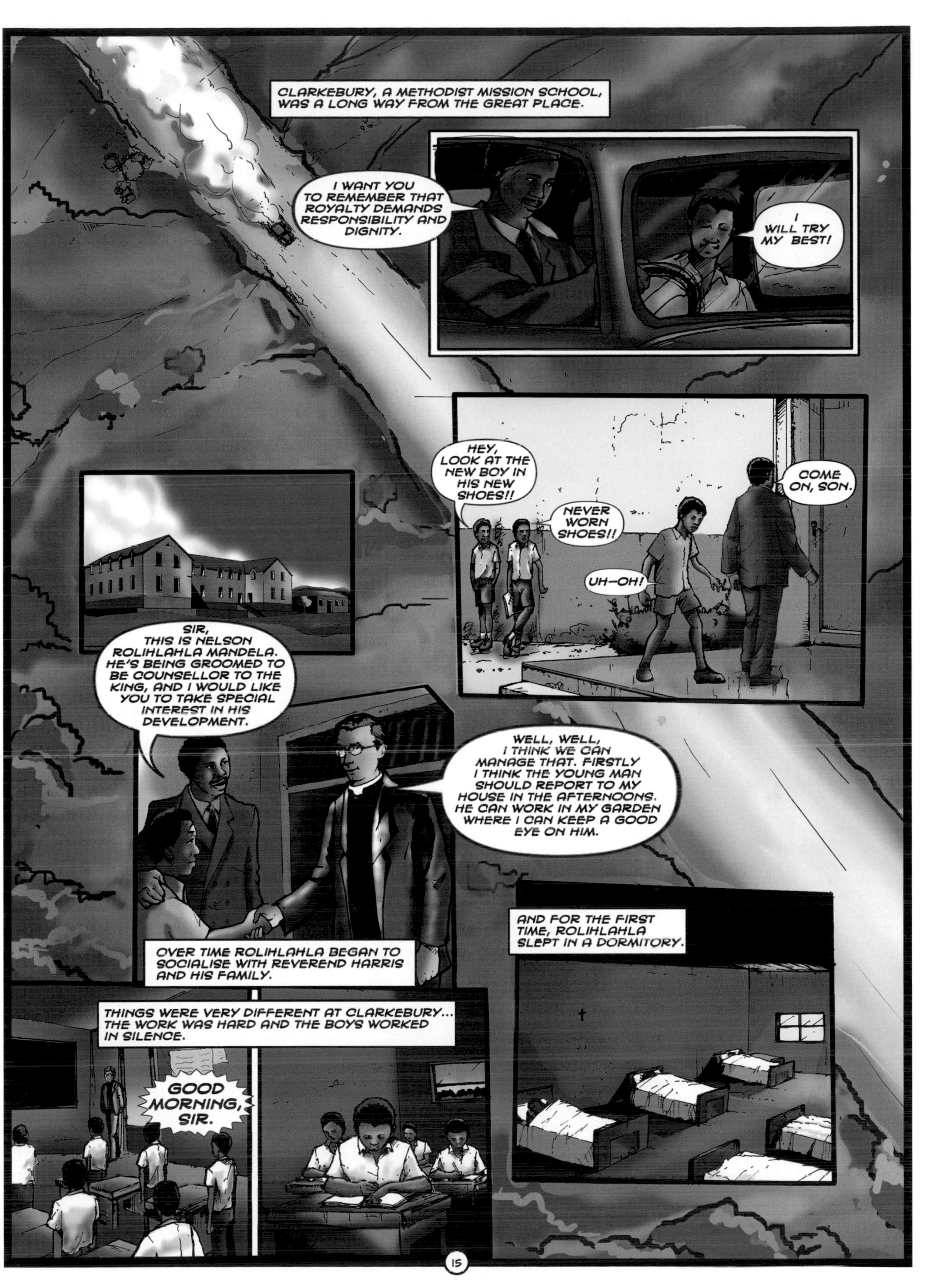
CLARKEBURY, A METHODIST MISSION SCHOOL, WAS A LONG WAY FROM THE GREAT PLACE.
I WANT YOU TO REMEMBER THAT ROYALTY DEMANDS RESPONSIBILITY AND DIGNITY.
I WILL TRY MY BEST!
HEY, LOOK AT THE NEW BOY IN HIS NEW SHOES!!
NEVER WORN SHOES!!
UH-OH!
COME ON, SON.
SIR, THIS IS NELSON ROLIHLAHLA MANDELA. HE'S BEING GROOMED TO BE COUNSELLOR TO THE KING, AND I WOULD LIKE YOU TO TAKE SPECIAL INTEREST IN HIS DEVELOPMENT.
WELL, WELL, I THINK WE CAN MANAGE THAT. FIRSTLY I THINK THE YOUNG MAN SHOULD REPORT TO MY HOUSE IN THE AFTERNOONS. HE CAN WORK IN MY GARDEN WHERE I CAN KEEP A GOOD EYE ON HIM.
OVER TIME ROLIHLAHLA BEGAN TO SOCIALISE WITH REVEREND HARRIS AND HIS FAMILY.
THINGS WERE VERY DIFFERENT AT CLARKEBURY... THE WORK WAS HARD AND THE BOYS WORKED IN SILENCE.
GOOD MORNING, SIR.
AND FOR THE FIRST TIME, ROLIHLAHLA SLEPT IN A DORMITORY.

IN 1937 ROLIHLAHLA LEFT CLARKEBURY FOR HEALDTOWN. IT WAS THE BIGGEST SCHOOL FOR AFRICANS IN THE COUNTRY.
ALL OF YOU CAN BE FUTURE LEADERS...
THESE ARE THE PREFECTS WHO WILL BE YOUR LEADERS THIS YEAR.
ROLIHLAHLA SOON MADE AN IMPRESSION, REALISING HIS SKILLS AND ABILITIES WERE AS IMPORTANT AS HIS HERITAGE...
PREFECT MANDELA ON DUTY ONE RAINY NIGHT...
STOP THAT!
THIS IS NOT A TOILET...
YOUR NAMES ARE GOING DOWN FOR DETENTION...
I TOLD YOU...
LATER THAT NIGHT...ANOTHER CULPRIT. THIS TIME A FELLOW PREFECT...
YOU ARE NOT GOING TO REPORT ME, ARE YOU?
AS A PREFECT YOU SHOULD KNOW BETTER...
WHO WILL GUARD THE GUARDIANS?
NO, NOBODY IS GETTING REPORTED...
IF I CANNOT REPORT YOU, I WON'T REPORT ANYBODY.

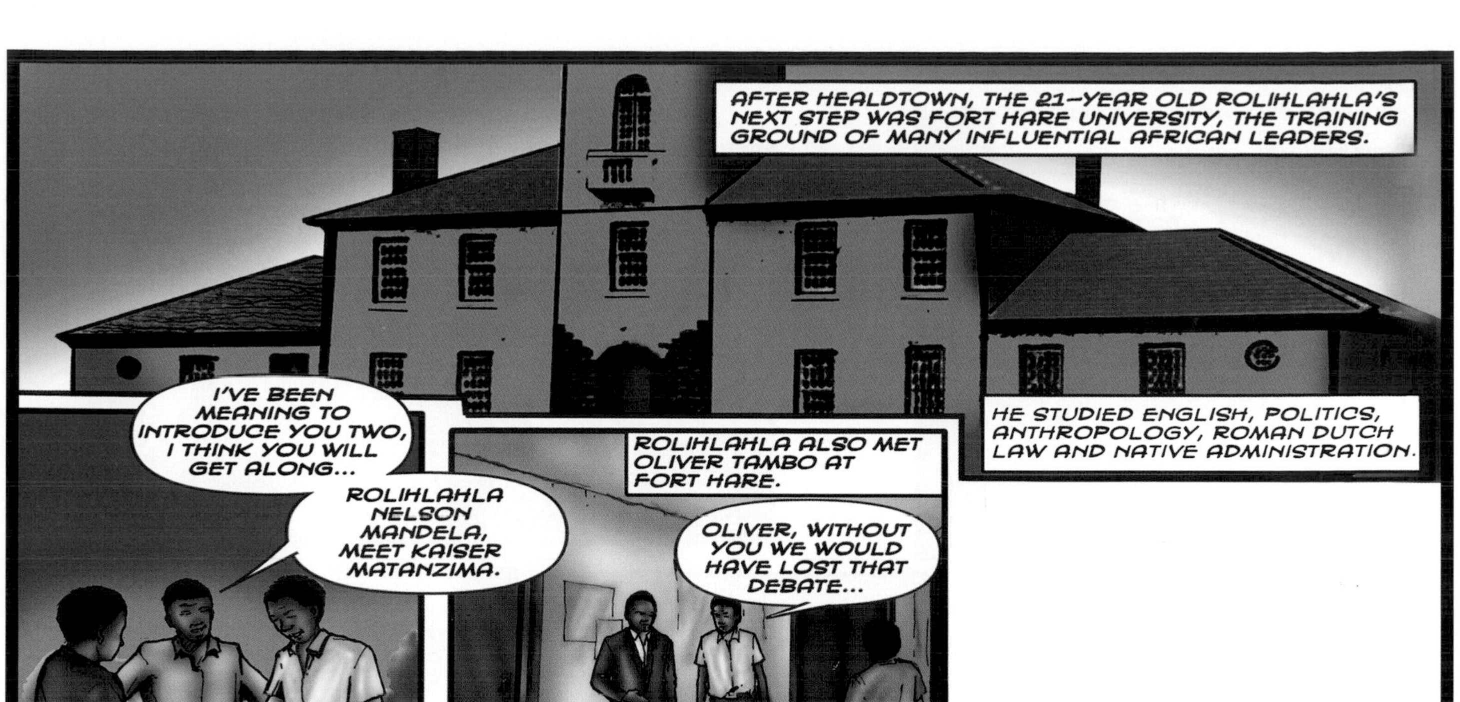
AFTER HEALDTOWN, THE 21-YEAR OLD ROLIHLAHLA'S NEXT STEP WAS FORT HARE UNIVERSITY, THE TRAINING GROUND OF MANY INFLUENTIAL AFRICAN LEADERS.
HE STUDIED ENGLISH, POLITICS, ANTHROPOLOGY, ROMAN DUTCH LAW AND NATIVE ADMINISTRATION.
I'VE BEEN MEANING TO INTRODUCE YOU TWO, I THINK YOU WILL GET ALONG...
ROLIHLAHLA NELSON MANDELA, MEET KAISER MATANZIMA.
KAISER MATANZIMA WAS A NEPHEW OF MANDELA'S AND MUCH LATER HE BECAME A POLITICAL OPPONENT. ROLIHLAHLA ADDRESSED HIM BY HIS CIRCUMCISION NAME, DALIWONGA.
ROLIHLAHLA ALSO MET OLIVER TAMBO AT FORT HARE.
OLIVER, WITHOUT YOU WE WOULD HAVE LOST THAT DEBATE...
HE LOVED BALLROOM DANCING, AND SOMETIMES ROLIHLAHLA AND HIS FRIENDS SNEAKED OUT TO PARTIES...
MAY I HAVE THIS DANCE?

YOU DANCE BEAUTIFULLY...
ON ONE OCCASION HE DISCOVERED THAT HE WAS DANCING WITH A UNIVERSITY PROFESSOR'S WIFE.

HE ENJOYED SOCIALISING WITH FRIENDS. DOING SIMPLE THINGS REMINDED HIM OF HOME...

HE PLAYED SOCCER, RAN CROSS COUNTRY, JOINED THE DRAMA SOCIETY AND GOT INVOLVED IN STUDENT POLITICS.

IN 1940, ROLIHLAHLA FACED A PERSONAL CRISIS.
THE ONLY WAY TO BRING ABOUT MEANINGFUL CHANGE IS TO BOYCOTT THE STUDENT COUNCIL ELECTIONS!
YES, WE WILL PLAY NO PART...

THE PRINCIPAL, DR ALEXANDER KERR, HAD OTHER IDEAS...
I WANT YOUR VOTES BY THE END OF THE DAY.

...AND THE MEMBERS OF THE COUNCIL ARE...
SIX OF THE STUDENTS WERE ELECTED TO THE COUNCIL.

KNOCK KNOCK
ROLIHLAHLA WAS SUMMONED TO DR KERR'S OFFICE...

MANDELA! IF YOU DON'T TAKE UP YOUR SEAT, YOU WILL HAVE TO LEAVE THE UNIVERSITY...
SORRY SIR, I WON'T BE TAKING UP THE SEAT. I AM STANDING WITH THE BOYCOTT OF THE ELECTION...
THINK ABOUT IT, AND LET ME KNOW TOMORROW.

DALIWONGA, I FEEL I AM RIGHT, ALTHOUGH ALL OF THE OTHERS ARE TAKING UP THEIR POSITIONS.
YES, BUT YOU CAN'T GIVE IN, AND THAT COULD BE THE END OF YOUR HOPES TO BE A LAWYER!

A UNIVERSITY EDUCATION WAS A RARE PRIVILEGE GRANTED TO FEW BLACK SOUTH AFRICANS.
BUT I JUST CAN'T DO IT!

YOU ARE MAKING A MISTAKE!
BUT GO AND SPEND THE SUMMER THINKING ABOUT THIS. IF YOU DON'T CHANGE YOUR MIND, DON'T BOTHER COMING BACK...

ROLIHLAHLA CONVEYED THE NEWS TO THE REGENT.
...SO HE SAID IF I DON'T TAKE UP MY SEAT IN THE COUNCIL I MUST LEAVE...
WHAT! I CAN'T BELIEVE WHAT I'M HEARING. YOU WILL GO BACK TO UNIVERSITY!
WHILE ROLIHLAHLA CONSIDERED HIS OPTIONS DURING THE HOLIDAYS, HE WAS RE-UNITED WITH JUSTICE.
HEY JUSTICE! WAIT!
SO HOW WAS CAPE TOWN?
BIG CITY, YOU HAVE TO SEE IT...!
SOON THEY WERE BACK TO THEIR OLD WAYS AGAIN...
...TRYING TO IMPRESS THE GIRLS...
...ATTENDING CHURCH ON SUNDAYS.
AFTER CHURCH ONE SUNDAY, THE REGENT HAD SOME INTERESTING NEWS FOR THE YOUNG MEN...

THINGS WERE ABOUT TO CHANGE...

THE REGENT HAD ARRANGED FOR THE TWO OF THEM TO GET MARRIED...
JUSTICE! ROLIHLAHLA! COME HERE, IT'S TIME WE TALK LIKE MEN!

WHAT!
NOO

THIS WAS A MOMENT FOR ROLIHLAHLA WHEN TRADITION CLASHED WITH PERSONAL DESTINY.
THIS IS HOW IT WILL BE... AND THAT'S FINAL.

THERE IS ONLY ONE THING TO DO... WE HAVE TO RUN AWAY.
TO JOHANNESBURG...

...WE'VE GOT NO TIME TO WASTE.

WHAT ABOUT MONEY?

DON'T WORRY, I HAVE AN IDEA!

I CAN'T BELIEVE WE ARE STEALING THE REGENT'S CATTLE...

WE'VE GOT NO CHOICE.

THEY SOLD THE CATTLE TO A LOCAL TRADER.

HE BELIEVED THAT WE WERE SENT BY THE REGENT TO SELL THEM!!!

I WON'T BE GOING BACK TO FORT HARE.

STATION

I AM SURE THE REGENT KNOWS WHAT IS GOING ON...

I THINK WE'RE OK!

BUT JUSTICE WAS RIGHT: THEY WERE NOT ALLOWED TO BUY TICKETS.

SORRY, THE REGENT SAYS YOU MAY BE RUNNING AWAY.

HUH, WHAT?

HE KNOWS WHAT WE ARE DOING!

WE HAVE TO GET TO THE NEXT STATION!!!

HERE IS SOME MONEY, PLEASE GET US TO THE NEXT STATION...

THERE'S THE TRAIN... FASTER!!!

TWO TICKETS TO QUEENSTOWN, PLEASE.

WE NEED TO GET TRAVEL DOCUMENTS. WITHOUT THEM WE COULD BE ARRESTED FOR LEAVING OUR DISTRICT!
WHAT ARE WE GOING TO DO?
EENSTOWN STATION
BLACK SOUTH AFRICANS NEEDED OFFICIAL PERMISSION TO TRAVEL ACROSS MAGISTERIAL DISTRICTS.

BUT LUCK WAS ON THEIR SIDE. FORTUNATELY THEY RAN INTO CHIEF MPONDOMBINI, THE REGENT'S BROTHER.
LET'S ASK HIM...

THINGS WENT SMOOTHLY UNTIL....
WE ARE ON AN ERRAND FOR THE REGENT, BUT WE NEED DOCUMENTATION.
NO PROBLEM, ANYTHING FOR MY BROTHER!! I WORK FOR THE MAGISTRATE, WE CAN GET IT ARRANGED.
THERE YOU ARE... HANG ON, LET ME JUST PHONE THE MTHATHA MAGISTRATE AND LET HIM KNOW.

LITTLE DID THEY KNOW THAT THE REGENT HAPPENED TO BE IN THE MAGISTRATE'S OFFICE IN MTHATHA.

WHAT? SEND THEM BACK!

YOU HEARD ME... ARREST THE BOYS!

I HAVE STUDIED THE LAW, AND I KNOW YOU HAVE NO RIGHT TO STOP US.

JUST GET OUT !

NOW WHAT?
I HAVE AN OLD FRIEND WORKING HERE, LET'S GO AND SEE HIM...
HE KNEW OF SOMEONE DRIVING TO JOHANNESBURG THE NEXT DAY...
...AND I THINK SHE WILL GIVE YOU A LIFT IF YOU PAY HER...
15 POUNDS! WE ARE PRETTY BROKE NOW, JUSTICE...
BUT AT LEAST WE WILL BE BROKE IN JOHANNESBURG.
I AM WATCHING YOU TWO.
YES, MADAM!
10 MILES
I CAN SEE WE ARE GETTING CLOSER...

FINALLY THEY ARRIVED IN THE BIG CITY... JOHANNESBURG.
THIS IS MUCH BIGGER THAN CAPE TOWN.
YES, THIS IS BIG...
YOU CAN SLEEP IN THE SERVANTS' QUARTERS TONIGHT.
THANK YOU VERY MUCH, MADAM.
I CAN'T SLEEP...
ME NEITHER...
WHAT CHALLENGES LIE AHEAD IN THE CITY OF GOLD? SEE THE NEXT CHAPTER TO FIND OUT.

2

BECOMING A LEADER

THESE ARE THE UNION BUILDINGS IN PRETORIA, WHERE A MARCH OF 20 000 WOMEN PROTESTING AGAINST THE PASS LAWS DELIVERED A PETITION TO PRIME MINISTER STRIJDOM.

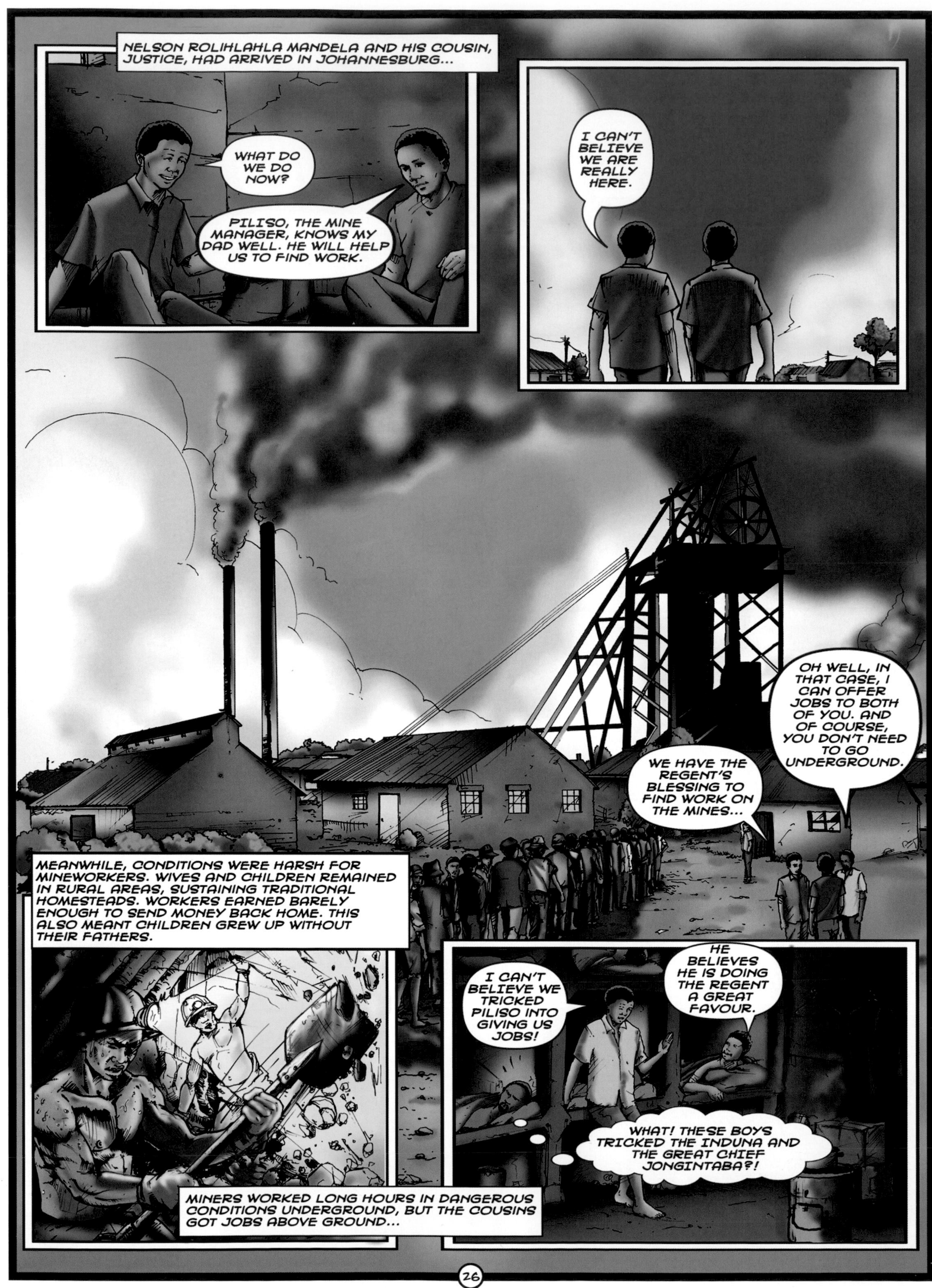
NELSON ROLIHLAHLA MANDELA AND HIS COUSIN, JUSTICE, HAD ARRIVED IN JOHANNESBURG...
WHAT DO WE DO NOW?
PILISO, THE MINE MANAGER, KNOWS MY DAD WELL. HE WILL HELP US TO FIND WORK.
I CAN'T BELIEVE WE ARE REALLY HERE.
WE HAVE THE REGENT'S BLESSING TO FIND WORK ON THE MINES...
OH WELL, IN THAT CASE, I CAN OFFER JOBS TO BOTH OF YOU. AND OF COURSE, YOU DON'T NEED TO GO UNDERGROUND.
MEANWHILE, CONDITIONS WERE HARSH FOR MINEWORKERS. WIVES AND CHILDREN REMAINED IN RURAL AREAS, SUSTAINING TRADITIONAL HOMESTEADS. WORKERS EARNED BARELY ENOUGH TO SEND MONEY BACK HOME. THIS ALSO MEANT CHILDREN GREW UP WITHOUT THEIR FATHERS.
MINERS WORKED LONG HOURS IN DANGEROUS CONDITIONS UNDERGROUND, BUT THE COUSINS GOT JOBS ABOVE GROUND...
I CAN'T BELIEVE WE TRICKED PILISO INTO GIVING US JOBS!
HE BELIEVES HE IS DOING THE REGENT A GREAT FAVOUR.
WHAT! THESE BOYS TRICKED THE INDUNA AND THE GREAT CHIEF JONGINTABA?!

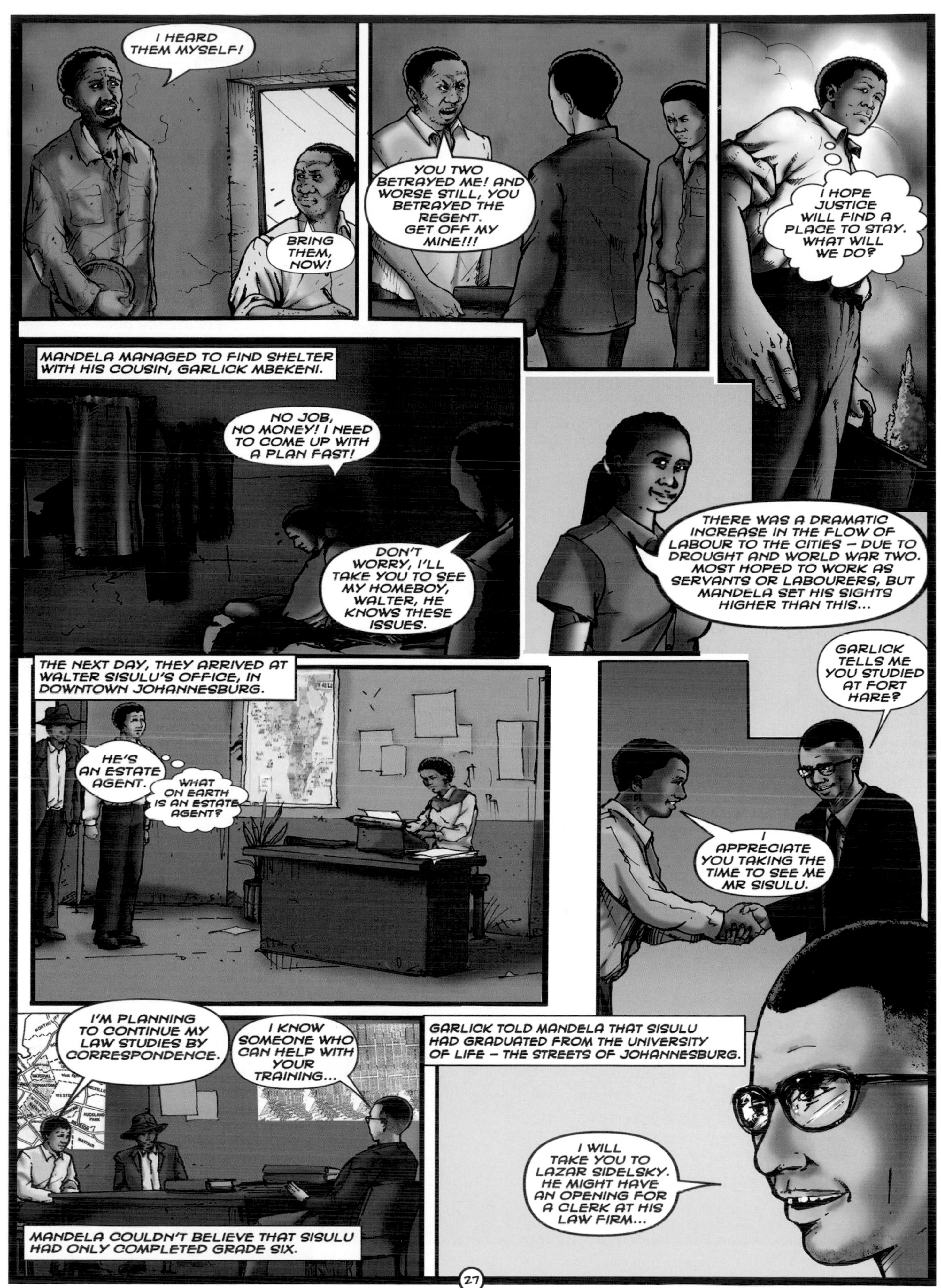
I HEARD THEM MYSELF!
BRING THEM, NOW!
YOU TWO BETRAYED ME! AND WORSE STILL, YOU BETRAYED THE REGENT. GET OFF MY MINE!!!
I HOPE JUSTICE WILL FIND A PLACE TO STAY. WHAT WILL WE DO?
MANDELA MANAGED TO FIND SHELTER WITH HIS COUSIN, GARLICK MBEKENI.
NO JOB, NO MONEY! I NEED TO COME UP WITH A PLAN FAST!
DON'T WORRY, I'LL TAKE YOU TO SEE MY HOMEBOY, WALTER, HE KNOWS THESE ISSUES.
THERE WAS A DRAMATIC INCREASE IN THE FLOW OF LABOUR TO THE CITIES – DUE TO DROUGHT AND WORLD WAR TWO. MOST HOPED TO WORK AS SERVANTS OR LABOURERS, BUT MANDELA SET HIS SIGHTS HIGHER THAN THIS...
THE NEXT DAY, THEY ARRIVED AT WALTER SISULU'S OFFICE, IN DOWNTOWN JOHANNESBURG.
HE'S AN ESTATE AGENT.
WHAT ON EARTH IS AN ESTATE AGENT?
GARLICK TELLS ME YOU STUDIED AT FORT HARE?
I APPRECIATE YOU TAKING THE TIME TO SEE ME MR SISULU.
I'M PLANNING TO CONTINUE MY LAW STUDIES BY CORRESPONDENCE.
I KNOW SOMEONE WHO CAN HELP WITH YOUR TRAINING...
MANDELA COULDN'T BELIEVE THAT SISULU HAD ONLY COMPLETED GRADE SIX.
GARLICK TOLD MANDELA THAT SISULU HAD GRADUATED FROM THE UNIVERSITY OF LIFE – THE STREETS OF JOHANNESBURG.
I WILL TAKE YOU TO LAZAR SIDELSKY. HE MIGHT HAVE AN OPENING FOR A CLERK AT HIS LAW FIRM...

MANDELA WAS GIVEN A JOB AT THE FIRM OF WITKIN, SIDELSKY AND EIDELMAN. HE RENTED A ROOM IN ALEXANDRA TOWNSHIP, CALLED THE DARK CITY BECAUSE IT HAD NO ELECTRICITY.
THIS IS ALL I NEED. TROUBLE WITH THE GANGSTERS AFTER WALKING SIX MILES FROM TOWN...
HOW WILL I KEEP THIS UP...I HAVE BARELY ENOUGH MONEY FOR FOOD, LET ALONE BUS FARE, RENT AND MY STUDIES.
MANDELA STUDIED BY CANDLE-LIGHT AT NIGHT TO COMPLETE HIS DEGREE.
Witkin, Sidel
& Eidelman
DON'T WORRY, THESE WHITE PEOPLE AND THEIR RACIST LAWS WON'T LAST LONG... THEN WE WILL CHASE THEM INTO THE SEA.
NELSON, DON'T LISTEN TO GAUR. POLITICS WILL ONLY MEAN TROUBLE FOR YOU.
DURING THE DAY HE WORKED ALONGSIDE GAUR RADEBE, AN OUTSPOKEN COMMUNIST AND TRADE UNION LEADER.
EVEN THOUGH MANDELA HAD A JOB, HE WAS NOT EXEMPT FROM THE LAWS AND CONDITIONS THAT APPLIED TO ALL AFRICAN PEOPLE...
...PASS LAWS, CURFEWS, HIGH TRANSPORT COSTS, SEPARATE POVERTY-STRICKEN COMMUNITIES, HIGH CRIME, AND NO FACILITIES...
EVEN AT THE OFFICE, THERE WAS SEPARATE TREATMENT FOR AFRICANS...
SEPARATE CUPS FOR AFRICANS... I'LL DRINK MY TEA IN THE KITCHEN, THIS IS HUMILIATING!
COME ON, NELSON, THE COMMUNISTS ARE NON-RACIAL, THEY STAND FOR EQUAL RIGHTS FOR ALL! IT IS TIME YOU BECAME INVOLVED.
MAYBE NEXT TIME, GAUR. THE REGENT IS IN TOWN AND HAS SENT WORD TO SEE ME.

REGENT!
ROLIHLAHLA, I HEAR YOU HAVE FOUND A HOME FOR YOURSELF...
THE REGENT VISITED JOHANNESBURG IN 1941.

AFTER I STOLE THE CATTLE, I WAS WORRIED THAT THE BOND BETWEEN US WAS BROKEN.
NO, ROLIHLAHLA, OUR BOND IS STRONG, AND I WILL SUPPORT YOU WHERE-EVER I CAN. BUT I NEED JUSTICE TO RETURN TO THE GREAT PLACE...I AM NOT WELL.

IN THE WINTER OF 1942 THE REGENT DIED. JUSTICE AND MANDELA READ OF HIS DEATH IN THE NEWSPAPER. THE TELEGRAM SENT TO THEM DID NOT ARRIVE.
WE MUST HURRY, WE MAY HAVE ALREADY MISSED THE FUNERAL.

HE LOOKED UNWELL WHEN HE VISITED. I SHOULD HAVE GONE HOME THEN...
YES, I SHOULD HAVE APPRECIATED THE REGENT MORE WHEN HE WAS ALIVE. HE TOOK CARE OF ME LIKE I WAS HIS SON.
SADLY, MANDELA AND JUSTICE ARRIVED AT THE GREAT PLACE A DAY AFTER THE REGENT'S FUNERAL...

AFTER A WEEK AT THE GREAT PLACE, MANDELA SAID GOODBYE TO HIS MOTHER AND TO JUSTICE, TO RETURN TO HIS LIFE IN THE BIG CITY. JUSTICE WAS TO SUCCEED THE REGENT.
STAY WELL.
BACK IN JOHANNESBURG, RADEBE WAS SURPRISED THAT MANDELA RETURNED.
IT IS GOOD TO BE BACK!
I STILL HAVE MANY RIVERS TO CROSS...

BUS FARES ARE UP AGAIN. YOU MAY WANT TO THINK OF JOINING THE ALEXANDRA BUS STRIKE?
YES. I CAN RELATE TO THAT. I CAN HARDLY GET BY NOW...
Increases
IN AUGUST 1943 MANDELA MARCHED WITH TEN THOUSAND OTHERS PROTESTING THE INCREASE IN BUS FARES, AND BOYCOTTED THE BUSES.
Bring Down The Fares!
We NOT RIDE!
AFTER NINE DAYS, THERE WAS VICTORY FOR THE COMMUTERS. THEIR UNITY HAD SUCCEEDED. IT SENT A POWERFUL MESSAGE TO THE PEOPLE OF SOUTH AFRICA.
NELSON, COME AND STAY AT OUR HOME UNTIL YOU CAN AFFORD YOUR OWN.
YOU ARE GOOD TO ME, WALTER.
MANDELA AND SISULU WERE BECOMING CLOSE FRIENDS AND DISCOVERING COMMON INTERESTS. MANDELA FELT THE IMMEDIATE WARMTH AND WELCOME AT THE SISULU HOME.
IT WAS THERE THAT MANDELA MET SISULU'S COUSIN, EVELYN MASE, A TRAINEE NURSE FROM ENGCOBO IN THE TRANSKEI. IT WAS LOVE AT FIRST SIGHT.

IN 1949, MANDELA GRADUATED WITH HIS BA DEGREE AT FORT HARE. HIS MOTHER, NOSEKENI, HIS NEPHEW, KAISER MATANZIMA, AND THE REGENT'S WIDOW, NO-ENGLAND, WERE THERE TO WISH HIM WELL.
DALIBHUNGA, YOU ARE NEEDED HERE NOW. WHY DON'T YOU STAY?
MANDELA DECLINED. HE RETURNED TO THE CITY TO CONTINUE HIS LAW STUDIES AT WITS UNIVERSITY. THIS WAS A DIFFICULT TIME FOR HIM, WITH MANY NEW FRIENDSHIPS, AND MANY HUMILIATIONS.

MANDELA ARRIVED LATE FOR CLASS ON OCCASION...
MANDELA, IF YOU CAN'T EVEN ARRIVE ON TIME, YOU CAN NEVER BE A LAWYER!
I CAN'T SIT NEXT TO HIM, WHO DOES HE THINK HE IS?

MANDELA WAS THE ONLY AFRICAN IN HIS CLASS. HE COULD NOT USE THE SPORTS FIELDS, SWIMMING POOL, CAFETERIA OR RESIDENCES. THESE WERE FOR WHITES ONLY!

MANDELA HAD A MIX OF EXPERIENCES AT WITS. HE WAS BEFRIENDED BY STUDENTS FROM OTHER RACE GROUPS LIKE RUTH FIRST, GEORGE BIZOS, JN SINGH AND ISMAIL MEER.
LET'S GO GET SOME LUNCH AT MY FLAT.

THEY BOARDED A TRAM RESERVED FOR WHITES AND INDIANS ONLY...

WE ARE NOT ALLOWED TO CARRY A KAFFIR!

WHAT DO YOU MEAN? DO YOU KNOW THE MEANING OF THAT WORD?
I WILL HAVE YOU ARRESTED AT THE NEXT STOP!

THEY WERE CHARGED WITH INTERFERING WITH THE TRANSPORT SERVICE. BRAM FISCHER, A COMMUNIST PARTY MEMBER, REPRESENTED THEM. FISCHER'S FATHER WAS THE JUDGE PRESIDENT IN THE FREE STATE. THE CASE WAS DISMISSED.
WE WERE LUCKY. THANK GOODNESS THE MAGISTRATE WAS SUCH AN ADMIRER OF BRAM'S FATHER.

IT WAS A TIME OF GREAT FRIENDSHIPS.
COME NELSON, THERE'S AN IMPORTANT MEETING. YOU HAVE TO BE THERE!
I WAS HOPING TO SEE EVELYN...
THERE IS PLENTY OF TIME TO SEE HER LATER...
OLIVER TAMBO, FUTURE HEAD OF THE AFRICAN NATIONAL CONGRESS (ANC), WHO HAD MET MANDELA AT FORT HARE.
WE KNOW THE AFRICAN NATIONAL CONGRESS. IT'S BEEN THERE SINCE 1912, BUT...
DR LIONEL MAJOMBOZI, HE CAME UP WITH THE IDEA OF A YOUTH LEAGUE.
THE PROBLEM WITH THE ANC IS THAT IT IS OUT OF TOUCH WITH THE NEEDS OF AFRICANS.
ANTON LEMBEDE, FIREBRAND ACTIVIST WITH A FERVOUR FOR AFRICAN NATIONALISM. HE BECAME THE FIRST LEADER OF THE YOUTH LEAGUE.
TOO MUCH TIME WASTED ON SENDING PETITIONS AND NOT TAKING DIRECT ACTION...
WILLIAM NKOMO, A STUDENT AT WITS, AND FORMER FORT HARE STUDENT.
AP MDA, A FUTURE LAWYER AND LEADER OF THE YOUTH LEAGUE.
WE NEED A NATIONAL MOVEMENT FOR ALL AFRICANS. AFRICANS HAVE TO RELY ON THEMSELVES, AND NOT BE FOOLED BY WHITE SUPPORTERS.
WE SHOULD FORM A YOUTH LEAGUE OF THE ANC, AND CHANGE THINGS FROM WITHIN.
WE HAVE TO DISCUSS THIS WITH DR XUMA...
CHAPS, I AGREE IN PRINCIPLE. BUT, WE DON'T NEED TO EXCLUDE EVERYONE ELSE...THE COMMUNISTS AND INDIANS CAN HELP US! AS LONG AS THE ANC LEADS...

DR XUMA, THE ANC PRESIDENT, OBJECTED TO THE YOUTHS' IDEAS OF MASS ACTION, BUT... IN APRIL 1944 THE YOUTH LEAGUE WAS FORMED WITH ANTON LEMBEDE AS ITS FIRST PRESIDENT...
WE MUST MAKE SURE THAT AFRICANS ARE AT THE FOREFRONT OF OUR STRUGGLE...
...NO FOREIGNER CAN EVER LEAD THE AFRICAN PEOPLE... OUR MANIFESTO SAYS THIS CLEARLY...
...THE NAMES OF OUR EXECUTIVE MEMBERS ARE OLIVER TAMBO, WALTER SISULU, NELSON MANDELA...

WHAT?!?

TAMBO AND SISULU KNEW WHY MANDELA WAS BEING CALLED UP....
IT'S A GOOD THING TO GET NELSON INVOLVED. HE IS A STRONG LEADER...

MANDELA'S ROMANCE WITH EVELYN GREW...
YOUR BROTHER HAS GIVEN ME PERMISSION TO REQUEST YOUR HAND IN MARRIAGE...

IT WAS A SIMPLE CEREMONY, HELD AT THE NATIVE COMMISSIONER'S OFFICE IN 1944. THEY COULDN'T AFFORD A BIG WEDDING.

...AT HOME IN ORLANDO, SOWETO.
...HE SAYS NOT TO WORRY ABOUT THE COMMUNISTS OVER-SHADOWING AFRICANS.
I DON'T UNDERSTAND ALL THIS POLITICS.

IN THE FIRST YEAR OF THEIR MARRIAGE EVELYN GAVE BIRTH TO THEIR SON, MADIBA THEMBEKILE – AFFECTIONATELY KNOWN AS THEMBI.
BUT WE NEED TO THINK OF OUR BABY'S FUTURE. THE GOVERNMENT'S LAWS HAVE STOLEN OUR LAND, CREATED SLUMS FOR US, DENIED US SKILLED WORK, AND ARE STOPPING US FROM VOTING. THEY EVEN RULE OUR KINGS.

THIS IS MADNESS! THE STRIKE WAS NON-VIOLENT, THEY WERE ASKING FOR A LIVING WAGE...AT LEAST NINE PEOPLE WERE KILLED.
RAND Daily Mail
Police open fire...
The communists, Rusty Bernstein, JB Marks, and Moses Kotane were arrested in connection with the strike.
"Their wild speeches and absurd demands could no longer be tolerated," a spokesman said.
Dr. Yusuf Dadoo from the TIC has also been arrested for his role in the strike.
70 000 downed tools.
"How can such people know anything of trade union procedure."
Glimmer of humanity as gunmen free children
NELSON, WE CAN BARELY MAKE ENDS MEET... WHAT WILL WE DO...
I'M TRYING FOR A LOAN. AND ONCE I FINISH MY LAW STUDIES, I WILL BRING IN A REASONABLE INCOME.
IN 1947 MAKAZIWE WAS BORN. SHE WAS A FRAIL AND SICKLY BABY.
I JUST WISH I KNEW WHAT IS WRONG WITH HER...
GET SOME REST, EVELYN, I WILL TAKE CARE OF HER TONIGHT...
DESPITE TIRELESS CARE, MAKAZIWE DIED AT ONLY NINE MONTHS.
I AM SO SORRY MY LOVE...
LATER THAT YEAR THEY SUFFERED ANOTHER LOSS. ANTON LEMBEDE, PRESIDENT OF THE YOUTH LEAGUE, COLLAPSED AND WAS RUSHED TO HOSPITAL BY SISULU AND MANDELA. HE DIED THAT NIGHT...
THIS DOES NOT MAKE ANY SENSE...HE WAS ONLY 33 YEARS OLD!
AP MDA SUCCEEDED LEMBEDE. HE SUPPORTED OPENING BRANCHES AT PLACES LIKE FORT HARE TO BRING IN NEW RECRUITS.

IN 1948, THE AFRIKANER NATIONAL PARTY, LED BY DR DANIEL FRANCOIS MALAN, CAME TO POWER.
FOR THE FIRST TIME SINCE THE UNION... SOUTH AFRICA IS OUR OWN!
Whites Only
WHY DO YOU NEVER SIT ON A BENCH NANA?
NEVER MIND, SISI.
THE GOVERNMENT STARTED TO ENFORCE SEGREGATION WITH VIGOUR – LEGISLATING SOCIAL INTERACTION AND THE USE OF PUBLIC SERVICES, AMONGST OTHERS...
AFRIKANER NATIONALISM WAS A POWERFUL POLITICAL AND SOCIAL FORCE. IT WAS DETERMINED TO DESTROY WHAT IT SAW AS ITS GREATEST ENEMIES – AFRICAN NATIONALISM, COMMUNISM AND WHITE LIBERALISM.
THE HOUR HAS COME...
AT THE SAME TIME BLACK SOUTH AFRICANS WERE PRAYING FOR A BETTER LIFE...
"LIFT US UP FROM THE SINKS OF IMPURITY..."
WHILE SOME FELT THE MALAN GOVERNMENT MADE THINGS EASIER BY BEING A CLEAR ENEMY, MANDELA WARNED THEY WERE UNDERESTIMATING THE AFRIKANERS' RESOLVE TO IMPLEMENT TOTAL SEGREGATION...
THE YOUTH LEAGUE REALISED IT WAS TIME FOR ACTION. A DOCUMENT THAT ADVOCATED NON-VIOLENT, ORGANISED MASS PROTESTS WAS DEVELOPED INTO A DETAILED PROGRAMME OF ACTION. THEY TOOK IT TO DR XUMA FOR APPROVAL.
YOUR IDEAS ARE PREMATURE; THEY WILL CRUSH US!!!
DR XUMA, WE NEED TO TAKE THE ROUTE OF NON-VIOLENT MASS ACTION...
IF YOU DON'T SUPPORT THIS PLAN, WE CANNOT RE-ELECT YOU.
YOU ARE TRYING TO BLACKMAIL ME! LEAVE!
MANDELA COULD NOT ATTEND THE ANC CONFERENCE IN BLOEMFONTEIN IN 1949 BUT HE COULD VOTE. HE, AP MDA, WALTER SISULU AND OLIVER TAMBO WERE THE KING-MAKERS. THEY ELECTED DR MOROKA AS THEIR NEW PRESIDENT. SISULU WAS ELECTED SECRETARY-GENERAL AT THE AGE OF 37.
I WISH I WAS THERE!!! SUCH A PITY I HAD TO WORK.
YES, BUT YOU ARE LUCKY TO HAVE SUCH A GOOD JOB!

LIFE IN SOPHIATOWN IN THE 1950'S WAS CROWDED, ITS PEOPLE MOSTLY POOR. BUT IT IS OFTEN DESCRIBED AS THE BEST OF TIMES...A TIME OF CULTURAL AWAKENING IN THE TOWNSHIPS...IT WAS ALSO A TIME WHEN MANY UNDERESTIMATED THE GOVERNMENT'S RESOLVE TO IMPOSE TOTAL SEGREGATION – APARTHEID.
MANDELA MADE FRIENDS WITH JAZZ LEGENDS LIKE THE MANHATTAN BROTHERS AND TOOK UP BOXING IN A MAKESHIFT GYM IN ORLANDO. BLACK AMERICAN BOXERS, MUSICIANS AND MOVIE STARS BECAME ROLE MODELS OF AFRICAN ACHIEVEMENT AND POWER IN TOWNSHIPS.
HE ENJOYED DINING AT THE FEW RESTAURANTS OPEN TO AFRICANS, AND HE BOUGHT A CAR...
BUT REPRESSION WAS GROWING...
THIS PASS IS NOT IN ORDER!
HURRY UP!
MOST AFRICANS WORKED LONG HOURS FOR A PITTANCE. THEY TRAVELLED LONG DISTANCES BETWEEN HOME AND WORK, AND BY 1952, PASS LAWS – WHICH MEANT CARRYING A DOCUMENT PROVING YOUR RIGHT TO BE IN A CERTAIN AREA – WERE EXTENDED TO WOMEN...
BEWARE, LOCK YOUR DOORS AT NIGHT...THE RED MENACE AND BLACK PERIL ARE HERE!
THE SUPPRESSION OF COMMUNISM ACT, UNDER WHICH ACTIVISTS COULD BE BANNED FROM POLITICAL ACTIVITIES, WAS ANNOUNCED.
STOP MARTIAL LAW
STOP POLICE RAIDS
STOP MARTIAL LAW
STOP MALAN TERROR
IN PROTEST AGAINST THE ACT OVER 10 000 PEOPLE GATHERED AT THE DEFEND FREE SPEECH CONVENTION IN JOHANNESBURG. THEY RESOLVED TO HAVE A ONE-DAY STRIKE ON 1 MAY 1950.

BUT THE CALL FOR THE MAY DAY STRIKE WAS MADE BY THE COMMUNIST AND INDIAN LEADERSHIP. ANC LEADERS FEARED OTHERS WOULD DOMINATE THE STRUGGLE.
THEY HAVE TO RESPECT US! WE ARE THE LEADERS OF THE STRUGGLE!
THEY ARE TRYING TO DOMINATE US!
IT WAS DECIDED BY THE ANC YOUTH LEAGUE TO DISRUPT THE STRIKE...
GO NOW!
MANDELA WAS SENT TO DISRUPT A COMMUNIST PARTY MEETING. JB MARKS, COMMUNIST PARTY AND TRADE UNION LEADER, HAD PLAYED A KEY ROLE IN THE 1946 MINEWORKERS' STRIKE.
WE NEED TO WORK TOGETHER!
I THINK EVERYONE HERE HAS HEARD ENOUGH! NOW IT IS MY TURN!
THERE ARE TWO BULLS IN THIS KRAAL. A BLACK BULL AND A WHITE BULL! HE WANTS THE WHITE ONE TO LEAD...
I SAY THE BLACK ONE SHOULD... WHAT DO YOU SAY?
BLACK BULL!
AHMED KATHRADA, A MEMBER OF THE TRANSVAAL INDIAN YOUTH CONGRESS, AND FRIEND, CONFRONTED NELSON ABOUT HIS BEHAVIOUR.
I AM ONLY AN INDIAN YOUTH, BUT IT IS CLEAR WHAT THE MASSES WANT...
I CHALLENGE YOU TO A PUBLIC DEBATE AND I GUARANTEE THAT I WILL WIN!
HOW DARE YOU THREATEN ME!
ALTHOUGH FRIENDS WITH MANY INDIANS AND COMMUNISTS, MANDELA AND OTHER ANC LEADERS WERE WARY OF JOINT ACTION...

1 MAY 1950. THE GOVERNMENT BANNED ALL GATHERINGS FOR THE DAY. IN ORLANDO A SMALL CROWD HAD GATHERED. PROTESTING PEACEFULLY. MANDELA AND SISULU WERE OBSERVING FROM THE SIDELINES.
DESPITE THE YOUTH LEAGUE'S OPPOSITION, MORE THAN HALF OF JOHANNESBURG'S WORKERS STAYED AT HOME THAT DAY...
NELSON! THE POLICE ARE HERE. THERE'S TROUBLE COMING!
THE POLICE ANNOUNCED THAT THE PROTESTORS HAD THREE MINUTES TO DISPERSE...
...WITHOUT FURTHER WARNING THEY OPENED FIRE.
MANDELA AND SISULU FOUND SHELTER IN A DORMITORY.
TAKE THAT!
...OTHERS WERE NOT SO LUCKY...
NOOO!!
EIGHTEEN PEOPLE WERE KILLED AND MANY OTHERS WOUNDED IN TOWNSHIPS AROUND THE CITY...

MANDELA AND SISULU HELPED TO TAKE THE INJURED TO HOSPITAL...
I CAN'T BELIEVE WE SURVIVED THAT!
THIS IS A FIERCE ENEMY WE ARE FACING.
THE MAY DAY TRAGEDY STIRRED THE ANC INTO ACTION. IT ASKED OTHER PARTIES TO JOIN IN A NATIONAL DAY OF MOURNING – A STAY-AWAY ON 26 JUNE 1950.
YES, WE ARE OPPOSING THE SUPPRESSION OF COMMUNISM ACT! WE ARE MOURNING FOR OUR BROTHERS AND SISTERS...
NELSON, EVELYN NEEDS YOU...
MAKGATHO LEWANIKA WAS BORN. HE WAS NAMED AFTER SEFAKO MAPOGO MAKGATHO, THE SECOND ANC PRESIDENT, WHO DEFIED THE LAWS THAT BARRED AFRICANS FROM WALKING ON PAVEMENTS IN PRETORIA... TO MANDELA HIS NAME WAS A SYMBOL OF COURAGE.
POLITICS WAS CAUSING MORE AND MORE FRICTION IN THE MANDELA HOME...
I WISH WE COULD GO BACK TO THE TRANSKEI... THEN WE WOULD SEE MORE OF YOU!
I'M SORRY EVELYN, BUT POLITICS IS NOT A DISTRACTION. IT IS MY LIFE WORK!
THE PROPOSED STAY-AWAY FAILED IN PARTS OF THE COUNTRY. FOR MANDELA THE STRUGGLE HAD BECOME ALL-CONSUMING. HE WAS ON THE EXECUTIVE OF THE ANC, WORKED AT LAW FIRMS IN THE CITY AND EVENTUALLY QUALIFIED AS AN ATTORNEY. EVELYN, ON THE OTHER HAND, WAS CONCENTRATING ON FAMILY, RELIGION AND NURSING...
JOE SLOVO, A COMMUNIST, TRIED TO CONVINCE THE ANC TO WORK WITH OTHER ORGANISATIONS IN A UNITED FRONT...
WE ARE GETTING THERE, JOE.

THE ANC WAS MOBILISING IN BLOEMFONTEIN, DECEMBER 1951...
WE HAVE TO START A MASS CAMPAIGN OF CIVIL DISOBEDIENCE... DEFYING UNJUST LAWS...AND GO TO PRISON IF WE NEED TO!
THIS WAS THE BIRTH OF THE DEFIANCE CAMPAIGN. MANDELA, ZK MATTHEWS, ISMAIL MEER AND JN SINGH WERE ASKED TO DRAFT A LETTER TO THE PRIME MINISTER, WARNING HIM OF THEIR PLANS, UNLESS SIX UNJUST LAWS WERE REPEALED...
6 UNJUST LAWS
Group Areas Act
Pass Laws
Suppression of Communism Act
Voters Act
Stock Limitation
Bantu Authorities
DR MALAN REACTED THE WAY THEY EXPECTED...
TELL THEM RACE DIFFERENCES ARE PERMANENT, NOT MAN-MADE! THE FULL WEIGHT OF THE STATE MACHINERY WILL BE USED TO CRUSH THEIR CAMPAIGN!!!
YOUR TIME HAS COME... YOU ARE OUR VOLUNTEER-IN-CHIEF. YOU HAVE TO TAKE CHARGE OF RECRUITING VOLUNTEERS TO THE CAMPAIGN!
OUR CAMPAIGN IS NON-VIOLENT AND DISCIPLINED. MAKE SURE ALL VOLUNTEERS FOLLOW THESE RULES!
ALL RACES UNITED AGAINST THE OPPRESSORS!
THE DEFIANCE CAMPAIGN DREW INSPIRATION FROM THE PASSIVE RESISTANCE STRATEGIES OF MK GANDHI.
WE ARE TIRED OF BEING HUMILIATED BY THE GOVERNMENT!
YES, BUT STILL NO VIOLENCE. WE MUST NOT RESIST ARREST. OUR AIM IS TO FILL THEIR JAILS.
WALTER SISULU, JB MARKS, YUSUF DADOO AND YUSUF CACHALIA MADE UP THE NATIONAL PLANNING COUNCIL. MANDELA WAS A VISIBLE PRESENCE THROUGHOUT THE CAMPAIGN, TRAVELLING FROM PLACE TO PLACE, AND MAKING SURE THAT ALL WAS RUNNING SMOOTHLY. FOR THE FIRST TIME, HE TOOK UP A NATIONAL LEADERSHIP ROLE. VOLUNTEERS WERE SIGNED UP, AND THEN ORGANISED INTO GROUPS TO BREAK THE LAWS TOGETHER.

FOUR DAYS BEFORE THE LAUNCH, 10 000 PEOPLE GATHERED IN DURBAN FOR "THE DAY OF THE VOLUNTEERS". MANDELA DELIVERED A SPEECH ON THE SAME STAGE AS CHIEF ALBERT LUTHULI, PRESIDENT OF THE NATAL ANC, AND DR NAICKER, PRESIDENT OF THE NATAL INDIAN CONGRESS.

WE WELCOME ALL TRUE-HEARTED VOLUNTEERS FROM ALL WALKS OF LIFE, WITHOUT THE CONSIDERATION OF COLOUR, RACE OR CREED...TO DEFY THESE UNJUST LAWS...

"I DO HEREBY PLEDGE TO BIND MYSELF TO SERVE MY COUNTRY AND MY PEOPLE... TO PARTICIPATE FULLY AND WITHOUT RESERVATIONS, TO THE BEST OF MY ABILITY..."

WHITES ONLY
SLEGS BLANKES
TICKET OFFICE
"¡Afrika! Mayibuye... let Africa come back!"

26 JUNE 1952, PORT ELIZABETH RAILWAY STATION. RAYMOND MHLABA LED VOLUNTEERS THROUGH A WHITES ONLY ENTRANCE...

ON THE SAME DAY IN BOKSBURG: SISULU AND NANA SITA LED VOLUNTEERS INTO A TOWNSHIP WITHOUT PERMITS.

"THINA SIZWE! GIVE US BACK OUR LAND!"
IF YOU ENTER, YOU WILL ALL BE ARRESTED!

THE VOLUNTEERS WERE ORDERLY AND WELCOMED ARREST.

OPEN UP THE JAILS, MALAN! WE ARE KNOCKING!
WHAT ARE THESE PEOPLE UP TO?

OVER THE NEXT SIX MONTHS, MORE THAN 8 000 PEOPLE WERE ARRESTED. THE JAILS WERE OVERFLOWING. EVEN THOUGH DEFIERS COULD PAY A FINE, THEY REFUSED, AND SERVED FULL SENTENCES – USUALLY 4 – 6 WEEKS. THE PEOPLE WERE BECOMING MORE POLITICISED, AND MEMBERSHIP OF THE ANC INCREASED FROM ABOUT 5 000 TO 100 000.

BUT ON 30 JULY 1952, POLICE RAIDED OFFICES AND HOMES OF ANC AND INDIAN CONGRESS MEMBERS. 20 LEADERS, INCLUDING MANDELA, WERE ARRESTED FOR VIOLATING THE SUPPRESSION OF COMMUNISM ACT.
MANDELA, YOU ARE UNDER ARREST!
GUILTY! BUT... STATUTORY COMMUNISM IS NOT THE SAME AS COMMUNISM AS IT IS COMMONLY KNOWN... NINE MONTHS WITH HARD LABOUR! SUSPENDED FOR TWO YEARS!
IN THE MIDST OF ALL THIS, MANDELA AND TAMBO OPENED A LAW FIRM IN CHANCELLOR HOUSE. ITS PRESENCE DEFIED SEGREGATION LAWS. SOON IT WAS CROWDED WITH PEOPLE IN TROUBLE BECAUSE OF THE MANY RACIST LAWS.
WE NEED MORE AFRICAN LAWYERS...
ON 2 DECEMBER 1952, MANDELA AND OTHER LEADERS WERE BANNED. THEY WERE NOT ALLOWED TO ATTEND MEETINGS OR TALK TO MORE THAN ONE PERSON AT A TIME, AND WERE NOT ALLOWED TO LEAVE THE AREAS IN WHICH THEY LIVED.
THEY FOLLOW ME ALL THE TIME...ISOLATING ME. I AM TREATED AS AN UNCONVICTED CRIMINAL! HOW WILL THE STRUGGLE OR MY JOB SURVIVE THIS SCRUTINY?
WORSE STILL, NEW LAWS SUCH AS THE PUBLIC SAFETY AND CRIMINAL LAW AMENDMENT ACTS PUT A FINAL STOP TO THE DEFIANCE CAMPAIGN. THESE LAWS ALLOWED FOR THREE-YEAR PRISON TERMS, AND FLOGGING REPLACED SHORTER TERMS.

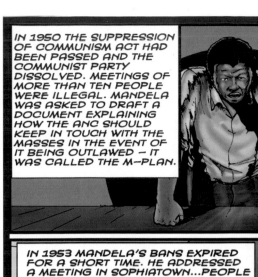

IN 1950 THE SUPPRESSION OF COMMUNISM ACT HAD BEEN PASSED AND THE COMMUNIST PARTY DISSOLVED. MEETINGS OF MORE THAN TEN PEOPLE WERE ILLEGAL. MANDELA WAS ASKED TO DRAFT A DOCUMENT EXPLAINING HOW THE ANC SHOULD KEEP IN TOUCH WITH THE MASSES IN THE EVENT OF IT BEING OUTLAWED – IT WAS CALLED THE M-PLAN.
IF YOU CANNOT HOLD MEETINGS PUBLICLY, THEN YOU MUST HOLD THEM IN THE FACTORIES, ON THE TRAMS AND BUSES...IN EVERY HOME, SHACK AND EVERY MUD STRUCTURE...WE MUST NEVER SURRENDER!

THE GOVERNMENT CONTINUED IMPLEMENTING APARTHEID. PLANS FOR BANTU EDUCATION LAWS – AN INFERIOR EDUCATION FOR AFRICANS – AND THE FORCED REMOVAL OF PEOPLE FROM THEIR HOMES IN SOPHIATOWN, AND OTHER AREAS, WERE BEING PUT IN PLACE.

THERE IS NOT A STRAND OF BARBED WIRE BETWEEN MY CONSTITUENCY AND THAT SLUM!

IN 1953 MANDELA'S BANS EXPIRED FOR A SHORT TIME. HE ADDRESSED A MEETING IN SOPHIATOWN...PEOPLE WERE OUTRAGED AT THE PROSPECT OF BEING FORCIBLY MOVED...
THESE ARE OUR ENEMIES!

YOU MUST REMEMBER TO EXERCISE DISCIPLINE, NELSON. MILITANCY WILL NOT HELP US NOW. WE HAVE TO AVOID BLOODSHED!
WE WONT MOVE!
IT IS DIFFICULT WHEN LIVING WITH THIS BRUTALITY EVERY DAY.

SISULU TRAVELLED TO CHINA IN 1953 AND EXPLORED THE OPTION OF AN ARMED STRUGGLE, BUT HAD BEEN ADVISED TO ONLY CONSIDER THIS WHEN THERE WERE NO OTHER OPTIONS LEFT.
THE BULLDOZERS AND POLICE ARE COMING!!
grrr!
BUT THE REMOVALS WENT AHEAD UNDER THE HEAVY HAND OF THE LAW. IN 1954 THE NATIVE RESETTLEMENT BILL WAS PASSED. IN FEBRUARY 1955, 2 000 POLICE ACCOMPANIED 86 TRUCKS AND STARTED LOADING UP SOPHIATOWN.

IT FEELS LIKE WE HAVE FAILED OUR PEOPLE...
WE DID WHAT WE COULD...

WE WILL NOT MOVE

FATHER TREVOR HUDDLESTON, A CHURCH MINISTER IN SOPHIATOWN, WAS A STAUNCH ALLY OF THE STRUGGLE. HE BECAME A LIFELONG FRIEND OF MANDELA'S. THE DESTRUCTION OF SOPHIATOWN WAS COMPLETED IN 1959.

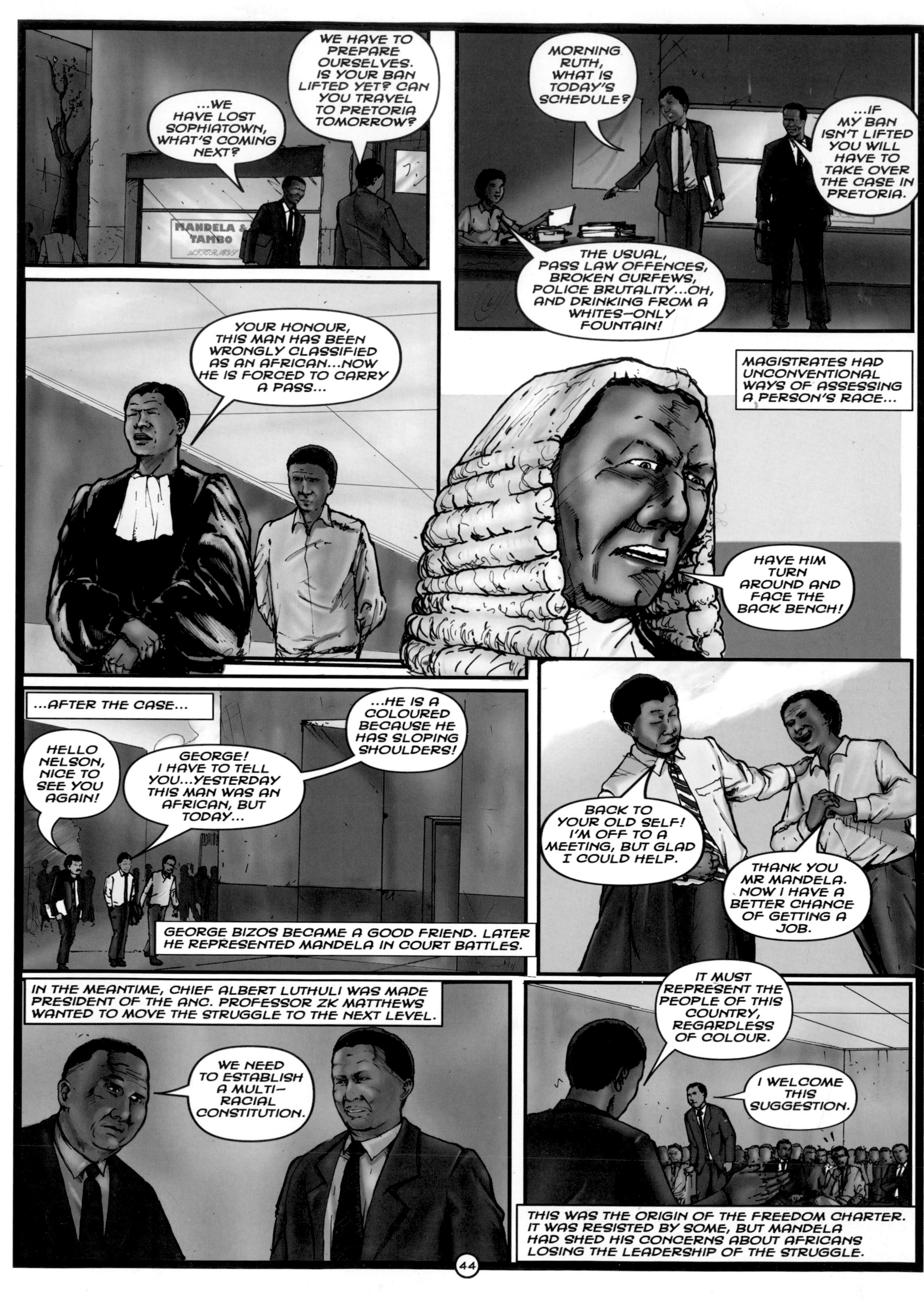
...WE HAVE LOST SOPHIATOWN, WHAT'S COMING NEXT?
WE HAVE TO PREPARE OURSELVES. IS YOUR BAN LIFTED YET? CAN YOU TRAVEL TO PRETORIA TOMORROW?
MANDELA & TAMBO
MORNING RUTH, WHAT IS TODAY'S SCHEDULE?
...IF MY BAN ISN'T LIFTED YOU WILL HAVE TO TAKE OVER THE CASE IN PRETORIA.
THE USUAL, PASS LAW OFFENCES, BROKEN CURFEWS, POLICE BRUTALITY...OH, AND DRINKING FROM A WHITES–ONLY FOUNTAIN!
YOUR HONOUR, THIS MAN HAS BEEN WRONGLY CLASSIFIED AS AN AFRICAN...NOW HE IS FORCED TO CARRY A PASS...
MAGISTRATES HAD UNCONVENTIONAL WAYS OF ASSESSING A PERSON'S RACE...
HAVE HIM TURN AROUND AND FACE THE BACK BENCH!
...AFTER THE CASE...
HELLO NELSON, NICE TO SEE YOU AGAIN!
GEORGE! I HAVE TO TELL YOU...YESTERDAY THIS MAN WAS AN AFRICAN, BUT TODAY...
...HE IS A COLOURED BECAUSE HE HAS SLOPING SHOULDERS!
GEORGE BIZOS BECAME A GOOD FRIEND. LATER HE REPRESENTED MANDELA IN COURT BATTLES.
BACK TO YOUR OLD SELF! I'M OFF TO A MEETING, BUT GLAD I COULD HELP.
THANK YOU MR MANDELA. NOW I HAVE A BETTER CHANCE OF GETTING A JOB.
IN THE MEANTIME, CHIEF ALBERT LUTHULI WAS MADE PRESIDENT OF THE ANC. PROFESSOR ZK MATTHEWS WANTED TO MOVE THE STRUGGLE TO THE NEXT LEVEL.
WE NEED TO ESTABLISH A MULTI–RACIAL CONSTITUTION.
IT MUST REPRESENT THE PEOPLE OF THIS COUNTRY, REGARDLESS OF COLOUR.
I WELCOME THIS SUGGESTION.
THIS WAS THE ORIGIN OF THE FREEDOM CHARTER. IT WAS RESISTED BY SOME, BUT MANDELA HAD SHED HIS CONCERNS ABOUT AFRICANS LOSING THE LEADERSHIP OF THE STRUGGLE.

FOUR ORGANISATIONS JOINED THE CAMPAIGN FOR A FREEDOM CHARTER – THE ANC, INDIAN CONGRESS, COLOURED PEOPLE'S ORGANISATION AND THE CONGRESS OF DEMOCRATS. TOGETHER THEY FORMED THE CONGRESS ALLIANCE, AND COLLECTED VIEWS FROM PEOPLE ACROSS THE COUNTRY.
ELECT YOUR DELEGATES
THIS CHAP WANTS TO HAVE PERMISSION TO HAVE 10 WIVES!
I'LL VOTE AGAINST THAT!

WE THE PEOPLE OF SOUTH AFRICA, DECLARE FOR ALL OUR COUNTRY AND THE WORLD TO KNOW THAT SOUTH AFRICA BELONGS TO ALL WHO LIVE IN IT, BLACK AND WHITE AND THAT NO GOVERNMENT CAN JUSTLY CLAIM AUTHORITY UNLESS IT IS BASED ON THE WILL OF THE PEOPLE.
ON 25 AND 26 JUNE 1955, THE CAMPAIGN CULMINATED IN A CONGRESS OF THE PEOPLE, ATTENDED BY THOUSANDS IN KLIPTOWN, SOWETO. THE FREEDOM CHARTER WAS ADOPTED.

MANDELA OBSERVED FROM A DISTANCE BECAUSE OF HIS BANNING ORDERS.

WE ARE INVESTIGATING A CASE OF TREASON, DO NOT LEAVE UNTIL WE HAVE YOUR NAME AND YOU HAVE BEEN SEARCHED!

EVERYONE WAS CHECKED BY THE POLICE.

WHILE THE AFRIKANERS ARE ENFORCING THEIR EXCLUSIVE POWER OVER ALL OTHER RACES, WE HAVE DECLARED ALL PEOPLE EQUAL!

YOU NO LONGER SPEND ANY TIME AT HOME...

I CANNOT BE PASSIVE IN THE FACE OF OPPRESSION!
YOU SHOULD SERVE GOD!
BY NOW THE COUPLE HAD ANOTHER BABY GIRL. THEY NAMED HER MAKAZIWE, TO HONOUR HER SISTER WHO DIED, BUT THEIR MARRIAGE WAS IN TROUBLE...

I MUST GO AND VISIT MY FAMILY.
MANDELA'S SECOND BAN EXPIRED AND HE TOOK THE OPPORTUNITY TO LEAVE JOHANNESBURG TO SEE HIS FAMILY IN THE TRANSKEI AND TO ORGANISE FOR THE ANC.

AFTER TRAVELLING THROUGH KWAZULU–NATAL MANDELA WENT TO THE GREAT PLACE LATE AT NIGHT.
WE THOUGHT IT WAS OUR CHIEF JUSTICE DALINDYEBO. YOU KNOW THE GOVERNMENT GOT RID OF HIM WHEN HE WOULD NOT LISTEN?
I KNOW. I CAME TO TALK TO DALIWONGA.
KAISER MATANZIMA WAS NOW A GOVERNMENT–APPOINTED CHIEF.
BLACK AND WHITE MUST WORK TOGETHER IN THE TRANSKEI.
DALIWONGA, YOU ARE NOW AT THE WHIM OF A POWERFUL ENEMY WHICH HAS BECOME YOUR MASTER!
MANDELA COULD NOT PERSUADE MATANZIMA OTHERWISE. HE HEADED TOWARDS PORT ELIZABETH, CONTINUING TO MEET WITH FELLOW ANC MEMBERS.
MY EDUCATION CAME FROM MISSIONARIES. NOW VERWOERD IS DOING AWAY WITH ALL OF THIS USING THE BANTU EDUCATION ACT.
HOW DARE VERWOERD SAY THERE IS NO PLACE FOR AFRICANS BEYOND CHEAP LABOUR!
HOW DID IT GO WITH THE SCHOOL BOYCOTT?
WE COULD NOT CONTINUE... VERWOERD WOULD HAVE KICKED ALL THE CHILDREN OUT OF SCHOOL.
IN PORT ELIZABETH, HE MET WITH GOVAN MBEKI, AN ANC LEADER.
I AM VERY CONCERNED ABOUT OUR CHILDREN'S EDUCATION...
NOW THIS IS A PLACE AN ARMY COULD FIGHT FROM! I MUST GET BACK AND REPORT ON ALL OF MY FINDINGS...
MANDELA CONTINUED HIS JOURNEY, GOING THROUGH THE KNYSNA FOREST.

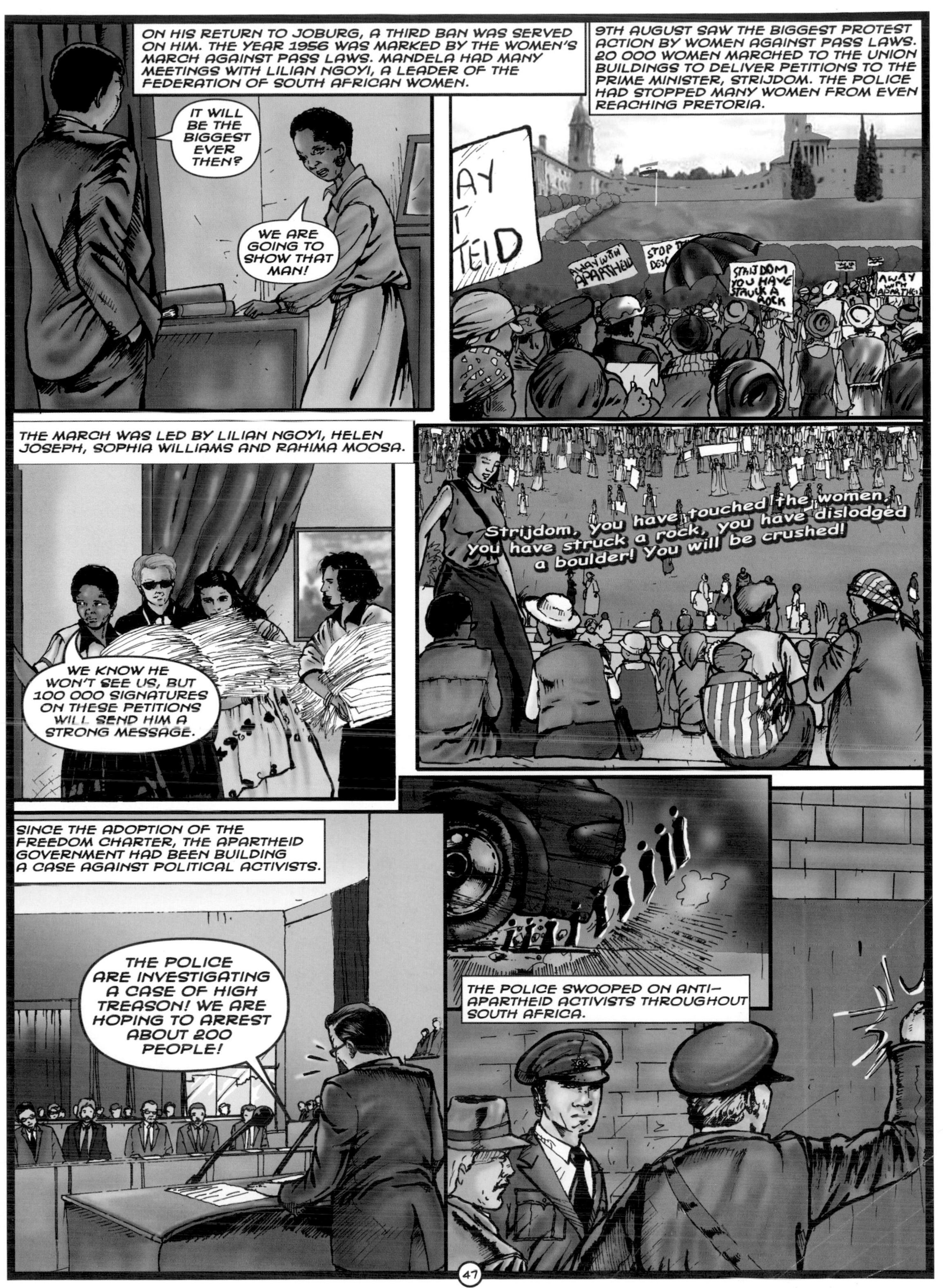
ON HIS RETURN TO JOBURG, A THIRD BAN WAS SERVED ON HIM. THE YEAR 1956 WAS MARKED BY THE WOMEN'S MARCH AGAINST PASS LAWS. MANDELA HAD MANY MEETINGS WITH LILIAN NGOYI, A LEADER OF THE FEDERATION OF SOUTH AFRICAN WOMEN.
IT WILL BE THE BIGGEST EVER THEN?
WE ARE GOING TO SHOW THAT MAN!
9TH AUGUST SAW THE BIGGEST PROTEST ACTION BY WOMEN AGAINST PASS LAWS. 20 000 WOMEN MARCHED TO THE UNION BUILDINGS TO DELIVER PETITIONS TO THE PRIME MINISTER, STRIJDOM. THE POLICE HAD STOPPED MANY WOMEN FROM EVEN REACHING PRETORIA.
AWAY WITH APARTHEID
STRIJDOM YOU HAVE STRUCK A ROCK
AWAY WITH APARTHEID
THE MARCH WAS LED BY LILIAN NGOYI, HELEN JOSEPH, SOPHIA WILLIAMS AND RAHIMA MOOSA.
WE KNOW HE WON'T SEE US, BUT 100 000 SIGNATURES ON THESE PETITIONS WILL SEND HIM A STRONG MESSAGE.
Strijdom, you have touched the women, you have struck a rock, you have dislodged a boulder! You will be crushed!
SINCE THE ADOPTION OF THE FREEDOM CHARTER, THE APARTHEID GOVERNMENT HAD BEEN BUILDING A CASE AGAINST POLITICAL ACTIVISTS.
THE POLICE ARE INVESTIGATING A CASE OF HIGH TREASON! WE ARE HOPING TO ARREST ABOUT 200 PEOPLE!
THE POLICE SWOOPED ON ANTI-APARTHEID ACTIVISTS THROUGHOUT SOUTH AFRICA.

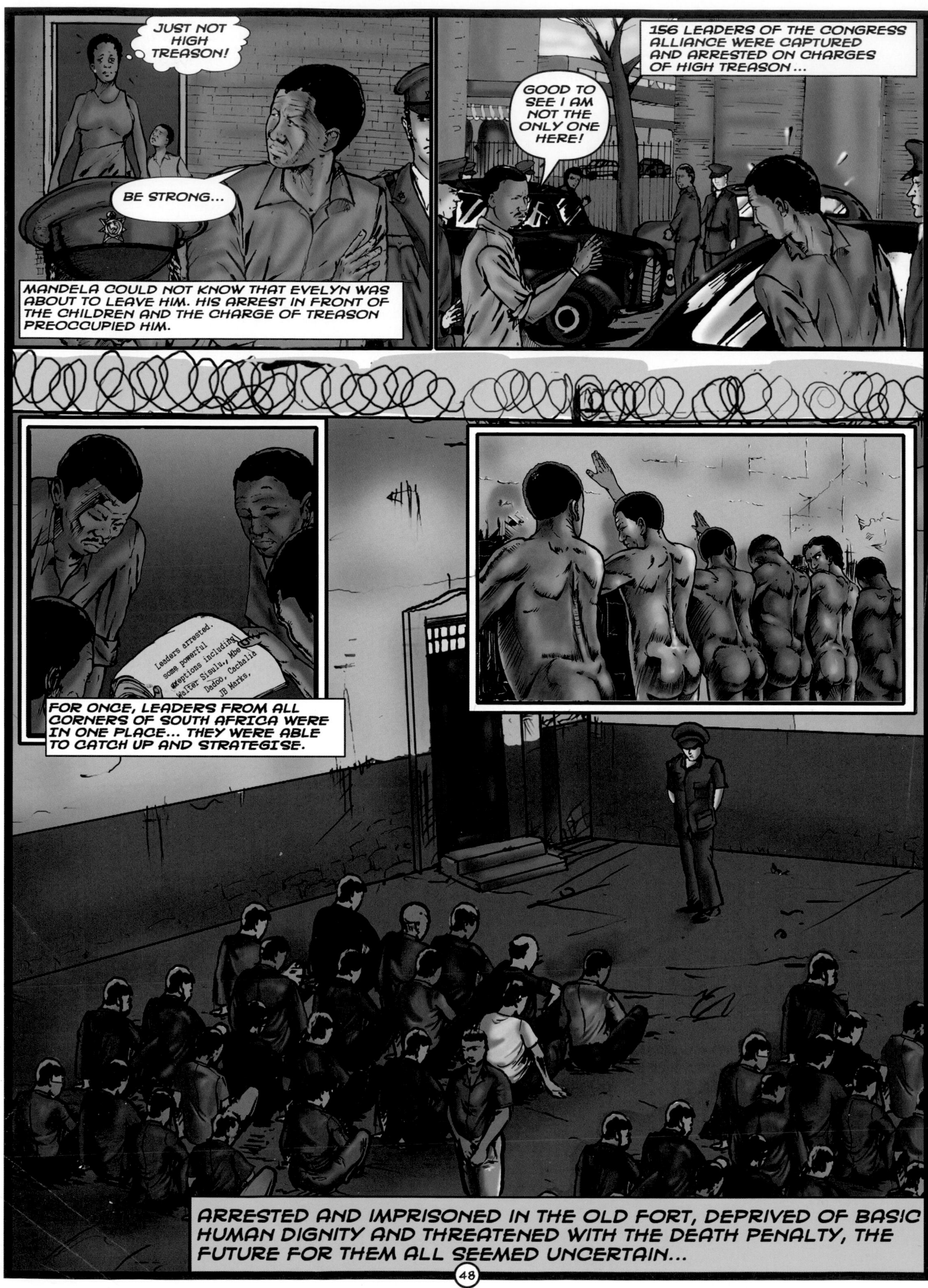
JUST NOT HIGH TREASON!
BE STRONG...
MANDELA COULD NOT KNOW THAT EVELYN WAS ABOUT TO LEAVE HIM. HIS ARREST IN FRONT OF THE CHILDREN AND THE CHARGE OF TREASON PREOCCUPIED HIM.
156 LEADERS OF THE CONGRESS ALLIANCE WERE CAPTURED AND ARRESTED ON CHARGES OF HIGH TREASON...
GOOD TO SEE I AM NOT THE ONLY ONE HERE!
Leaders arrested.
some powerful
exeptions including
Walter Sisulu, Mbe
Dadoo, Cachalia
JB Marks,
FOR ONCE, LEADERS FROM ALL CORNERS OF SOUTH AFRICA WERE IN ONE PLACE... THEY WERE ABLE TO CATCH UP AND STRATEGISE.
ARRESTED AND IMPRISONED IN THE OLD FORT, DEPRIVED OF BASIC HUMAN DIGNITY AND THREATENED WITH THE DEATH PENALTY, THE FUTURE FOR THEM ALL SEEMED UNCERTAIN...

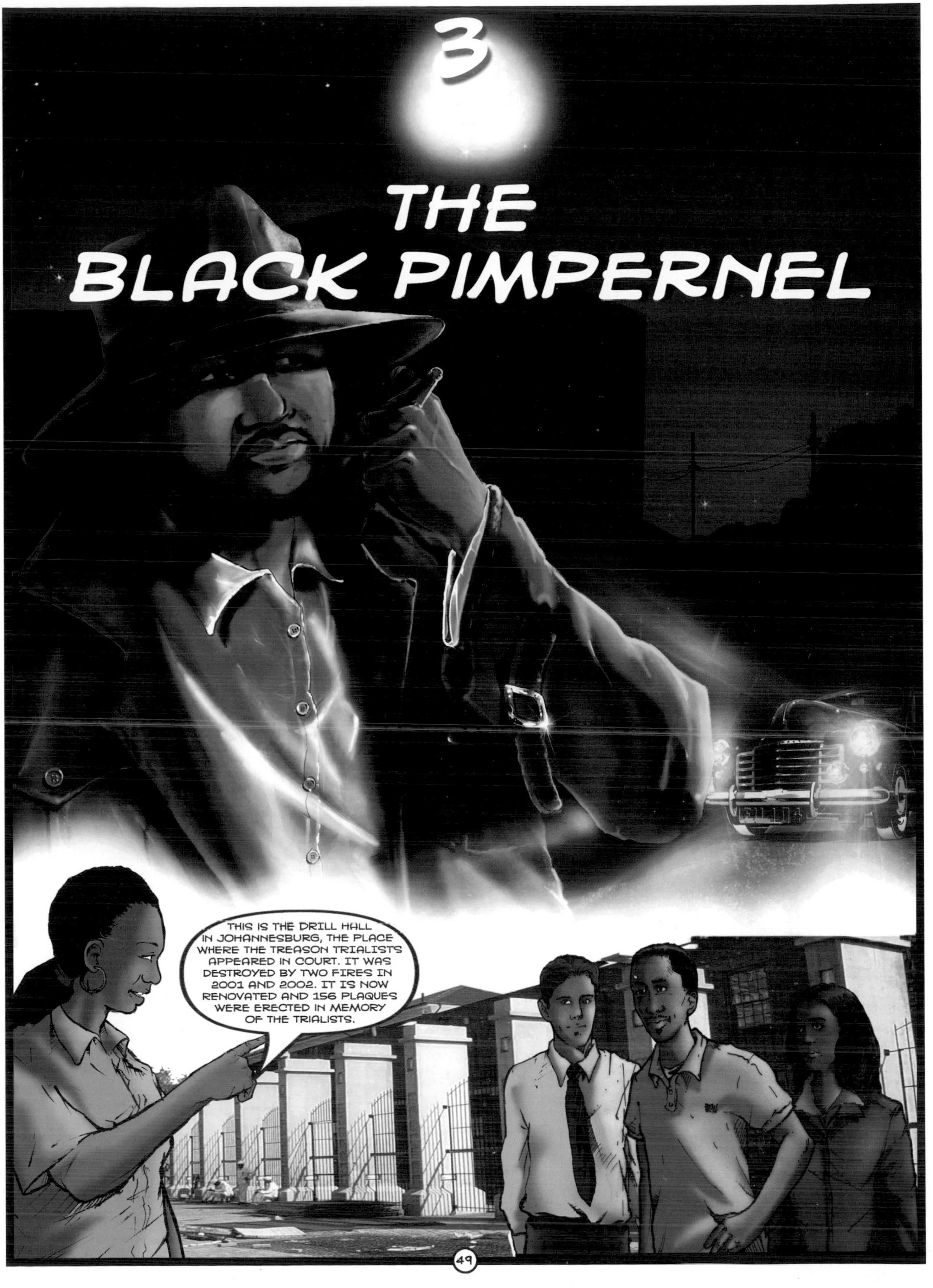

3

THE BLACK PIMPERNEL

THIS IS THE DRILL HALL IN JOHANNESBURG, THE PLACE WHERE THE TREASON TRIALISTS APPEARED IN COURT. IT WAS DESTROYED BY TWO FIRES IN 2001 AND 2002. IT IS NOW RENOVATED AND 156 PLAQUES WERE ERECTED IN MEMORY OF THE TRIALISTS.

19 DECEMBER 1956: AFTER TWO WEEKS IN PRISON, THE 156 ACCUSED WERE TAKEN TO THE OLD DRILL HALL IN JOHANNESBURG. IT HAD BEEN TURNED INTO A MAKESHIFT COURTROOM CONTAINING A LARGE CAGE TO HOLD THE DEFENDANTS. THIS WAS THE PREPARATORY EXAMINATION THAT WOULD DETERMINE WHETHER THE CHARGES OF HIGH TREASON WERE SUFFICIENT TO BE HEARD IN THE SUPREME COURT.
ON DAY TWO, THE CHIEF PROSECUTOR READ AN 18 000-WORD INDICTMENT.
YOUR WORSHIP, WE WILL PROVE THE DEFENDANTS' PLANS TO OVERTHROW THE GOVERNMENT WITH THE USE OF VIOLENCE!
YOUR HONOUR! MY CLIENTS ARE CAGED LIKE ANIMALS! THIS IS OUTRAGEOUS!
THEY HAD A FORMIDABLE DEFENCE TEAM: ISRAEL MAISELS, NORMAN ROSENBERG, VERNON BERRANGE, MAURICE FRANKS, BRAM FISCHER, GEORGE BIZOS AND ARTHUR CHASKALSON.
WE STAND BY OUR LEADERS
WE STAND BY OUR LEADERS
WE STAND BY OUR LEADERS
OUTSIDE, SUPPORTERS SHOWED SOLIDARITY.

THE CAGE WAS REMOVED. WHILE THE TRIAL WENT AHEAD INSIDE, POLICE AND SUPPORTERS CLASHED OUTSIDE: 22 PEOPLE WERE INJURED.
WE STAND BY OUR LEADERS
WE STAND BY OUR LEADERS
WE STAND BY OUR LEADERS
THE DRILL HALL SITE IS NOW A MUSEUM.
ON THE FOURTH DAY OF THE TRIAL, THE PRISONERS WERE RELEASED ON BAIL. 25 POUNDS FOR AFRICANS, 100 POUNDS FOR INDIANS, AND 250 POUNDS FOR WHITES... DEMONSTRATING PETTY APARTHEID...
I SEE I AM 75 POUNDS MORE VALUABLE TO THE COURTS THAN YOU!
WHAT NEXT!
BY NOW, THE MANDELA MARRIAGE WAS OVER...
IT'S NOT TOO LATE TO SAVE YOUR MARRIAGE...
NO, WALTER! IT'S OVER.

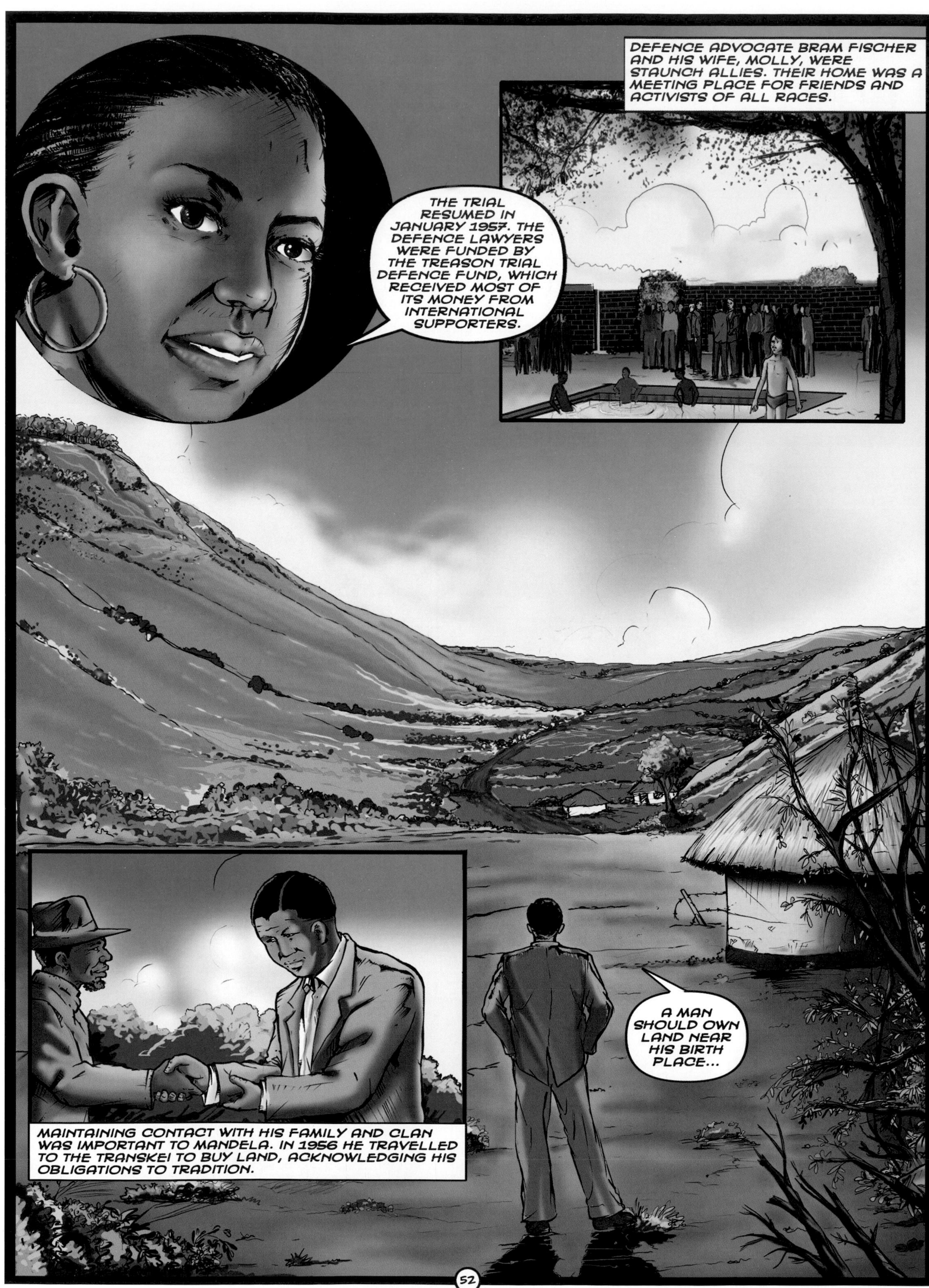
THE TRIAL RESUMED IN JANUARY 1957. THE DEFENCE LAWYERS WERE FUNDED BY THE TREASON TRIAL DEFENCE FUND, WHICH RECEIVED MOST OF ITS MONEY FROM INTERNATIONAL SUPPORTERS.
DEFENCE ADVOCATE BRAM FISCHER AND HIS WIFE, MOLLY, WERE STAUNCH ALLIES. THEIR HOME WAS A MEETING PLACE FOR FRIENDS AND ACTIVISTS OF ALL RACES.
MAINTAINING CONTACT WITH HIS FAMILY AND CLAN WAS IMPORTANT TO MANDELA. IN 1956 HE TRAVELLED TO THE TRANSKEI TO BUY LAND, ACKNOWLEDGING HIS OBLIGATIONS TO TRADITION.
A MAN SHOULD OWN LAND NEAR HIS BIRTH PLACE...

BACK IN JOHANNESBURG, MANDELA RACED BETWEEN HIS LAW FIRM AND THE TRIAL, TRYING TO KEEP THE LAW PRACTICE GOING...
WHO IS THAT!
A FEW WEEKS LATER, MANDELA WAS SURPRISED TO SEE THE SAME BEAUTIFUL WOMAN IN A DELI SHOP WITH ADELAIDE AND OLIVER TAMBO.
IT'S HER...
WE ARE FRIENDS FROM BIZANA.
THIS IS WINNIE MADIKIZELA. WINNIE, THIS IS NELSON MANDELA.
WINNIE WAS THE FIRST AFRICAN SOCIAL WORKER AT BARAGWANATH HOSPITAL IN SOWETO.
SOON AFTERWARD, MANDELA INVITED HER TO LUNCH. THEY DISCUSSED RAISING FUNDS FOR THE ANC...
BUT, I ALSO WANTED TO SEE YOU AGAIN.
MANDELA LEARNT THAT WINNIE'S GREAT GRANDFATHER WAS AN IMPORTANT 19TH CENTURY CHIEF IN THE MPONDO KINGDOM.
THERE WAS A POWERFUL CONNECTION BETWEEN THEM. LIFE WAS TO TEST IT SEVERELY.

BY DECEMBER 1957 CHARGES AGAINST 61 OF THE ACCUSED HAD BEEN WITHDRAWN. THE REST OF THE ACCUSED HOPED THAT THE ENTIRE CASE WOULD BE DISMISSED, BUT THE MAGISTRATE RULED THAT THERE WAS SUFFICIENT EVIDENCE TO ALLOW THE TRIAL TO GO AHEAD.

WINNIE, I WOULD LIKE YOU TO MEET CHIEF LUTHULI...

I WONDER WHAT HIS INTENTIONS ARE?

GOLDEN CITY POST

MANDELA KNEW WHAT HIS INTENTIONS WERE. HE STARTED WEDDING PLANS, AND GETTING THE BLESSING OF WINNIE'S FATHER AND PAYING LOBOLA. AN ENGAGEMENT NOTICE WAS PLACED IN THE NEWSPAPER.

THE BLESSING FROM WINNIE'S FATHER CAME WITH A WARNING THAT MARRYING "MANDELA FROM THE ANC" WOULD NOT BE EASY.

MANDELA'S BANNING ORDERS WERE RELAXED FOR A FEW DAYS, SO THAT HE COULD TRAVEL TO THE TRANSKEI FOR THE WEDDING.

DON'T WORRY, MKHULU, I WILL STAY AWAY FROM HIM!

AT THE BRIDE'S PLACE, MBONGWENI, THEY WERE SEPARATED AS TRADITION REQUIRED.

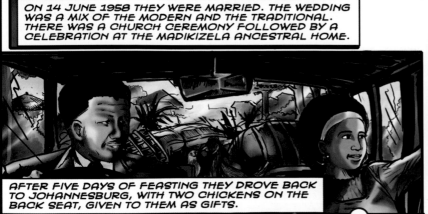

ON 14 JUNE 1958 THEY WERE MARRIED. THE WEDDING WAS A MIX OF THE MODERN AND THE TRADITIONAL. THERE WAS A CHURCH CEREMONY FOLLOWED BY A CELEBRATION AT THE MADIKIZELA ANCESTRAL HOME.
LATER, THEY CELEBRATED AT THE BIZANA TOWN HALL. WINNIE'S FATHER, COLUMBUS MADIKIZELA, DELIVERED A SPEECH.
...THIS MARRIAGE IS THREATENED FROM ALL SIDES...BE LIKE YOUR HUSBAND AND HIS PEOPLE...

AFTER FIVE DAYS OF FEASTING THEY DROVE BACK TO JOHANNESBURG, WITH TWO CHICKENS ON THE BACK SEAT, GIVEN TO THEM AS GIFTS.

THE CHICKENS ESCAPED WHEN THEY STOPPED FOR LUNCH ALONG THE ROADSIDE.

THE NEWLY-WEDS WERE WELCOMED IN ORLANDO WITH ANOTHER CELEBRATION...

AND A FEW WEEKS LATER MEMBERS OF THE MADIBA CLAN ARRIVED TO OFFICIALLY WELCOME WINNIE INTO THE CLAN.
YOUR NEW CLAN NAME IS NOBANDLA.

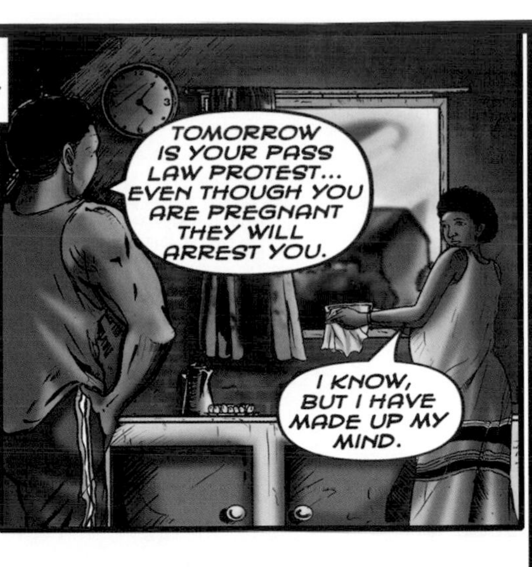

TOMORROW IS YOUR PASS LAW PROTEST... EVEN THOUGH YOU ARE PREGNANT THEY WILL ARREST YOU.
I KNOW, BUT I HAVE MADE UP MY MIND.

MORE THAN A THOUSAND WOMEN WERE ARRESTED IN OCTOBER 1958, AND IMPRISONED FOR TWO WEEKS. WINNIE MANDELA, LILIAN NGOYI AND ALBERTINA SISULU WERE AMONGST THOSE ARRESTED.

OH ALBERTINA! I HOPE THAT THESE TERRIBLE CONDITIONS WILL NOT HARM MY BABY!

WINNIE, YOU HAVE TO BELIEVE YOUR BABY WILL BE FINE...

WE ARE ORGANISING LEGAL COUNSEL FOR ALL OF YOU...

NELSON, THIS PLACE IS OVERCROWDED...WE ARE SLEEPING ON MATS AND THE SMELL IS UNBEARABLE...BUT WE ARE VERY STRONG.

THE ANC PAID THEIR FINES, BUT WINNIE LOST HER JOB AT THE HOSPITAL. MONEY WORRIES FORCED MANDELA TO SELL HIS LAND IN THE TRANSKEI. BUT A NEW ARRIVAL BROUGHT THEM JOY!

SO, MY DARLING, WHAT HAVE YOU BROUGHT TO THE WORLD? YES, LET US CALL HER ZENANI*.

* ZENANI MEANS "WHAT HAVE YOU BROUGHT TO THE WORLD".

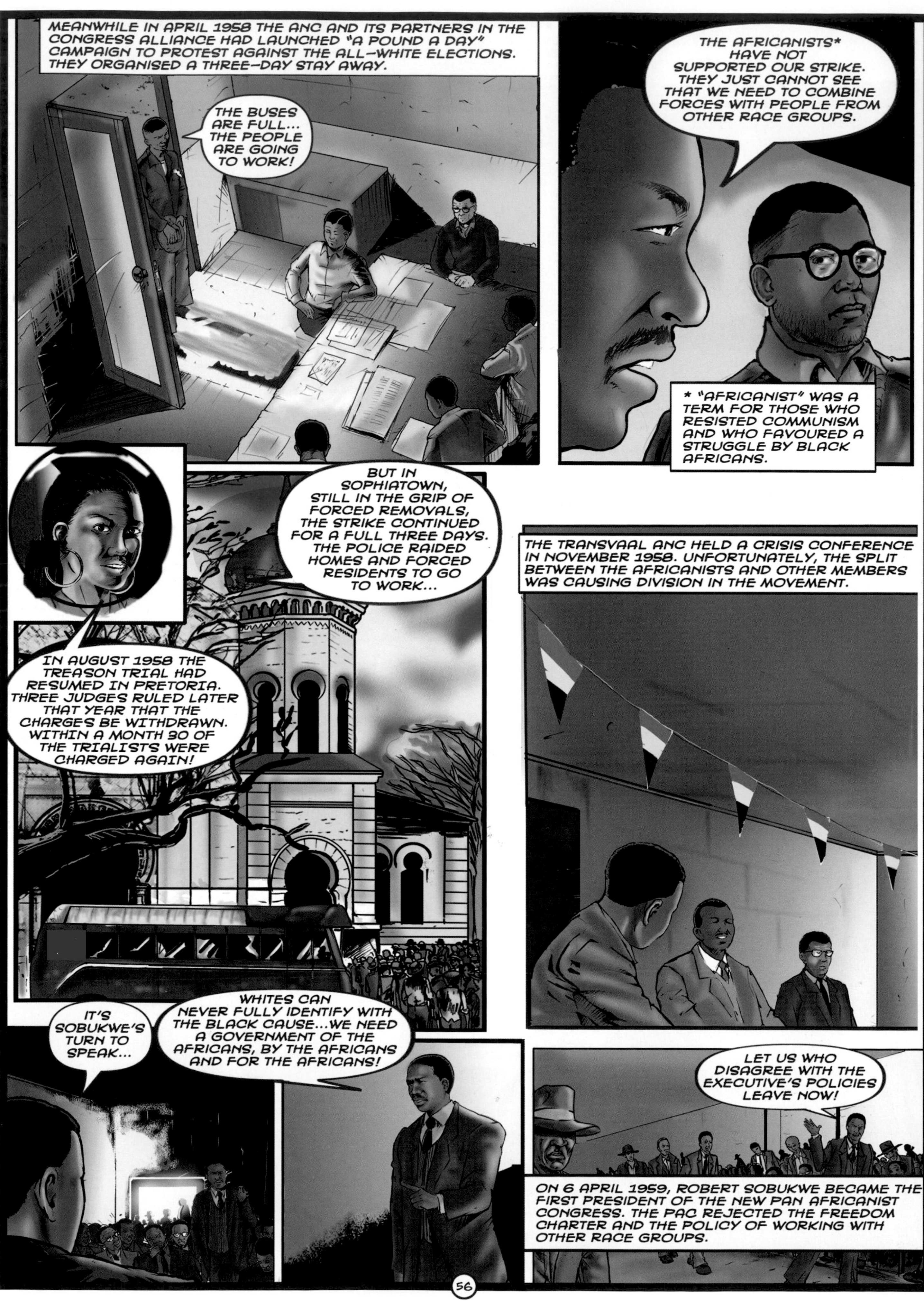
MEANWHILE IN APRIL 1958 THE ANC AND ITS PARTNERS IN THE CONGRESS ALLIANCE HAD LAUNCHED "A POUND A DAY" CAMPAIGN TO PROTEST AGAINST THE ALL-WHITE ELECTIONS. THEY ORGANISED A THREE-DAY STAY AWAY.
THE BUSES ARE FULL... THE PEOPLE ARE GOING TO WORK!
THE AFRICANISTS* HAVE NOT SUPPORTED OUR STRIKE. THEY JUST CANNOT SEE THAT WE NEED TO COMBINE FORCES WITH PEOPLE FROM OTHER RACE GROUPS.
* "AFRICANIST" WAS A TERM FOR THOSE WHO RESISTED COMMUNISM AND WHO FAVOURED A STRUGGLE BY BLACK AFRICANS.
BUT IN SOPHIATOWN, STILL IN THE GRIP OF FORCED REMOVALS, THE STRIKE CONTINUED FOR A FULL THREE DAYS. THE POLICE RAIDED HOMES AND FORCED RESIDENTS TO GO TO WORK...
IN AUGUST 1958 THE TREASON TRIAL HAD RESUMED IN PRETORIA. THREE JUDGES RULED LATER THAT YEAR THAT THE CHARGES BE WITHDRAWN. WITHIN A MONTH 30 OF THE TRIALISTS WERE CHARGED AGAIN!
THE TRANSVAAL ANC HELD A CRISIS CONFERENCE IN NOVEMBER 1958. UNFORTUNATELY, THE SPLIT BETWEEN THE AFRICANISTS AND OTHER MEMBERS WAS CAUSING DIVISION IN THE MOVEMENT.
IT'S SOBUKWE'S TURN TO SPEAK...
WHITES CAN NEVER FULLY IDENTIFY WITH THE BLACK CAUSE...WE NEED A GOVERNMENT OF THE AFRICANS, BY THE AFRICANS AND FOR THE AFRICANS!
LET US WHO DISAGREE WITH THE EXECUTIVE'S POLICIES LEAVE NOW!
ON 6 APRIL 1959, ROBERT SOBUKWE BECAME THE FIRST PRESIDENT OF THE NEW PAN AFRICANIST CONGRESS. THE PAC REJECTED THE FREEDOM CHARTER AND THE POLICY OF WORKING WITH OTHER RACE GROUPS.

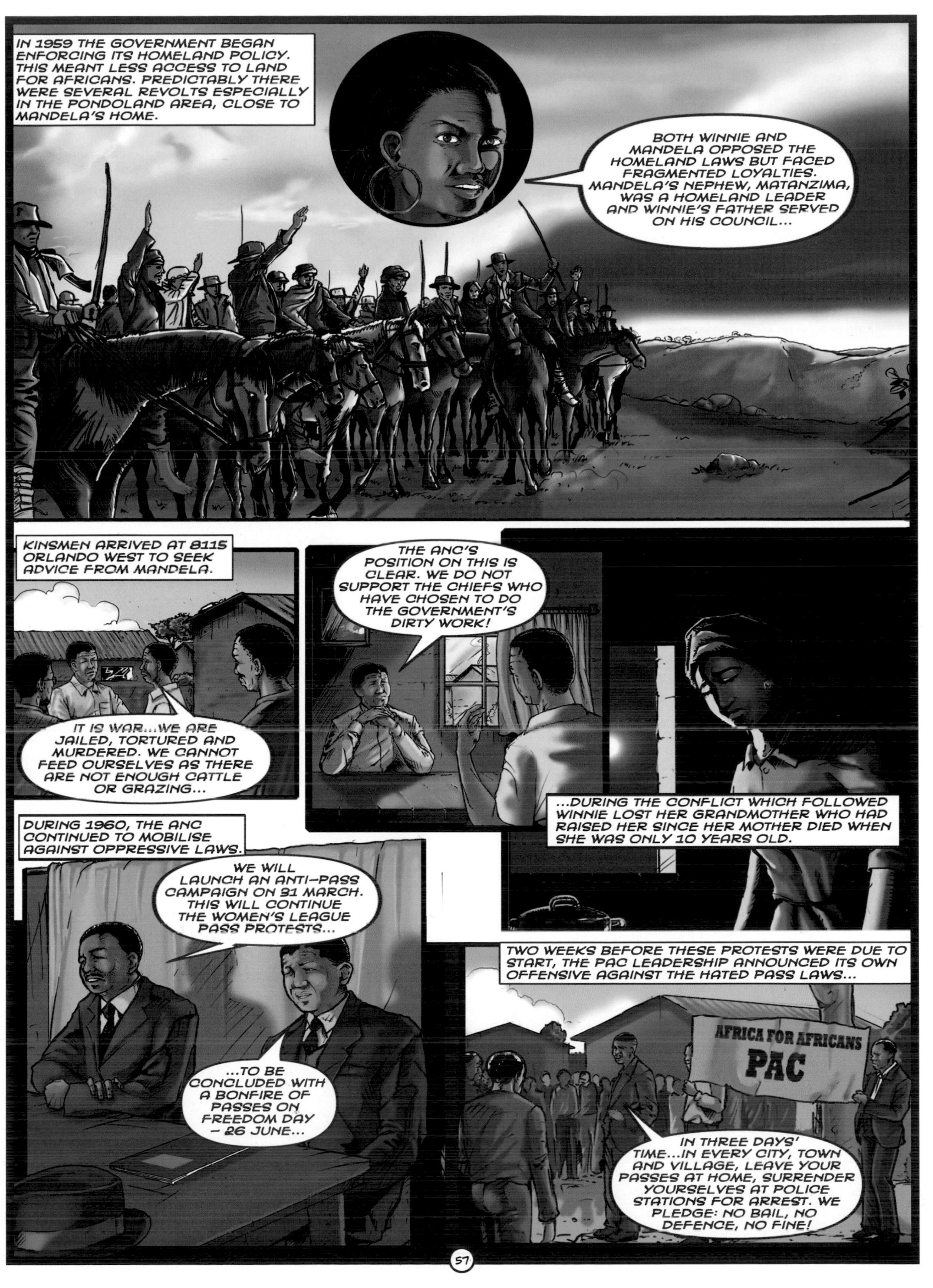
IN 1959 THE GOVERNMENT BEGAN ENFORCING ITS HOMELAND POLICY. THIS MEANT LESS ACCESS TO LAND FOR AFRICANS. PREDICTABLY THERE WERE SEVERAL REVOLTS ESPECIALLY IN THE PONDOLAND AREA, CLOSE TO MANDELA'S HOME.
BOTH WINNIE AND MANDELA OPPOSED THE HOMELAND LAWS BUT FACED FRAGMENTED LOYALTIES. MANDELA'S NEPHEW, MATANZIMA, WAS A HOMELAND LEADER AND WINNIE'S FATHER SERVED ON HIS COUNCIL...
KINSMEN ARRIVED AT 8115 ORLANDO WEST TO SEEK ADVICE FROM MANDELA.
IT IS WAR...WE ARE JAILED, TORTURED AND MURDERED. WE CANNOT FEED OURSELVES AS THERE ARE NOT ENOUGH CATTLE OR GRAZING...
THE ANC'S POSITION ON THIS IS CLEAR. WE DO NOT SUPPORT THE CHIEFS WHO HAVE CHOSEN TO DO THE GOVERNMENT'S DIRTY WORK!
...DURING THE CONFLICT WHICH FOLLOWED WINNIE LOST HER GRANDMOTHER WHO HAD RAISED HER SINCE HER MOTHER DIED WHEN SHE WAS ONLY 10 YEARS OLD.
DURING 1960, THE ANC CONTINUED TO MOBILISE AGAINST OPPRESSIVE LAWS.
WE WILL LAUNCH AN ANTI-PASS CAMPAIGN ON 31 MARCH. THIS WILL CONTINUE THE WOMEN'S LEAGUE PASS PROTESTS...
...TO BE CONCLUDED WITH A BONFIRE OF PASSES ON FREEDOM DAY – 26 JUNE...
TWO WEEKS BEFORE THESE PROTESTS WERE DUE TO START, THE PAC LEADERSHIP ANNOUNCED ITS OWN OFFENSIVE AGAINST THE HATED PASS LAWS...
AFRICA FOR AFRICANS
PAC
IN THREE DAYS' TIME...IN EVERY CITY, TOWN AND VILLAGE, LEAVE YOUR PASSES AT HOME, SURRENDER YOURSELVES AT POLICE STATIONS FOR ARREST. WE PLEDGE: NO BAIL, NO DEFENCE, NO FINE!

ON 21 MARCH 1960 PAC-ORGANISED ANTI-PASS MARCHES TOOK PLACE IN SHARPEVILLE, ORLANDO, VANDERBIJL PARK, LANGA AND NYANGA.
COME PEOPLE, THIS WAY!
AT SHARPEVILLE POLICE STATION ABOUT 5 000 PEOPLE GATHERED PEACEFULLY...
BY MID-AFTERNOON TENSION WAS MOUNTING...
A MINOR INCIDENT CAUSED THE CROWD TO SURGE AGAINST THE FENCE...
THE POLICE STARTED SHOOTING...
...KILLING AT LEAST 69 AND WOUNDING NEARLY 200 PEOPLE. MOST OF THOSE KILLED HAD BEEN SHOT IN THE BACK. IN LANGA, CAPE TOWN, THE PROTESTERS WERE MET BY A BATON CHARGE AND TWO PEOPLE WERE KILLED.

THE NEWS REACHED THE TREASON TRIALISTS SOON ENOUGH...THE ANC LEADERSHIP GATHERED AT JOE SLOVO'S HOUSE TO DECIDE ON A PATH OF ACTION.
WE CAN'T SIT AROUND TALKING NON-VIOLENCE AFTER WHAT HAS HAPPENED!
THEY HAVE GONE TOO FAR!
THEY DECIDED TO PUSH ON WITH A NATIONAL PASS-BURNING CAMPAIGN, A STAY-AWAY AND DAY OF MOURNING ON 28 MARCH.
THE ANC KNEW THAT REPRESSION FROM THE GOVERNMENT WOULD ONLY INCREASE. OLIVER TAMBO WAS SMUGGLED OUT OF THE COUNTRY TO BUILD THE ANC FROM OUTSIDE...
TJ 4001

ON 31 MARCH 1960 A STATE OF EMERGENCY WAS DECLARED, GIVING THE GOVERNMENT SWEEPING POWERS TO CRUSH ALL OPPOSITION. THOUSANDS OF PEOPLE WERE DETAINED, INCLUDING ALMOST EVERY KNOWN ACTIVIST IN THE COUNTRY...THE MANDELA HOUSE WAS RAIDED AFTER MIDNIGHT....

WHERE ARE YOUR WARRANTS? WHERE ARE YOU TAKING HIM?
MIND YOUR OWN BUSINESS!

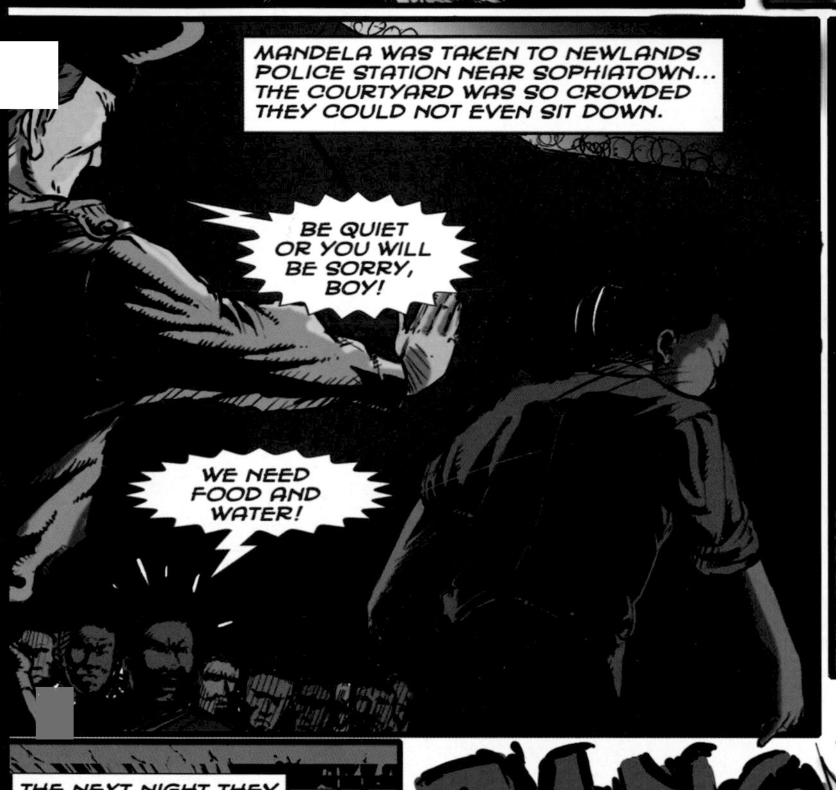
MANDELA WAS TAKEN TO NEWLANDS POLICE STATION NEAR SOPHIATOWN... THE COURTYARD WAS SO CROWDED THEY COULD NOT EVEN SIT DOWN.
BE QUIET OR YOU WILL BE SORRY, BOY!
WE NEED FOOD AND WATER!

THEY WERE GIVEN A THIN MAIZE LIQUID TO EAT AND BLOOD-STAINED BLANKETS COVERED IN LICE AND COCKROACHES.

THE NEXT NIGHT THEY WERE RELEASED...

BANG
...FOR A FEW SECONDS, AND THEN FORMALLY ARRESTED UNDER EMERGENCY REGULATIONS.
MANDELA AND SOME OTHERS WERE TRANSFERRED TO PRETORIA LOCAL PRISON.

ON 8 APRIL 1960 THE ANC AND PAC WERE BANNED. NEWSPAPERS SMUGGLED IN, GAVE THE PRISONERS THE NEWS.
WE CANNOT DEFEND YOU FAIRLY UNDER THE EMERGENCY LAWS!
I AGREE WITH YOU BRAM..
THE LAWYERS WITHDREW FROM THE CASE ...

MANDELA AND ANOTHER LAWYER, DUMA NOKWE, ADVISED THEIR FELLOW DETAINEES ABOUT THEIR DEFENCE IN THE TREASON TRIAL.
DO NOT WORRY, YOU ARE WELL PREPARED, KATHY*...
* KATHY WAS THE NAME THEY USED FOR AHMED KATHRADA.
BY THIS TIME, THE MANDELA AND TAMBO LAW FIRM HAD REACHED THE END OF ITS TEN-YEAR EXISTENCE. MANDELA WAS ESCORTED BY POLICE TO JOHANNESBURG OVER WEEKENDS TO TIE UP THE LAST BUSINESS OF THE FIRM.
AFTER FIVE MONTHS THOSE ARRESTED WERE RELEASED, AND IN AUGUST THE STATE OF EMERGENCY ENDED.
I'VE MISSED YOU.
WE HAVE DECIDED TO DISSOLVE THE YOUTH AND WOMEN'S LEAGUES AND SET UP A SMALL WORKING COMMITTEE.
THE BANNED ANC NOW HAD TO OPERATE ALONG THE LINES OF THE M-PLAN, RELYING ON A SECRET UNDERGROUND NETWORK OF ACTIVISTS.
YOU KNOW WE WILL HAVE ANOTHER MOUTH TO FEED SOON.
YES, I WILL HAVE TO FIND A PLACE TO WORK FROM FOR US TO SURVIVE. KATHY WILL LET ME USE HIS FLAT.

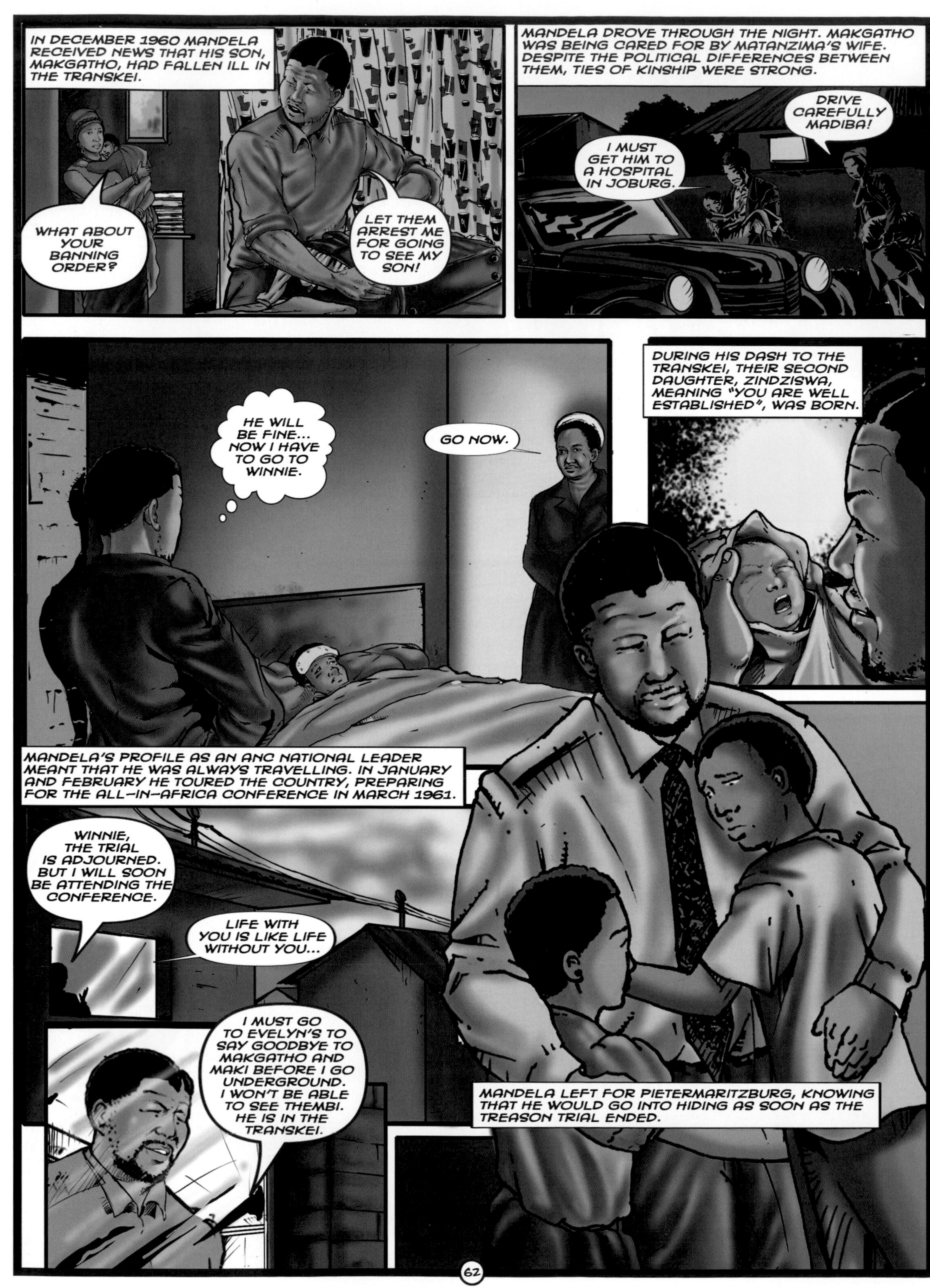
IN DECEMBER 1960 MANDELA RECEIVED NEWS THAT HIS SON, MAKGATHO, HAD FALLEN ILL IN THE TRANSKEI.
WHAT ABOUT YOUR BANNING ORDER?
LET THEM ARREST ME FOR GOING TO SEE MY SON!
MANDELA DROVE THROUGH THE NIGHT. MAKGATHO WAS BEING CARED FOR BY MATANZIMA'S WIFE. DESPITE THE POLITICAL DIFFERENCES BETWEEN THEM, TIES OF KINSHIP WERE STRONG.
I MUST GET HIM TO A HOSPITAL IN JOBURG.
DRIVE CAREFULLY MADIBA!
HE WILL BE FINE... NOW I HAVE TO GO TO WINNIE.
GO NOW.
DURING HIS DASH TO THE TRANSKEI, THEIR SECOND DAUGHTER, ZINDZISWA, MEANING "YOU ARE WELL ESTABLISHED", WAS BORN.
MANDELA'S PROFILE AS AN ANC NATIONAL LEADER MEANT THAT HE WAS ALWAYS TRAVELLING. IN JANUARY AND FEBRUARY HE TOURED THE COUNTRY, PREPARING FOR THE ALL-IN-AFRICA CONFERENCE IN MARCH 1961.
WINNIE, THE TRIAL IS ADJOURNED. BUT I WILL SOON BE ATTENDING THE CONFERENCE.
LIFE WITH YOU IS LIKE LIFE WITHOUT YOU...
I MUST GO TO EVELYN'S TO SAY GOODBYE TO MAKGATHO AND MAKI BEFORE I GO UNDERGROUND. I WON'T BE ABLE TO SEE THEMBI. HE IS IN THE TRANSKEI.
MANDELA LEFT FOR PIETERMARITZBURG, KNOWING THAT HE WOULD GO INTO HIDING AS SOON AS THE TREASON TRIAL ENDED.

MANDELA MADE HIS FIRST PUBLIC SPEECH IN FIVE YEARS AT THE CONFERENCE.
WE CALL FOR AFRICAN UNITY WHERE ALL SOUTH AFRICANS CREATE A NEW CONSTITUTION...
POWER IS OURS
IF THE GOVERNMENT REFUSES TO LISTEN WE WILL START WITH MORE MILITANT CAMPAIGNS! WE WILL GET SUPPORT FROM OUTSIDE SOUTH AFRICA!
AMANDLA NGAWETHU!
OUR PEOPLE ARE READY FOR A PROLONGED STRUGGLE.
MANDELA WROTE TO VERWOERD REQUESTING A NATIONAL MEETING ABOUT A CONSTITUTION. THERE WAS NO REPLY. A STRIKE WAS PLANNED TO COINCIDE WITH THE GOVERNMENT'S PROCLAMATION OF SOUTH AFRICA AS A REPUBLIC. MANDELA ORGANISED IT.
ON 29 MARCH 1961, AFTER FIVE YEARS, THE TREASON TRIAL ENDED. JUSTICE RUMPFF HANDED DOWN HIS VERDICT.
NOT GUILTY! THE ANC DID NOT TRY TO OVERTHROW THE STATE WITH VIOLENCE... THE PROSECUTION FAILED TO PROVE THEY ARE COMMUNISTS.
DESPITE THE RELIEF, MANDELA KNEW HE WOULD NOW LIVE IN THE SHADOWS – ORGANISING THE ANC FROM UNDERGROUND – A LONELY AND DANGEROUS LIFE...
MAY THE GODS OF AFRICA BE WITH HIM...

SOON AFTER MANDELA WENT UNDERGROUND, ANOTHER WARRANT FOR HIS ARREST WAS ISSUED. BY THIS TIME, HE WAS TRAVELLING SECRETLY AROUND THE COUNTRY. IN PORT ELIZABETH, HE MET WITH GOVAN MBEKI AND RAYMOND MHLABA.
SOME ARE UNHAPPY WITH THIS NEW CORE LEADERSHIP. WHAT MUST WE TELL THEM?
WE MUST REMEMBER THE ANC IS NOW ILLEGAL AND WE NEED NEW METHODS OF ORGANISING.
YES, CREATING SMALL UNDERGROUND CELLS IS WORKING WELL...
WE HAVE TO REACH THE WORKERS!
HE MET WITH RELIGIOUS GROUPS IN THE CAPE, RALLYING THEIR SUPPORT.
WE WROTE TO VERWOERD EXPLAINING THE NEED FOR A NON-RACIAL CONSTITUTION. HE HAS IGNORED US!
WE ARE CALLING FOR A STAY-AWAY FROM WORK ON REPUBLIC DAY. NO PUBLIC DEMONSTRATIONS. WE DON'T WANT MORE POLICE VIOLENCE.
IN NATAL HE VISITED SUGAR WORKERS...
WE STILL STAND FOR NON-VIOLENCE...
IN LONDON, OLIVER TAMBO WARNED THAT IF THE STAY-AWAY WAS CRUSHED, IT WOULD BE THE LAST TIME THE ANC WOULD CAMPAIGN PEACEFULLY.
MANDELA CONTACTED JOURNALISTS AROUND THE COUNTRY, INCLUDING BENJAMIN POGRUND OF THE RAND DAILY MAIL. MANDELA WAS UNDERGROUND, UNTRACEABLE AND MYSTERIOUS, THE BLACK PIMPERNEL...
I'LL KEEP YOU INFORMED. THE STAY-AWAY IS GOING AHEAD... PEACEFULLY...
THE GOVERNMENT SAYS OTHERWISE...
THAT IS AN ATTEMPT TO SMEAR OUR CAMPAIGN. WE REMAIN OPPOSED TO VIOLENCE.

BEFORE THE STRIKE EVEN STARTED THE GOVERNMENT BANNED MEETINGS, RAIDED HOMES, ARRESTED 10 000 PEOPLE, AND HAD THE LARGEST MILITARY CALL UP SINCE WORLD WAR TWO...DURING THE STAY-AWAY, MANDELA AND MEMBERS OF THE ACTION COMMITTEE STAYED AT A "SAFE HOUSE".
I CANNOT BELIEVE THIS! THE PRESS IS DOWNPLAYING THE STRIKE...
WHY ARE YOU DOWNPLAYING THE STRIKE? THE PEOPLE HEEDED OUR CALL...EVEN WITH THE PAC TRYING TO SABOTAGE OUR EFFORTS.
WE HAVE NEW REPORTS THAT THE STRIKE HAD 50% SUCCESS.
ON THE DAY OF THE STRIKE RUTH FIRST ARRANGED MANDELA'S FIRST TELEVISION INTERVIEW. HE MET WITH A REPORTER FROM BRITAIN'S ITN CHANNEL. BUT THE NEXT DAY IT WAS AGREED TO CALL THE STRIKE OFF.
THE AFRICANS REQUIRE THE FRANCHISE ON THE BASIS OF ONE MAN ONE VOTE. WE WANT POLITICAL INDEPENDENCE.
THERE ARE MANY PEOPLE WHO FEEL THAT IT IS FUTILE FOR US TO CONTINUE TALKING PEACE AND NON-VIOLENCE AGAINST A GOVERNMENT WHOSE REPLY IS ONLY SAVAGE ATTACKS ON AN UNARMED AND DEFENCELESS PEOPLE.
NOT ALL IN THE ANC AGREED WITH THE PROPOSAL TO TAKE UP ARMS. A FULL MEETING OF THE NATIONAL EXECUTIVE DISCUSSED THE ISSUE IN JULY 1961.
THE TIME HAS COME FOR US TO CONSIDER WHETHER THE METHODS WHICH WE HAVE APPLIED SO FAR ARE ADEQUATE.

THE EXECUTIVE MEETING TOOK PLACE ON A SUGARCANE FARM IN KWAZULU–NATAL...THE FORMATION OF A MILITARY WING WAS ON THE AGENDA. THERE WERE RESERVATIONS ABOUT THE USE OF VIOLENCE...
WE DO NOT WANT TO HARM CIVILIANS... LET US PURSUE A PROGRAMME OF SABOTAGE OF GOVERNMENT STRUCTURES...
AFTER MUCH DISCUSSION, MANDELA WAS APPOINTED AS COMMANDER–IN–CHIEF OF THE SPEAR OF THE NATION, UMKHONTO WE SIZWE. HE WOULD RECRUIT MEMBERS AND APPOINT ITS LEADERSHIP.
BUT NON–VIOLENCE HAS NOT FAILED US, WE HAVE FAILED NON–VIOLENCE...
THE SABOTAGE MUST BE CAREFULLY CONTROLLED.
IT WAS DECIDED THAT THE MILITARY WING WOULD OPERATE SEPARATELY FROM THE ANC, BUT ULTIMATELY REPORT TO THE ANC. IN THE DAYS THAT FOLLOWED, THE REST OF THE CONGRESS ALLIANCE HAD TO BE PERSUADED TO ACCEPT THE DECISION.
I AM GOING TO NEED PEOPLE TO HELP ME.
STILL IN HIDING, MANDELA ENDED UP AT A FLAT IN YEOVILLE WITH WOLFIE KODESH, A JOURNALIST FROM THE LEFTIST NEW AGE NEWSPAPER...
I NEED TO EXERCISE, BUT IT'S TOO RISKY TO GO RUNNING IN THE MORNING...

WHAT ARE YOU DOING!?! IT'S FIVE 'O'CLOCK IN THE MORNING!
WELL, YOU SHOULD COME AND JOIN ME.
EVENTUALLY WOLFIE DECIDED TO JOIN IN EVERY MORNING.
HOW WILL YOU KEEP BUSY WHILE I AM AT WORK?
I BELIEVE I CAN LEARN A LOT FROM THIS BOOK...
ON WAR
YES, CLAUSEWITZ WAS TO WAR WHAT SHAKESPEARE WAS TO LITERATURE.
COMMANDO
WHAT IS THAT SOUR MILK DOING IN THE WINDOW. THERE MUST BE AN AFRICAN LIVING THERE!
NELSON, IT'S GETTING TOO RISKY. YOU HAVE TO MOVE ON.
The Star
THE BLACK PIMPERNEL
CLEANERS IN THE BUILDING BECAME SUSPICIOUS...

USING THE ALIAS DAVID MOTSAMAYI, AND STAYING IN MANY SAFE HOUSES, MANDELA EVENTUALLY MOVED TO LILIESLEAF FARM IN RIVONIA. IT WAS OWNED BY THE COMMUNIST PARTY, AND USED AS A "SAFE HOUSE" BY ACTIVISTS WORKING UNDERGROUND.
HE HAD TO LEARN HOW TO BECOME A REVOLUTIONARY. THIS HE DID BY READING AND TALKING TO EXPERTS.
ACTS OF SABOTAGE ARE VERY IMPORTANT... TERRORISM IS DIFFERENT... IT MAKES VICTIMS OF INNOCENT PEOPLE!
UMKHONTO NEEDED A CONSTITUTION. MANDELA, RAYMOND MHLABA AND JOE SLOVO DREW UP A MANIFESTO.
RAY, WE'VE ARRANGED FOR YOUR MILITARY TRAINING IN CHINA.
I AM READY.
WHO CAN THAT BE?
DAD!
THE MANDELA HOME WAS CONSTANTLY UNDER POLICE SURVEILLANCE. WITH THE HELP OF FRIENDS, WINNIE MANAGED TO VISIT WITH THE CHILDREN OCCASIONALLY.
HOW IS YOUR JOB AT CHILD WELFARE GOING?
I AM DOING FINE. AND YOU, MY DEAR, HAVE BECOME THE MOST WANTED MAN IN THE COUNTRY!
IT WAS NOT EASY BEING A FATHER, HUSBAND, REVOLUTIONARY LEADER AND FUGITIVE FROM THE LAW.

WHEN ARE YOU COMING HOME?

MANDELA POSED AS A GARDENER ON THE PROPERTY.

...BUT ALSO ATTENDED MEETINGS.

JOE SLOVO AND JACK HODGSON, WHO HAD SERVED IN WORLD WAR TWO, WERE AMONGST THOSE MANDELA MET WITH...

JACK HAS COME TO HELP US WITH SOME IDEAS FOR SABOTAGE.

NOW, IF WE TARGET THESE KEY AREAS, WE CAN DAMAGE THE LINKS BETWEEN MAJOR CENTRES IN THE COUNTRY...
YES, I SEE! MINIMUM MANPOWER, MAXIMUM EFFECT...

MANDELA, KODESH AND HODGSON WENT TO TEST THEIR HOMEMADE EXPLOSIVES AT AN UNUSED BRICKYARD.
RIGHT, LET'S DO THIS!
IT WORKED!
BOOM!!...
SO, DO YOU THINK WE ARE READY?
YES, WE HAVE FOUR REGIONS FOR TRAINING RECRUITS...THE M-PLAN IS WORKING.
I KNOW THIS IS NOT EASY ON YOU.
LET'S LISTEN TO THE RADIO... CHIEF LUTHULI IS ACCEPTING THE NOBEL PEACE PRIZE...
WINNIE VISITED MANDELA AS OFTEN AS POSSIBLE. SOME THOUGHT THEY WERE BECOMING TOO CARELESS...

...CHIEF ALBERT LUTHULI, NATIONAL LEADER OF THE ANC IN SOUTH AFRICA, HAS JUST ACCEPTED THE NOBEL PEACE PRIZE IN OSLO, NORWAY...
NOW... THIS GIVES THE ANC REAL INTERNATIONAL ENDORSEMENT!
IT IS IRONIC THAT THE CHIEF IS RECEIVING A PRIZE FOR PEACE, JUST DAYS BEFORE OUR FIRST PLANNED ACTS OF SABOTAGE!
THE WORLD IS BEHIND US NOW! THE GOVERNMENT HAS TO LISTEN.
ON 16 DECEMBER 1961, ELECTRICAL SUBSTATIONS AND GOVERNMENT BUILDINGS IN JOHANNESBURG AND PORT ELIZABETH BECAME THE TARGETS OF UMKHONTO SABOTAGE.
UMKHONTO WE SIZWE
SPEAR OF THE NATION
THE TIME COMES IN THE LIFE OF ANY NATION WHEN THERE REMAIN ONLY TWO CHOICES SUBMIT OR FIGHT!
THAT TIME HAS NOW COME TO SOUTH AFRICA
UMKHONTO WE SIZWE
SPEAR OF THE NATION
THE TIME COMES IN THE LIFE OF ANY NATION WHEN THERE REMAIN ONLY TWO CHOICES SUBMIT OR FIGHT!
THAT TIME HAS N
COME TO SOUTH AFR
UMKHONTO WE SIZWE
SPEAR OF THE NATION
THE TIME COMES IN THE LIFE OF ANY NATION WHEN THERE REMAIN ONLY TWO CHOICES SUBMIT OR FIGHT!
THAT TIME HAS NOW COME TO SOUTH AFRICA

THE ANC WAS INVITED TO ATTEND THE PAN-AFRICAN FREEDOM MOVEMENT FOR EAST, CENTRAL AND SOUTHERN AFRICA CONFERENCE IN ADDIS ABABA, ETHIOPIA. MANDELA WAS ASKED TO REPRESENT THE ANC.
CHIEF LUTHULI, I WILL BE LEAVING SOON. I WILL NEED ALL THE SUPPORT I CAN GET.
BUT OF COURSE. WE NEED A STRONG LEADER TO REPRESENT US IN AFRICA!
I DON'T KNOW WHEN I WILL RETURN.
THE JOURNEY BEGAN WITH A TRIP OUT OF THE COUNTRY, TO BECHUANALAND (BOTSWANA) IN JANUARY 1962...
WHAT LIES AHEAD? WILL THE BLACK PIMPERNEL RETURN?

4

THE TRIALIST

MANDELA: TO LIVE OR DIE ?

THIS IS THE PALACE OF JUSTICE – THE HIGH COURT – WHERE THE RIVONIA TRIAL TOOK PLACE. THE BUILDING WAS RESTORED TO ITS ORIGINAL STATE IN 2002.

MANDELA, STILL ON THE RUN, LEFT JOHANNESBURG ON 10 JANUARY 1962 TO LEAD THE ANC'S DELEGATION AT THE PAFMECSA* CONFERENCE IN ADDIS ABABA, ETHIOPIA. THE FIRST STOP ON HIS JOURNEY WAS TANZANIA.
* PAN AFRICAN FREEDOM MOVEMENT FOR EAST, CENTRAL AND SOUTHERN AFRICA.
...FOR THE FIRST TIME, I AM NOT JUDGED BY THE COLOUR OF MY SKIN...
HIS JOURNEY HAD ANOTHER PURPOSE: TO PERSUADE AFRICAN GOVERNMENTS TO PROVIDE WEAPONS AND TRAINING TO UMKHONTO WE SIZWE (MK).
BUT HE SOON FOUND THAT MANY AFRICAN LEADERS WERE NOT AS SUPPORTIVE OF MK AS HE HAD HOPED. THEY OBJECTED TO THE ANC'S ALLIANCE WITH OTHER RACE GROUPS.
THE ANC AND PAC SPLIT IS A GRAVE CONCERN. AFRICAN FREEDOM FIGHTERS MUST BE UNITED!
WE CAN'T EXCLUDE PEOPLE FROM THE STRUGGLE BECAUSE OF THEIR SKIN COLOUR...
HE MET WITH PRESIDENT JULIUS NYERERE, WHO SUGGESTED TO MANDELA THAT THE ARMED STRUGGLE BE POSTPONED UNTIL THE PAC'S ROBERT SOBUKWE WAS RELEASED FROM PRISON.
GOOD TO SEE YOU, OLIVER!
I COULD NOT BE CERTAIN YOU WOULD ARRIVE.
MANDELA THEN FLEW TO WEST AFRICA, AND WAS REUNITED WITH OLIVER TAMBO IN NIGERIA.
I HAVE TO BRIEF YOU ABOUT MK. I KNOW IT MAKES YOUR JOB OUTSIDE THE COUNTRY EVEN MORE DIFFICULT...
YES, OUR INTERNATIONAL PROFILE IS IMPORTANT. BUT WE'LL REMIND THE WESTERN WORLD THAT THE WAR AGAINST THE NAZIS WAS A JUST WAR, JUST LIKE THE WAR AGAINST THE EVILS OF APARTHEID!

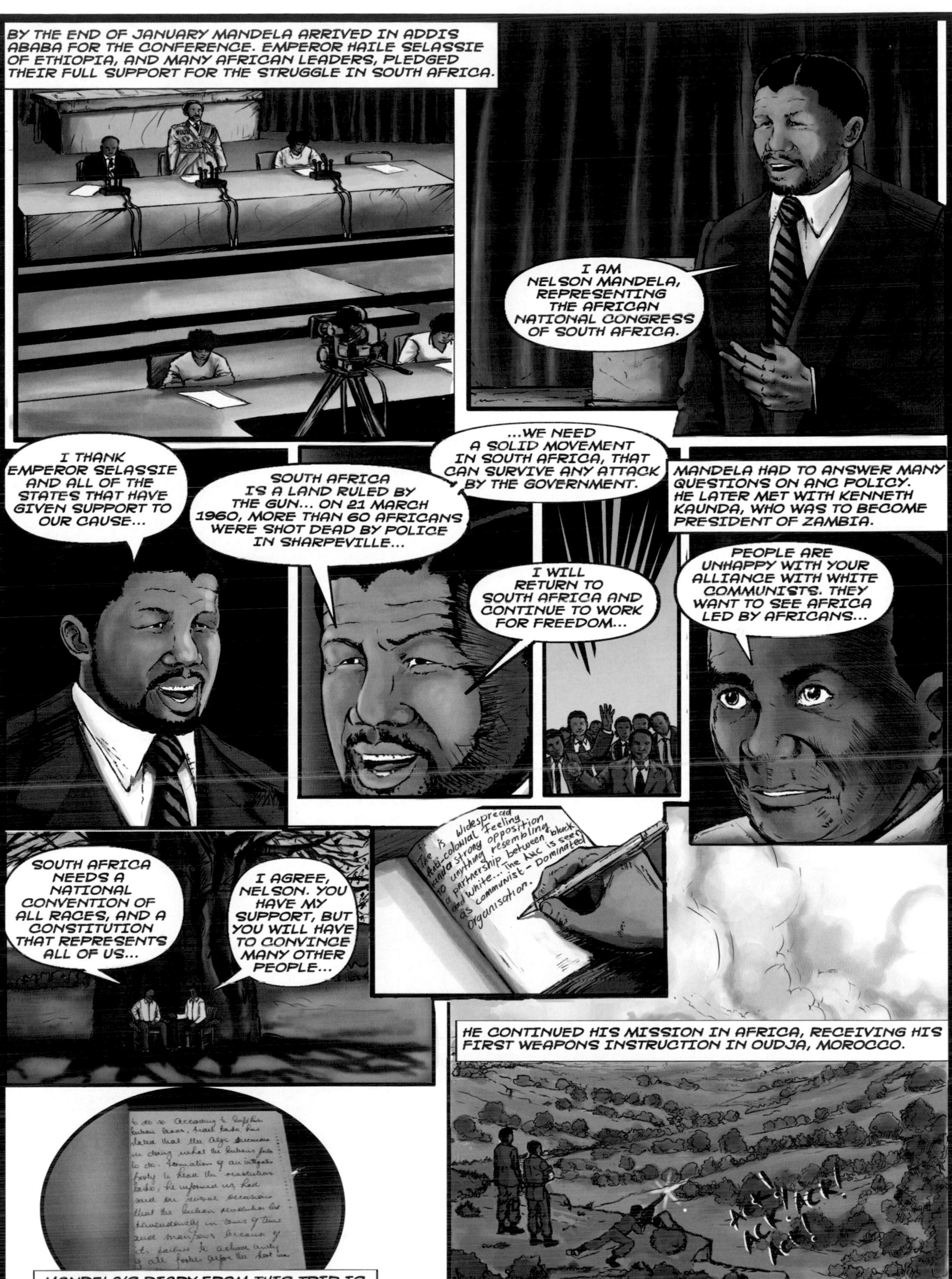

BY THE END OF JANUARY MANDELA ARRIVED IN ADDIS ABABA FOR THE CONFERENCE. EMPEROR HAILE SELASSIE OF ETHIOPIA, AND MANY AFRICAN LEADERS, PLEDGED THEIR FULL SUPPORT FOR THE STRUGGLE IN SOUTH AFRICA.
I AM NELSON MANDELA, REPRESENTING THE AFRICAN NATIONAL CONGRESS OF SOUTH AFRICA.
I THANK EMPEROR SELASSIE AND ALL OF THE STATES THAT HAVE GIVEN SUPPORT TO OUR CAUSE...
SOUTH AFRICA IS A LAND RULED BY THE GUN... ON 21 MARCH 1960, MORE THAN 60 AFRICANS WERE SHOT DEAD BY POLICE IN SHARPEVILLE...
...WE NEED A SOLID MOVEMENT IN SOUTH AFRICA, THAT CAN SURVIVE ANY ATTACK BY THE GOVERNMENT.
I WILL RETURN TO SOUTH AFRICA AND CONTINUE TO WORK FOR FREEDOM...
MANDELA HAD TO ANSWER MANY QUESTIONS ON ANC POLICY. HE LATER MET WITH KENNETH KAUNDA, WHO WAS TO BECOME PRESIDENT OF ZAMBIA.
PEOPLE ARE UNHAPPY WITH YOUR ALLIANCE WITH WHITE COMMUNISTS. THEY WANT TO SEE AFRICA LED BY AFRICANS...
SOUTH AFRICA NEEDS A NATIONAL CONVENTION OF ALL RACES, AND A CONSTITUTION THAT REPRESENTS ALL OF US...
I AGREE, NELSON. YOU HAVE MY SUPPORT, BUT YOU WILL HAVE TO CONVINCE MANY OTHER PEOPLE...
The is widespread Anti-colonial Feeling and a strong opposition to anything resembling a partnership between black and white... The ANC is seen as communist - Dominated organisation.
HE CONTINUED HIS MISSION IN AFRICA, RECEIVING HIS FIRST WEAPONS INSTRUCTION IN OUDJA, MOROCCO.
MANDELA'S DIARY FROM THIS TRIP IS HELD AT THE BRENTHURST LIBRARY IN JOHANNESBURG.

HE TRAVELLED TO MANY PARTS OF AFRICA. IN SENEGAL, HE AND TAMBO MET WITH PRESIDENT LEOPOLD SENGHOR.
COUGH!! COUGH!! COUGH!!
YOU'RE SICK, OLIVER, WE SHOULD GET YOU BACK TO THE HOTEL...
NO, THE MEETING IS TOO IMPORTANT...
I WILL CARRY YOU!
WE HAVE GREAT RESPECT FOR CHIEF LUTHULI. WE WILL DO ALL WE CAN TO ASSIST...
TAMBO WAS BEDRIDDEN FOR A FEW DAYS, AND AS SOON AS HE WAS FIT ENOUGH, THEY TRAVELLED TO LONDON FOR MEETINGS WITH BRITISH POLITICIANS, JOURNALISTS, SOUTH AFRICAN ACTIVISTS AND INTERNATIONAL SUPPORTERS...
ONE OF THESE MEETINGS WAS WITH CANON JOHN COLLINS... INTERNATIONAL FUNDRAISER AND A LEADER OF THE ANTI-APARTHEID CAMPAIGN.
IT'S GOOD TO SEE YOU, NELSON.
WE COULD NOT HAVE CONTINUED WITHOUT YOUR SUPPORT...
WE WILL SEE TODD AND ESME MATSHIKIZA FROM SOWETO!
TODD, A JOURNALIST AND COMPOSER OF THE AFRICAN MUSICAL HIT, KING KONG, AND HIS WIFE LIVED IN EXILE IN LONDON...
WHY GO BACK TO SUCH A LIFE, NELSON?
THE POLICE HAVE BEEN HUNTING ME FOR TEN MONTHS NOW...
I NEED TO BE PART OF THE STRUGGLE BACK HOME...
BEFORE LEAVING LONDON, MANDELA MET WITH OLD FRIEND AND INDIAN CONGRESS LEADER, YUSUF DADOO...
YUSUF, OUR POLICY OF MULTI-RACIALISM IS NOT ACCEPTED BY MANY LEADERS IN AFRICA. WE HAVE TO CHANGE OUR IMAGE!
ARE YOU SUGGESTING WE CHANGE OUR POLICY?!?
NO! BUT WE HAVE TO TAKE THESE VIEWS SERIOUSLY, AND PERHAPS EVEN CHANGE THE PUBLIC FACE OF THE ANC...

AFTER TEN DAYS IN LONDON, MANDELA WENT BACK TO AFRICA FOR SIX MONTHS' MILITARY TRAINING IN ETHIOPIA.
BOOM!!!
...BUT HIS STAY LASTED ONLY TWO WEEKS. AN URGENT TELEGRAM ASKED HIM TO RETURN HOME... MK NEEDED ITS COMMANDER-IN-CHIEF.
MANDELA ARRIVED BACK AT LILIESLEAF ON 24 JULY 1962.
I HAD BETTER HIDE THIS WEAPON WELL!
WINNIE HAD HEARD OF HIS ARRIVAL, AND WAS TAKEN TO LILIESLEAF IN AN AMBULANCE, POSING AS A PREGNANT WOMAN...TO EVADE THE POLICE...
AMBULANCE
WEE-WAAA!
WEE-WAAA
THEY WOULDN'T STOP AN AMBULANCE?!?
I AM SO HAPPY TO SEE YOU ARE SAFE!

AT LILIESLEAF, MANDELA REPORTED TO THE ANC NATIONAL WORKING COMMITTEE.
I HAVE TO TELL CHIEF LUTHULI ABOUT THE PROBLEMS I ENCOUNTERED.
IT'S NOT SAFE TO TRAVEL NOW...
KATHY, I HAVE TO GO. THE CHIEF THINKS I'VE ABANDONED OUR POLICIES!
POSING AS A CHAUFFEUR TO CECIL WILLIAMS, A CONGRESS ALLIANCE ACTIVIST, MANDELA DROVE TO KWAZULU-NATAL TO SEE CHIEF LUTHULI.
CHIEF LUTHULI WAS NOT HAPPY WHEN HE HEARD THE OPINIONS OF THE OTHER AFRICAN LEADERS.
THEY HAVE NO RIGHT TO DICTATE TO US!
THEY ARE NOT DICTATING TO US... THIS IS THE WAY THAT MANY AFRICAN LEADERS VIEW THE ANC...
ON 5 AUGUST 1962 MANDELA AND WILLIAMS LEFT FOR JOHANNESBURG...THIS TIME WILLIAMS DROVE.
WE'VE GOT TROUBLE!!
POLICE! ALL THESE MONTHS OF FREEDOM... ENDED!
MANDELA HURRIEDLY HID A GUN AND TRAVEL DIARY UNDER THE SEAT.

¡¡¡¡¡¡¡!
SURROUNDED, MANDELA CONTEMPLATED AN ESCAPE, BUT WAS QUICKLY APPROACHED BY THE POLICE...
NAME?
DAVID MOTSAMAYI.
WE KNOW YOU ARE NELSON MANDELA!
THEY ARRESTED MANDELA OUTSIDE HOWICK, KWAZULU-NATAL. THE "BLACK PIMPERNEL" HAD EVADED CAPTURE FOR 17 MONTHS...
IT'S TOO SOON!
HE WAS TRANSFERRED TO A PRISON IN JOHANNESBURG WHERE HE WAS ALLOWED TO CONSULT WITH OLD FRIEND JOE SLOVO, A LAWYER. AT THE SAME TIME SISULU HAD BEEN ARRESTED...
I'VE BEEN TOLD THAT THEY HAVE...
PLEASE ENSURE MY DIARIES AT LILIESLEAF HAVE BEEN REMOVED.
I WILL CONDUCT MY OWN DEFENCE, BUT I WILL NEED YOU, JOE...
THE FREE MANDELA COMMITTEE WAS SET UP, WITH KATHRADA AS ITS SECRETARY. PROTEST MEETINGS WERE HELD THROUGHOUT THE COUNTRY.
NO MORE CHAINS
FREE MANDELA.
FREE US!
MANDELA IS IN PRISON the PEOPLE ARE IN CHAINS

IN PRISON MANDELA REGISTERED FOR A LAW DEGREE THROUGH THE UNIVERSITY OF LONDON.
HOW ARE YOU AND THE CHILDREN DOING, WINNIE?
THINGS ARE DIFFICULT, BRAM, BUT WE'RE COPING.
CONDITIONS WERE TOUGH FOR WINNIE AND BRAM FISCHER ADVISED HER TO LEAVE THE COUNTRY.
BUT WINNIE'S COMMITMENT TO THE STRUGGLE WAS STRONG. SHE WAS INVITED TO SPEAK TO THE INDIAN YOUTH CONGRESS. THIS WAS HER FIRST PUBLIC APPEARANCE.
I SPEAK FOR MY HUSBAND, WHO CANNOT BE HERE...
I AM VERY PROUD OF YOU!
YOU HAVE BEEN ELECTED AS HONORARY PRESIDENT OF THE INDIAN YOUTH CONGRESS!
THE OLD FORT STILL STANDS IN JOHANNESBURG AND HAS BEEN TURNED INTO A MUSEUM.
AFTER HER SPEECH, WINNIE WENT TO THE OLD FORT TO VISIT MANDELA.

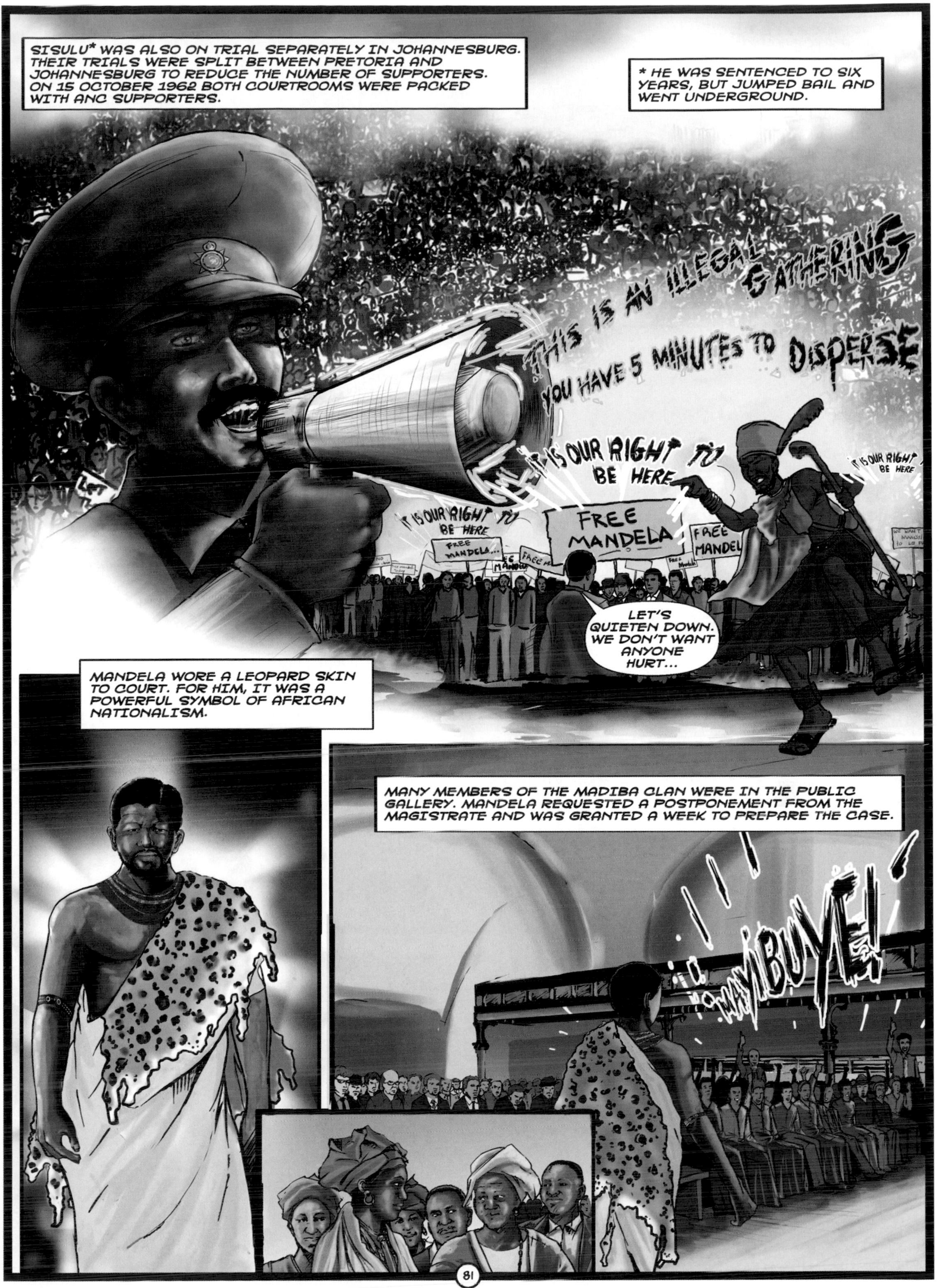
SISULU* WAS ALSO ON TRIAL SEPARATELY IN JOHANNESBURG. THEIR TRIALS WERE SPLIT BETWEEN PRETORIA AND JOHANNESBURG TO REDUCE THE NUMBER OF SUPPORTERS. ON 15 OCTOBER 1962 BOTH COURTROOMS WERE PACKED WITH ANC SUPPORTERS.
* HE WAS SENTENCED TO SIX YEARS, BUT JUMPED BAIL AND WENT UNDERGROUND.
THIS IS AN ILLEGAL GATHERING
YOU HAVE 5 MINUTES TO DISPERSE
IT IS OUR RIGHT TO BE HERE
IT IS OUR RIGHT TO BE HERE
IT IS OUR RIGHT TO BE HERE
FREE MANDELA
FREE MANDELA...
FREE MANDEL
LET'S QUIETEN DOWN. WE DON'T WANT ANYONE HURT...
MANDELA WORE A LEOPARD SKIN TO COURT. FOR HIM, IT WAS A POWERFUL SYMBOL OF AFRICAN NATIONALISM.
MANY MEMBERS OF THE MADIBA CLAN WERE IN THE PUBLIC GALLERY. MANDELA REQUESTED A POSTPONEMENT FROM THE MAGISTRATE AND WAS GRANTED A WEEK TO PREPARE THE CASE.
MAYIBUYE!

THE AUTHORITIES TRIED TO CONFISCATE MANDELA'S LEOPARD SKIN KAROSS.
THE COLONEL HAS ORDERED YOU TO HAND OVER THAT BLANKET!
TELL YOUR BOSS HE CANNOT HAVE MY KAROSS. IF YOU TOUCH IT, I WILL TAKE YOU TO COURT!
WHY AM I FACING A WHITE MAGISTRATE... A WHITE PROSECUTOR... WHITE ORDERLIES? ...I AM A BLACK MAN IN A WHITE MAN'S COURT.
DID YOU GIVE THIS LETTER TO THE PRIME MINISTER?
YES.
THE PROSECUTION CALLED MORE THAN 100 WITNESSES. MANDELA DID NOT DISPUTE THE CHARGES, BUT VIGOROUSLY CROSS-EXAMINED MR BARNARD, SECRETARY TO PRIME MINISTER VERWOERD.
HE DID NOT REPLY TO THE LETTER. NOW WILL YOU AGREE THAT THIS LETTER RAISES MATTERS OF VITAL CONCERN?
I DO NOT AGREE.
IN THE LETTER MANDELA HAD DEMANDED A NATIONAL CONVENTION OF ALL RACES...
WOULD YOU AGREE THAT IN ANY CIVILISED COUNTRY IT WOULD BE SCANDALOUS FOR A PRIME MINISTER TO FAIL TO REPLY TO A LETTER RAISING VITAL ISSUES AFFECTING THE MAJORITY OF ITS CITIZENS?
I DON'T AGREE!

IS THAT ALL YOU HAVE TO SAY?
I PLEAD NOT GUILTY.
MY PLEA IS THAT I WAS MADE, BY THE LAW, A CRIMINAL, NOT BECAUSE OF WHAT I HAD DONE, BUT BECAUSE OF WHAT I STOOD FOR, BECAUSE OF WHAT I THOUGHT, BECAUSE OF MY CONSCIENCE.
...NO MAN IN HIS RIGHT SENSES WOULD CHOOSE THE LIFE OF A MAN HUNTED CONTINUOUSLY BY POLICE...
I SENTENCE YOU TO THREE YEARS' IMPRISONMENT FOR INCITING WORKERS TO STRIKE AND TWO YEARS FOR LEAVING THE COUNTRY ILLEGALLY.
AMANDLA!!...
POWER!!...
ITS OURS
KE A RONA!!
ON THE SAME DAY THERE WERE EXPLOSIONS IN PORT ELIZABETH AND DURBAN, IN PROTEST AGAINST MANDELA'S SENTENCING.

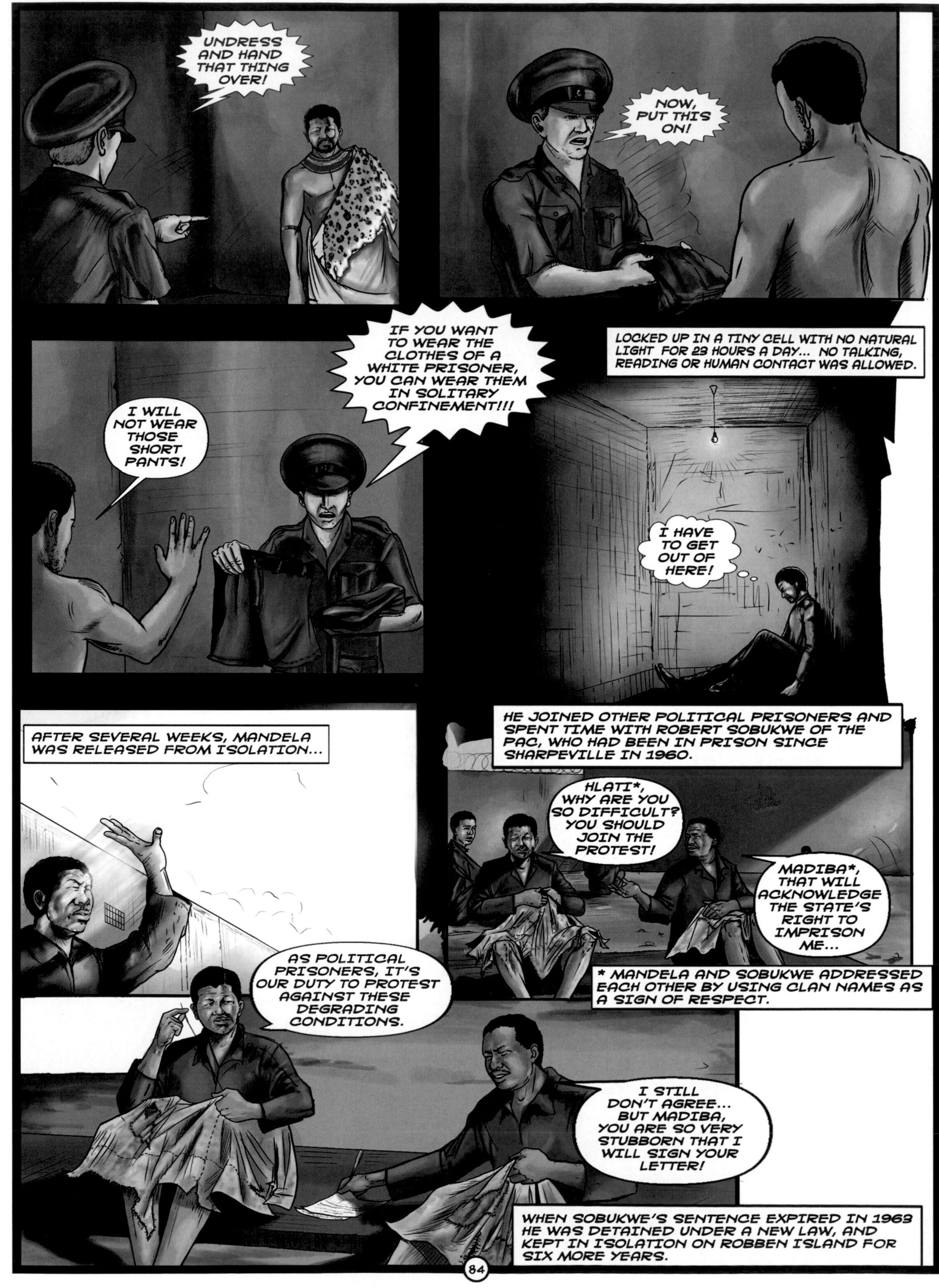
UNDRESS AND HAND THAT THING OVER!
NOW, PUT THIS ON!
I WILL NOT WEAR THOSE SHORT PANTS!
IF YOU WANT TO WEAR THE CLOTHES OF A WHITE PRISONER, YOU CAN WEAR THEM IN SOLITARY CONFINEMENT!!!
LOCKED UP IN A TINY CELL WITH NO NATURAL LIGHT FOR 23 HOURS A DAY... NO TALKING, READING OR HUMAN CONTACT WAS ALLOWED.
I HAVE TO GET OUT OF HERE!
AFTER SEVERAL WEEKS, MANDELA WAS RELEASED FROM ISOLATION...
HE JOINED OTHER POLITICAL PRISONERS AND SPENT TIME WITH ROBERT SOBUKWE OF THE PAC, WHO HAD BEEN IN PRISON SINCE SHARPEVILLE IN 1960.
HLATI*, WHY ARE YOU SO DIFFICULT? YOU SHOULD JOIN THE PROTEST!
MADIBA*, THAT WILL ACKNOWLEDGE THE STATE'S RIGHT TO IMPRISON ME...
* MANDELA AND SOBUKWE ADDRESSED EACH OTHER BY USING CLAN NAMES AS A SIGN OF RESPECT.
AS POLITICAL PRISONERS, IT'S OUR DUTY TO PROTEST AGAINST THESE DEGRADING CONDITIONS.
I STILL DON'T AGREE... BUT MADIBA, YOU ARE SO VERY STUBBORN THAT I WILL SIGN YOUR LETTER!
WHEN SOBUKWE'S SENTENCE EXPIRED IN 1963 HE WAS DETAINED UNDER A NEW LAW, AND KEPT IN ISOLATION ON ROBBEN ISLAND FOR SIX MORE YEARS.

ON 24 MAY, WITHOUT WARNING, MANDELA WAS MOVED TO ROBBEN ISLAND. EIGHT MILES OFF THE COAST OF CAPE TOWN, THE ISLAND HAD, AMONGST OTHER USES, SERVED AS A PRISON FOR XHOSA CHIEFS IN THE 19TH CENTURY, A LEPER COLONY, A MENTAL ASYLUM, A WORLD WAR TWO BASE AND A PRISON. PRISONERS INCLUDED POLITICAL AND RELIGIOUS LEADERS FROM THE EAST INDIES WHO HAD FOUGHT AGAINST DUTCH COLONIAL RULE.

MOVE! MOVE! THIS IS NOT PRETORIA!

PUT TO WORK, MANDELA SAW HIS NEPHEW DIGGING A DITCH.
NQABENI, IS THAT YOU?
MADIBA!

MANDELA'S DISCUSSIONS DURING HIS RECENT AFRICA TRIP HAD STARTED RUMOURS...
UNCLE, I HEAR YOU HAVE JOINED THE PAC?
NO, THAT'S NOT TRUE.

IN THE MEANTIME, THE REST OF MK'S LEADERSHIP CONTINUED TO GATHER AT LILIESLEAF. THIS WAS INCREASINGLY RISKY, SINCE THE GOVERNMENT PLACED ADVERTISEMENTS IN NEWSPAPERS OFFERING LARGE SUMS OF MONEY TO INFORMERS...
WE NEED ONE MORE MEETING HERE AT LILIESLEAF TO DISCUSS OPERATION MAYIBUYE*...
EVERYONE SHOULD BE MORE CAREFUL!!
LILIESLEAF IS NO LONGER SAFE FOR US... TOO MANY PEOPLE KNOW ABOUT IT.
* OPERATION MAYIBUYE WAS A PROPOSAL FOR THE START OF GUERRILLA OPERATIONS WHICH WERE NEVER FORMALLY ENDORSED BY THE ANC.
MK'S SABOTAGE CAMPAIGN CONTINUED IN A BID TO BRING THE GOVERNMENT TO ITS SENSES ...
WHITES ONLY
SLEGS BLANKES
Be brave my love...
remember now that I am in
prison you have an important
position in the community...
Be careful of people who
will try to trick you...
SUNDAY POST
SABOTAGE ROCKS S.A
MANDELA AND WINNIE WERE DUE TO HAVE THEIR FIRST VISIT IN APRIL 1963. THEIR HOPES WERE DASHED IN DECEMBER 1962 WHEN WINNIE WAS BANNED. ALSO, AUTHORITIES DID NOT INFORM HER WHEN MANDELA WAS MOVED TO ROBBEN ISLAND.

ON 11 JULY 1963, THE FINAL MEETING WAS HELD AT LILIESLEAF IN RIVONIA...
MINUTES AFTER THE MEETING STARTED, THE POLICE SWOOPED.

GO! GO!

THEY ARRESTED EVERYONE PRESENT – WALTER SISULU, AHMED KATHRADA, GOVAN MBEKI, RAYMOND MHLABA, BOB HEPPLE, DENIS GOLDBERG AND RUSTY BERNSTEIN.
DOEF
DOEF

WHOOF!
WHOOF!

MOST OF THE MEN WERE IN DISGUISE. SISULU TRIED TO ESCAPE THROUGH A WINDOW AND KATHRADA ALSO TRIED TO GET AWAY.
GRR
STOP OR WE SHOOT!

ARTHUR GOLDREICH WAS ALSO ARRESTED AT LILIESLEAF, BUT NOT AT THE SAME TIME AS THE FIRST GROUP. ELIAS MOTSOALEDI, ANDREW MLANGENI, JAMES KANTOR AND HAROLD WOLPE WERE ARRESTED ELSEWHERE.

MANDELA WAS TRANSFERRED BACK TO PRETORIA UNAWARE OF THE ARRESTS AT LILIESLEAF. AGAIN, HE WAS ISOLATED IN A SINGLE CELL. HE WAS UNAWARE THAT HIS TRAVEL DIARY AND MANY DOCUMENTS IN HIS HANDWRITING WERE SEIZED AT THE FARM – THE DOCUMENTS HAD NOT BEEN REMOVED AS HE HAD REQUESTED.
THOMAS MASHIFANE!?!
IF THEY GOT THOMAS, THEY MUST HAVE GOT TO LILIESLEAF!

THOSE ARRESTED AT LILIESLEAF WERE DETAINED AT PRETORIA PRISON UNDER THE NINETY-DAY DETENTION LAW... MOOSA MOOLA, ABDULHAY JASSAT, HAROLD WOLPE AND ARTHUR GOLDREICH, WHO WERE HELD AT MARSHALL SQUARE POLICE STATION, MANAGED TO ESCAPE...

AFTER THEIR ORDEAL IN SOLITARY CONFINEMENT THEY WERE FINALLY CHARGED AND WERE ALLOWED TO MEET EACH OTHER AND THE LAWYERS THEIR FAMILIES HAD ARRANGED.

NELSON! YOU'VE LOST WEIGHT!
IT IS THE COLD PORRIDGE!
THIS IS SERIOUS! THE STATE WILL ASK FOR THE DEATH PENALTY...

THEY WERE TO BE DEFENDED BY BRAM FISCHER, VERNON BERRANGE, JOEL JOFFE, GEORGE BIZOS AND ARTHUR CHASKALSON...BUT JIMMY KANTOR AND BOB HEPPLE'S SITUATIONS WERE NOT SO EASY TO DEAL WITH...

I HAVE TO SEPARATE MY TRIAL FROM THE REST. I AM ONLY HERE BECAUSE MY BROTHER-IN-LAW, WOLPE, ESCAPED!
... AND I HAVE BEEN ASKED TO BE A STATE WITNESS... I AM STILL CONSIDERING WHAT TO DO...

THE STATE VERSUS THE NATIONAL HIGH COMMAND AND OTHERS BEGAN AT THE PALACE OF JUSTICE, THE SUPREME COURT IN PRETORIA, ON 9 OCTOBER 1963. MANDELA, THE CONVICTED PRISONER, WAS KEPT SEPARATELY FROM THE OTHERS.
THEY HAVE GIVEN US THE JUDGE-PRESIDENT, QUARTUS DE WET! I'VE HEARD HE IS CONSERVATIVE BUT HE DOES NOT LIKE THE GOVERNMENT TELLING HIM WHAT TO DO!
DR PERCY YUTAR, THE DEPUTY ATTORNEY GENERAL OF THE TRANSVAAL PROVINCE, WAS TO PROSECUTE THE MEN...
ON BEHALF OF THE PROSECUTION I DELIVER THIS INDICTMENT TO PROVE THE GUILT OF ALL THOSE CHARGED.
FOR THE DEFENCE, WE SEE THAT MR MANDELA IS CHARGED WITH 156 ACTS OF SABOTAGE, ALL OF WHICH OCCURRED WHILE HE WAS IN PRISON...THEY COULD NOT HAVE BEEN COMMITTED BY MY CLIENT.
THE COURT ADJOURNED FOR THREE WEEKS TO ALLOW THE DEFENCE TO STUDY THE INDICTMENT. IT WAS A VAGUE, UNCLEAR DOCUMENT HASTILY PUT TOGETHER BY YUTAR.
I EARNESTLY BEG YOUR LORDSHIP, NAY, CRAVE YOUR LORDSHIP, NOT TO QUASH THE INDICTMENT!
IT IS OBVIOUSLY DEFECTIVE. I ORDER IT QUASHED!
RAW
WE'RE FREE!
WE ARE ARRESTING EACH OF YOU ON A CHARGE OF SABOTAGE!
YUTAR'S EFFORTS WERE DISMISSED BY THE JUDGE, AND FOR A FEW MOMENTS THE DEFENDANTS WERE FREE...
WITHIN MINUTES THEY WERE ALL RE-ARRESTED!

THE TRIAL BECAME KNOWN AS THE RIVONIA TRIAL. MANDELA WAS ACCUSED NO. 1...WINNIE DID NOT GET PERMISSION TO ATTEND THE FIRST DAY OF THE TRIAL – SHE APPEALED AND LATER GOT PERMISSION TO ATTEND AS LONG AS SHE DID NOT WEAR TRADITIONAL DRESS.
HOW DO YOU PLEAD?
THE GOVERNMENT SHOULD BE IN THE DOCK, NOT ME. I PLEAD NOT GUILTY.
I DON'T WANT ANY POLITICAL SPEECHES HERE. YOU MAY PLEAD GUILTY OR NOT GUILTY, BUT NOTHING ELSE!
IT IS THE GOVERNMENT THAT IS GUILTY, NOT ME.
IT IS THE GOVERNMENT THAT IS RESPONSIBLE FOR WHAT IS HAPPENING IN THIS COUNTRY. I PLEAD NOT GUILTY!
A PLOT TO COMMIT SABOTAGE, VIOLENCE AND DESTRUCTION... THE VIOLENT OVERTHROW OF THE GOVERNMENT WAS PLANNED...
THOMAS MASHIFANE, THE FOREMAN AT LILIESLEAF, WAS CALLED TO TESTIFY...
YES, I HAVE SEEN THE ACCUSED AT LILIES-LEAF...
...BUT, I'VE DONE NOTHING WRONG. WHY WAS I DETAINED AND TORTURED BY THE POLICE?
YUTAR'S STAR WITNESS, MR X, GAVE DAMNING EVIDENCE.
MANDELA IS THE COMMANDER-IN-CHIEF OF MK...
OH NO! IT'S BRUNO MTOLO...MK IN NATAL...

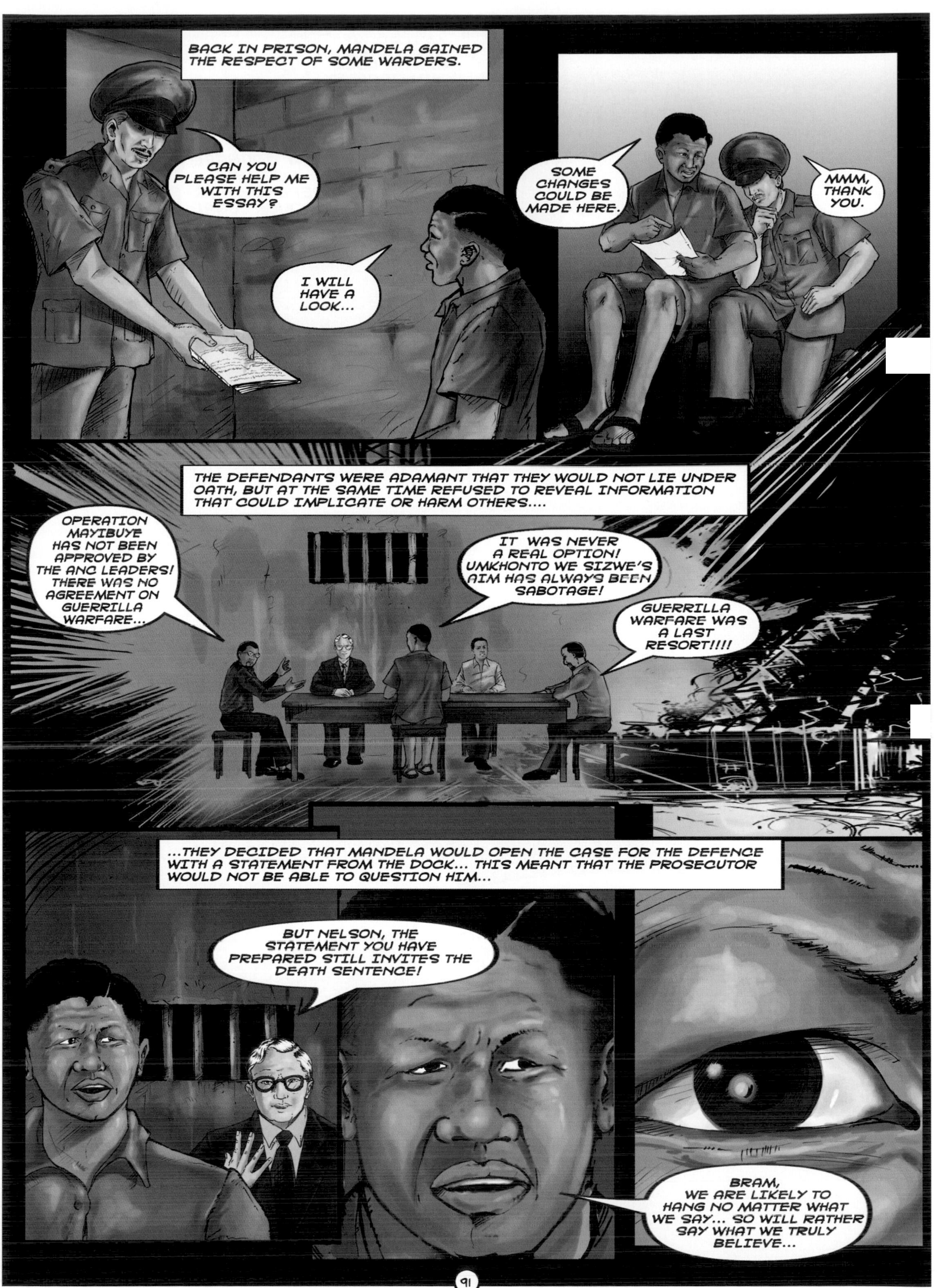
BACK IN PRISON, MANDELA GAINED THE RESPECT OF SOME WARDERS.
CAN YOU PLEASE HELP ME WITH THIS ESSAY?
I WILL HAVE A LOOK...
SOME CHANGES COULD BE MADE HERE.
MMM, THANK YOU.
THE DEFENDANTS WERE ADAMANT THAT THEY WOULD NOT LIE UNDER OATH, BUT AT THE SAME TIME REFUSED TO REVEAL INFORMATION THAT COULD IMPLICATE OR HARM OTHERS....
OPERATION MAYIBUYE HAS NOT BEEN APPROVED BY THE ANC LEADERS! THERE WAS NO AGREEMENT ON GUERRILLA WARFARE...
IT WAS NEVER A REAL OPTION! UMKHONTO WE SIZWE'S AIM HAS ALWAYS BEEN SABOTAGE!
GUERRILLA WARFARE WAS A LAST RESORT!!!!
...THEY DECIDED THAT MANDELA WOULD OPEN THE CASE FOR THE DEFENCE WITH A STATEMENT FROM THE DOCK... THIS MEANT THAT THE PROSECUTOR WOULD NOT BE ABLE TO QUESTION HIM...
BUT NELSON, THE STATEMENT YOU HAVE PREPARED STILL INVITES THE DEATH SENTENCE!
BRAM, WE ARE LIKELY TO HANG NO MATTER WHAT WE SAY... SO WILL RATHER SAY WHAT WE TRULY BELIEVE...

THE DEFENCE, MY LORD, WILL COMMENCE WITH A STATEMENT FROM THE DOCK BY MR NELSON MANDELA.
MY LORD, MY LORD! A STATEMENT FROM THE DOCK DOES NOT CARRY THE SAME WEIGHT AS EVIDENCE UNDER OATH!
I THINK THAT COUNSEL FOR THE DEFENCE HAS ENOUGH LEGAL EXPERIENCE TO ADVISE!
I AM A CONVICTED PRISONER, SERVING FIVE YEARS...
...I HAVE DONE WHATEVER I DID, BOTH AS AN INDIVIDUAL AND AS A LEADER OF MY PEOPLE... BECAUSE OF MY OWN PROUDLY FELT AFRICAN BACKGROUND, AND NOT BECAUSE OF WHAT ANY OUTSIDER MIGHT HAVE SAID...
...I LISTENED TO THE ELDERS OF MY TRIBE TELLING STORIES OF THE OLD DAYS... I HOPED THEN THAT LIFE MIGHT OFFER ME THE OPPORTUNITY TO SERVE MY PEOPLE AND MAKE MY OWN HUMBLE CONTRIBUTION TO THEIR FREEDOM STRUGGLE...
...I WAS ONE OF THE PERSONS WHO HELPED TO FORM UMKHONTO WE SIZWE... WE OF THE ANC HAD ALWAYS STOOD FOR A NON-RACIAL DEMOCRACY...
...WE DID NOT WANT TO BE COMMITTED TO CIVIL WAR...
...OUR FIGHT IS AGAINST REAL AND NOT IMAGINARY HARDSHIPS...WE FIGHT AGAINST...POVERTY AND LACK OF HUMAN DIGNITY...
...ABOVE ALL, WE WANT EQUAL POLITICAL RIGHTS...
DURING MY LIFETIME I HAVE DEDICATED MYSELF TO THIS STRUGGLE OF THE AFRICAN PEOPLE. I HAVE FOUGHT AGAINST WHITE DOMINATION, AND I HAVE FOUGHT AGAINST BLACK DOMINATION. I HAVE CHERISHED THE IDEAL OF A DEMOCRATIC AND FREE SOCIETY IN WHICH ALL PERSONS LIVE TOGETHER IN HARMONY...
...AND WITH EQUAL OPPORTUNITIES. IT IS AN IDEAL WHICH I HOPE TO LIVE FOR AND TO ACHIEVE. BUT IF NEEDS BE, IT IS AN IDEAL FOR WHICH I AM PREPARED TO DIE.

THE DEFENCE MAY CALL ITS NEXT WITNESS NOW...
ACCUSED NO. 2, WALTER SISULU, WAS CALLED. HIS CROSS-EXAMINATION LASTED FIVE DAYS. DURING THIS TIME YUTAR ENSURED THAT HE WAS ISOLATED FROM THE REST OF THE ACCUSED.
WHO WAS THE MEMBER OF UMKHONTO WHO DRAFTED THIS PAMPHLET?
YOU ARE NOT PREPARED TO ANSWER!?
I AM NOT MENTIONING ANY NAMES!
IT DOES NOT HELP TO INSIST ON A NAME... I EXPLAINED THAT ... I WILL CERTAINLY NOT ANSWER!
KATHRADA'S CROSS EXAMINATION FOLLOWED. HE DECIDED NOT TO DISCLOSE HIS FULL INVOLVEMENT IN MK, AND LIKE SISULU, REFUSED TO IMPLICATE OTHERS...
THEN HOW AM I TO TEST YOUR STORY?
IF I KNEW ANYTHING ABOUT MK, I WOULD NOT TELL YOU!
I DON'T NEED YOUR SYMPATHY! HOW WILL HIS LORDSHIP TEST THE ACCURACY OF YOUR EVIDENCE?
I FEEL SORRY FOR YOU DR YUTAR. I AM UNABLE TO HELP YOU THERE...
I AM AFRAID I DO NOT HAVE ANY SUGGESTIONS!

BERNSTEIN, MBEKI, GOLDBERG AND MHLABA'S CROSS-EXAMINATION FOLLOWED. THE DEFENCE DECIDED NOT TO CALL MOTSOALEDI AND MLANGENI AS THEY WERE NOT PART OF THE ANC LEADERSHIP.
INSTEAD THEY DELIVERED STATEMENTS FROM THE DOCK...BOTH TESTIFIED TO BEING TORTURED DURING THEIR NINETY-DAY DETENTION...
...I KNOW THAT YOU, MY LORD, HAVE TO ADMINISTER THE LAW, BUT WHEN YOU DO SO, I ASK YOU TO REMEMBER THAT WE, THE AFRICANS AND NON-WHITE PEOPLE, HAVE TO SUFFER...
I HAVE SUFFERED MANY ASSAULTS IN POLICE DETENTION, AND CAN SHOW YOU EVIDENCE OF THE PHYSICAL TORTURE PEOPLE HAVE SUFFERED...
THIS IS A CLASSIC CASE OF AN INTENTION TO OVERTHROW THE GOVERNMENT BY FORCE AND VIOLENCE!
AT LAST, ON 11 JUNE 1964, THE JUDGE DELIVERED HIS VERDICT TO A PACKED COURTROOM, DESPITE ATTEMPTS BY POLICE TO KEEP SUPPORTERS AWAY...
STOP!! HAND ME YOUR PASSES
STOP
NKOSI SIKELEL' I'AFRIKA!!
WE STAND BY OUR LEADERS!!
ALL BUT RUSTY BERNSTEIN WERE FOUND GUILTY. THE MEN WERE DRIVEN BACK TO PRISON AND THEIR DEFENCE TEAM SET OFF TO PREPARE PLEAS IN MITIGATION OF SENTENCE... THE NEXT DAY THE JUDGE WOULD RULE ON WHETHER THEY WOULD LIVE OR DIE...

THE SENTENCE IN THE CASE OF ALL THOSE FOUND GUILTY WILL BE ONE OF LIFE IMPRISONMENT.
GOODBYE MY SON
GOODBYE MADIBA
DAD!
AMANDLA!!...
NGAWETHU!...
FREE MANDELA
WE STAND BY OUR LEADER
LONG LIVE MANDELA
LATER THAT NIGHT THE PRISONERS, HANDCUFFED AND SHACKLED, WERE LOADED INTO A PLANE...
MOVE! THIS IS ROBBEN ISLAND!!! HERE YOU WILL DIE!
THE TIMES
RIVONIA TRIALISTS GET LIFE IMPRISONMENT
THE PICTURE THAT EMERGES IS OF MEN GOADED BEYOND ENDURANCE..
THE VERDICT OF HISTORY WILL BE THAT THE ULTIMATE GUILTY PARTY IS THE GOVERNMENT IN POWER AND THAT ALREADY IS THE VERDICT OF WORLD OPINION...
AMANDLA!!..
NGAWETHU!..

THE REALITY OF LIFE IN PRISON SOON SET IN. AFTER TWO WEEKS IN CELLS MEASURING SIX FEET SQUARE THEY WERE VISITED BY JOEL JOFFE AND BRAM FISCHER.
WILL YOU NOT APPEAL YOUR SENTENCE!?!
NO, WE ARE COMMITTED TO OUR DECISION.
THE PRISONERS WERE EAGER TO HEAR NEWS OF FAMILY AND FRIENDS...
HOW IS MOLLY DOING, BRAM?
FISCHER LEFT THE ROOM WITHOUT ANSWERING, LEAVING A CONFUSED MANDELA BEHIND...
!?..
MR FISCHER ASKED THAT WE TELL YOU THAT HIS WIFE DIED IN A CAR CRASH ON THEIR WAY DOWN HERE...
MOLLY FISCHER HAD BEEN A FRIEND AND COMRADE TO THE PRISONERS. IN THE DAYS THAT FOLLOWED, MANDELA WROTE A LETTER OF CONDOLENCE TO THE FISCHER FAMILY. IT WAS NEVER DELIVERED...
WILL MANDELA AND HIS COMRADES EVER SEE THE OUTSIDE WORLD AGAIN?

5

PRISONER 466/64

ROBBEN ISLAND IS NOW A WORLD HERITAGE SITE, AND A SYMBOL OF RESISTANCE TO OPPRESSION.

ROBBEN ISLAND, 1964. MANDELA AND 19 OTHERS WERE PLACED IN THE 'OLD JAIL' BEFORE THEY WERE MOVED TO B SECTION – A NEWLY BUILT BLOCK FOR POLITICAL PRISONERS...
... WARDERS WOKE THEM AT FIVE–THIRTY EACH MORNING TO CLEAN THEIR CELLS, EMPTY THEIR SANITARY BUCKETS, AND TO EAT A BREAKFAST OF COLD CORN MEAL PORRIDGE. AFTERWARDS THEY CRUSHED STONE TO GRAVEL IN THE COURTYARD...
REMEMBER MADIBA SAID "IT'S ABOUT BALANCE NOT STRENGTH"...
MAKE THAT WHEELBARROW MOVE!
A LIFE SENTENCE IS NOT A DEATH SENTENCE.
THEY LABOURED TOGETHER, ATE LUNCH OF CORNCOBS AND BOILED TURNIPS AND YEAST DRINK. THEY WASHED UNDER COLD SHOWERS AND ATE SUPPER IN THE SOLITUDE OF THEIR SINGLE CELLS. THEY WERE TO FIGHT LONG STRUGGLES TO END RACIAL DISCRIMINATION RELATING TO FOOD AND CLOTHING.
"...I AM THE MASTER OF MY FATE; I AM THE CAPTAIN OF MY SOUL."*
466/64
MANDELA WAS PRISONER 466 OF 1964. HE WAS FORTY–SIX YEARS OLD, INCARCERATED IN A CELL OF TWO BY THREE METRES. THE ONLY COMFORT IN A FREEZING WINTER – A SISAL MAT AND THREE THIN BLANKETS...
* QUOTE FROM "INVICTUS" BY W E HENLEY.

AFTER A FEW WEEKS THEIR ROUTINE WAS INTERRUPTED...
TRRR
MEND THOSE JERSEYS! MOVE, MOVE!!
MANDELA, COME, YOU WILL TALK NOW!
THEY ARE HIDING THE TRUTH! WE HAVE BEEN HAMMERING STONES FOR WEEKS!
THESE PEOPLE ARE FROM THE DAILY TELEGRAPH IN LONDON. GIVE YOUR CO-OPERATION!
...CONDITIONS ARE APPALLING, THE FOOD IS INADEQUATE, COLD AND MONOTONOUS. WE DO HARD LABOUR AND OUR CELLS ARE FREEZING AND DAMP.

THAT WENT WELL, NOW BACK TO NORMAL!
THE PARTY IS OVER! MOVE MOVE! GIVE US A BUCKET OF GRAVEL!
MANDELA, YOU AND SISULU WILL HAVE VISITORS TOMORROW.
MAYBE WINNIE AND ALBERTINA...
...THE CHILDREN ARE WELL BUT I LOST MY JOB...
MY BANS ARE RESTRICTING ME TO ORLANDO WEST!
I AM SO SORRY ZAMI*...
*ZAMI IS A SHORTENING OF WINNIE'S FIRST NAME, NOMZAMO, MEANING: SHE WHO WILL ENDURE TRIALS.
AS A CATEGORY D PRISONER, MANDELA WAS ALLOWED ONE VISITOR AND ONE LETTER EVERY SIX MONTHS.
STAY STRONG...
I WILL, OUR CAUSE IS JUST...
TIME UP !!! 30 MINUTES !!!
HOW LONG WILL IT BE BEFORE I SEE HER AGAIN? I WISH I COULD PROTECT HER AND MY CHILDREN...
OH, ALBERTINA, HE IS SO THIN!
YOU KNOW WINNIE, OUR MEN ARE SHRINKING HERE, BUT THEIR SPIRITS ARE STRONG...
1964
ONLY FAMILY MEMBERS OLDER THAN 16 YEARS COULD VISIT. VISITORS WERE ALLOWED TO SPEAK ONLY ENGLISH OR AFRIKAANS, AND ONLY FINANCIAL AND FAMILY MATTERS COULD BE DISCUSSED.

PRISONERS WERE NOT ALLOWED TO WEAR WATCHES. ROUTINE WAS MARKED BY A SERIES OF BELLS, COMMANDS AND WHISTLES. MANDELA MADE A CALENDAR TO HELP HIM KEEP TRACK OF TIME.
FROM JANUARY 1965 THEY STARTED WORKING IN THE LIME QUARRY A FEW KILOMETRES AWAY.
DING!..
DONG.....
DING..
DONG!!
DING
SLOWER, SLOWER... WE WILL NOT RUN FOR THEM...
FASTER!
THE HEAT AND THE GLARE FROM THE LIME STONE ARE UNBEARABLE. WE NEED SUNGLASSES!
MOVE!
FOR THE FIRST FEW MONTHS AT THE QUARRY THE PRISONERS WERE NOT ALLOWED TO TALK.

NO COMPLAINTS! AND CALL ME BOSS!!!
PRRRR!!
I WILL NEVER CALL YOU BOSS... AND I WILL GET SUNGLASSES!
THEY HAD LUNCH AT A SHED IN THE QUARRY WHERE THEY COULD SOMETIMES TALK...
IT IS IMPORTANT TO TRY TO LEARN TO SPEAK THEIR LANGUAGE...
THESE WARDERS ARE ALL BRUTAL!, THE OTHER DAY THEY BURIED SOME CHAPS AND URINATED ON THEIR HEADS!
IF YOU ARE DECENT TO A WARDER, YOU CAN LATER GET A BLANKET. YOU CANNOT GET A BLANKET FROM THE MINISTER OF JUSTICE!
WALKING TO AND FROM THE QUARRY THEY PASSED THE HOUSE WHERE ROBERT SOBUKWE, LEADER OF THE PAC, WAS KEPT IN ISOLATION FOR SIX YEARS...
ISOLATION LIKE THAT IS INHUMAN... I WONDER HOW HLATI IS COPING? AT LEAST WE ARE TOGETHER.
KATHY,WE CAN USE THE MATCHBOXES TO SMUGGLE MESSAGES TO THE GENERAL SECTION. WE CAN DROP THEM AT THE CROSSROADS.
LET'S DISCUSS IT IN THE HIGH ORGAN*.
1965
* AN ORGANISED LEADERSHIP STRUCTURE OF SENIOR ANC MEN WAS SET UP IN 1965. THE FIRST MEMBERS WERE MANDELA, MBEKI, MHLABA AND SISULU. LATER WILTON MKWAYI, KATHRADA AND LALOO CHIBA WERE INVITED TO JOIN AS ROTATING MEMBERS. COMMITTEES WERE FORMED IN THE GENERAL SECTION TO ADDRESS DISCIPLINE, EDUCATION, STUDY AND COMMUNICATION.

CONTACT BETWEEN THE GENERAL PRISONERS IN COMMUNAL CELLS AND B SECTION WAS STRICTLY FORBIDDEN.

BUT THE HIGH ORGAN SET UP A COMMUNICATIONS COMMITTEE TO FIND WAYS OF MAKING CONTACT. APART FROM USING MATCHBOXES WITH FALSE BOTTOMS THEY ALSO RECEIVED NOTES WRAPPED IN PLASTIC INSIDE FOOD DRUMS WHICH MOVED FROM THE KITCHEN TO B SECTION.

IT WAS ESSENTIAL TO KEEP IN TOUCH WITH EACH OTHER AND THE OUTSIDE...

IN JULY 1966, A SECRET MESSAGE INFORMED THE PRISONERS OF A HUNGER STRIKE IN THE GENERAL SECTION. B SECTION JOINED IN.

*On hunger strike - general section

A FEW DAYS LATER THE COMMANDING OFFICER SPOKE TO MANDELA.

WHY STRIKE? YOU DON'T EVEN KNOW WHY THE OTHERS ARE NOT EATING!

WE SEE ANY ACTION OF PROTEST TO ALTER PRISON CONDITIONS AS PART OF THE STRUGGLE AGAINST APARTHEID.

PRISONERS WERE GETTING WEAK FROM LACK OF NOURISHMENT COMBINED WITH HARD LABOUR.

MANY MEN FROM THE GENERAL SECTION ENDED UP IN HOSPITAL...

COMRADES WILL START DYING SOON!
EVENTUALLY THE AUTHORITIES NEGOTIATED AND THE STRIKE ENDED.

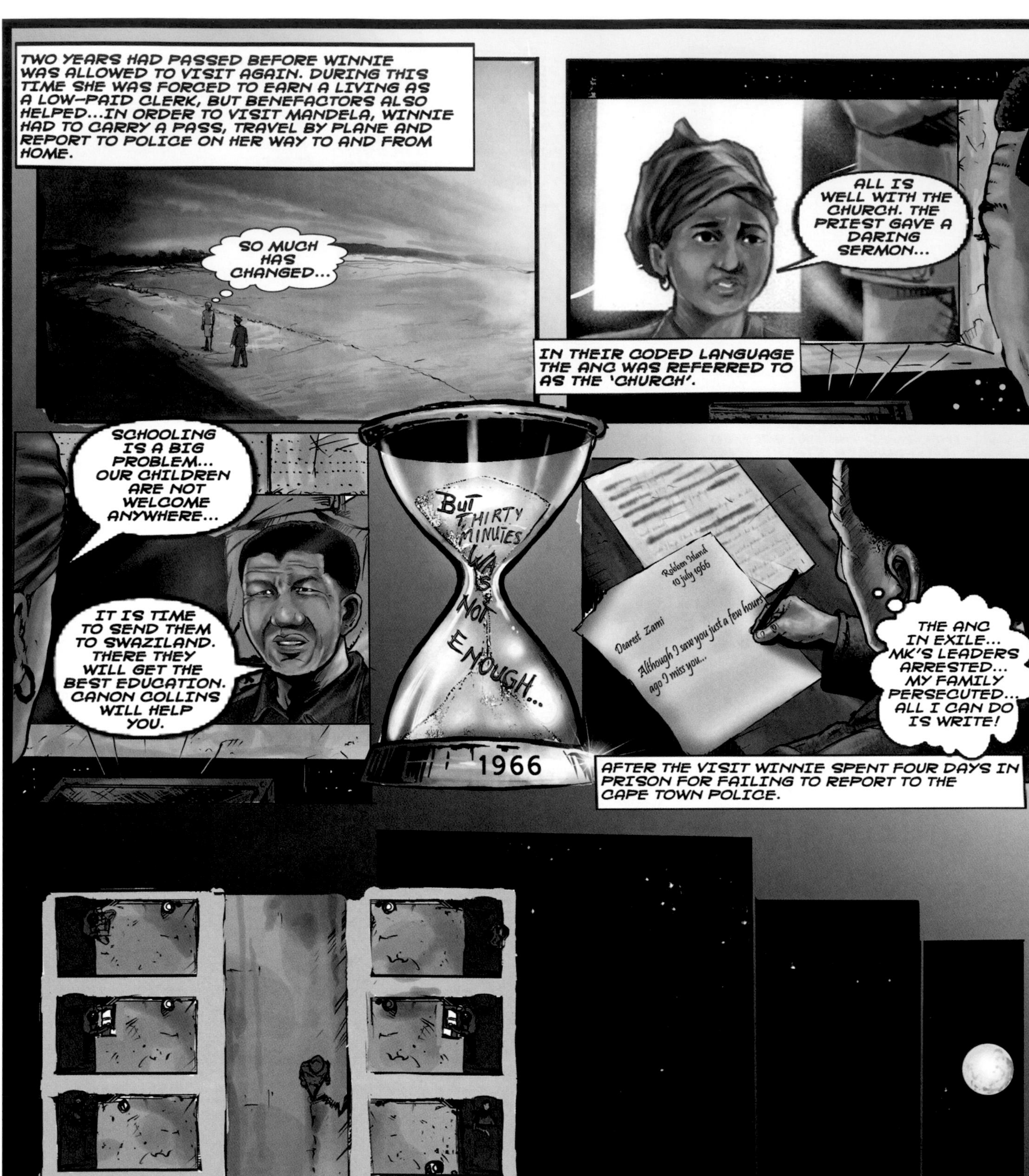
TWO YEARS HAD PASSED BEFORE WINNIE WAS ALLOWED TO VISIT AGAIN. DURING THIS TIME SHE WAS FORCED TO EARN A LIVING AS A LOW-PAID CLERK, BUT BENEFACTORS ALSO HELPED...IN ORDER TO VISIT MANDELA, WINNIE HAD TO CARRY A PASS, TRAVEL BY PLANE AND REPORT TO POLICE ON HER WAY TO AND FROM HOME.
SO MUCH HAS CHANGED...
ALL IS WELL WITH THE CHURCH. THE PRIEST GAVE A DARING SERMON...
IN THEIR CODED LANGUAGE THE ANC WAS REFERRED TO AS THE 'CHURCH'.
SCHOOLING IS A BIG PROBLEM... OUR CHILDREN ARE NOT WELCOME ANYWHERE...
IT IS TIME TO SEND THEM TO SWAZILAND. THERE THEY WILL GET THE BEST EDUCATION. CANON COLLINS WILL HELP YOU.
BUT THIRTY MINUTES WAS NOT ENOUGH...
1966
Robben Island
10 July 1966
Dearest Zami
Although I saw you just a few hours ago I miss you...
THE ANC IN EXILE... MK'S LEADERS ARRESTED... MY FAMILY PERSECUTED... ALL I CAN DO IS WRITE!
AFTER THE VISIT WINNIE SPENT FOUR DAYS IN PRISON FOR FAILING TO REPORT TO THE CAPE TOWN POLICE.
NIGHTS WERE SOLITARY, A TIME OF INTROSPECTION. THE PRISONERS WERE LOCKED IN THEIR CELLS FROM 6PM TO 5.30AM. THEY USED THE TIME TO STUDY, AND MANY, LIKE EDDIE DANIELS AND MICHAEL DINGAKE, EARNED NUMEROUS DEGREES WHILE IN PRISON.

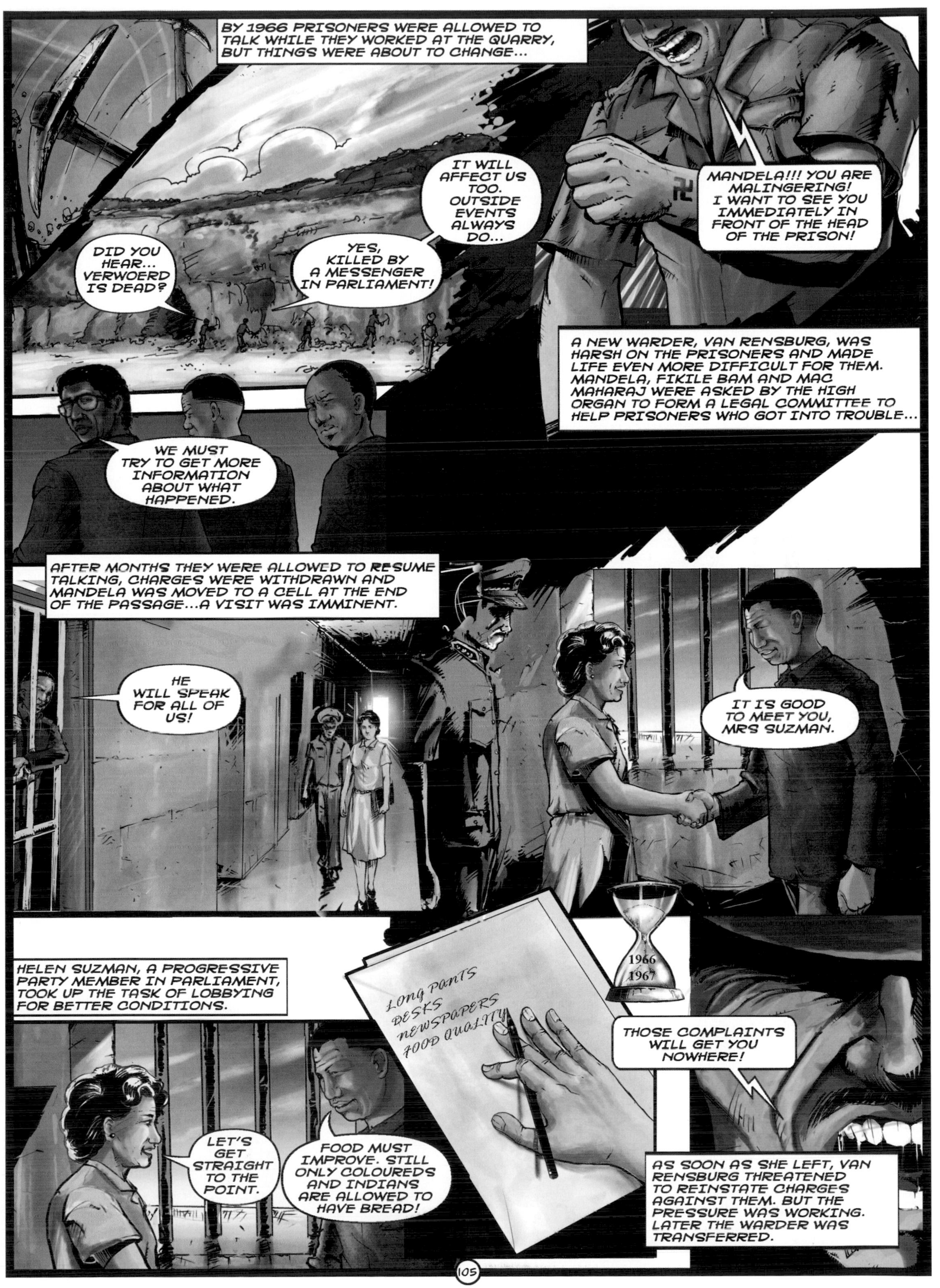
BY 1966 PRISONERS WERE ALLOWED TO TALK WHILE THEY WORKED AT THE QUARRY, BUT THINGS WERE ABOUT TO CHANGE...
DID YOU HEAR... VERWOERD IS DEAD?
YES, KILLED BY A MESSENGER IN PARLIAMENT!
IT WILL AFFECT US TOO. OUTSIDE EVENTS ALWAYS DO...
WE MUST TRY TO GET MORE INFORMATION ABOUT WHAT HAPPENED.
MANDELA!!! YOU ARE MALINGERING! I WANT TO SEE YOU IMMEDIATELY IN FRONT OF THE HEAD OF THE PRISON!
A NEW WARDER, VAN RENSBURG, WAS HARSH ON THE PRISONERS AND MADE LIFE EVEN MORE DIFFICULT FOR THEM. MANDELA, FIKILE BAM AND MAC MAHARAJ WERE ASKED BY THE HIGH ORGAN TO FORM A LEGAL COMMITTEE TO HELP PRISONERS WHO GOT INTO TROUBLE...
AFTER MONTHS THEY WERE ALLOWED TO RESUME TALKING, CHARGES WERE WITHDRAWN AND MANDELA WAS MOVED TO A CELL AT THE END OF THE PASSAGE...A VISIT WAS IMMINENT.
HE WILL SPEAK FOR ALL OF US!
IT IS GOOD TO MEET YOU, MRS SUZMAN.
HELEN SUZMAN, A PROGRESSIVE PARTY MEMBER IN PARLIAMENT, TOOK UP THE TASK OF LOBBYING FOR BETTER CONDITIONS.
LET'S GET STRAIGHT TO THE POINT.
FOOD MUST IMPROVE. STILL ONLY COLOUREDS AND INDIANS ARE ALLOWED TO HAVE BREAD!
LONG PANTS
DESKS
NEWSPAPERS
FOOD QUALITY
1966
1967
THOSE COMPLAINTS WILL GET YOU NOWHERE!
AS SOON AS SHE LEFT, VAN RENSBURG THREATENED TO REINSTATE CHARGES AGAINST THEM. BUT THE PRESSURE WAS WORKING. LATER THE WARDER WAS TRANSFERRED.

IN JULY 1967 CHIEF ALBERT LUTHULI, THE PRESIDENT-GENERAL OF THE ANC, WAS KILLED BY A TRAIN NEAR HIS HOME IN KWAZULU-NATAL WHERE HE LIVED AS A BANNED PERSON. THE PRISONERS UNITED AT A MEMORIAL SERVICE FOR THE CHIEF...
THE CHIEF COMMANDED RESPECT FROM BOTH BLACK AND WHITE...HE WAS A HUMBLE MAN. A NOBEL PEACE PRIZE WINNER IN A TIME OF WAR...
SHORTLY AFTERWARDS, IN 1968, MANDELA'S MOTHER, NOSEKENI DIED. SHE CAME TO SEE HER SON A FEW WEEKS BEFORE WITH TWO OF HIS CHILDREN, MAKGATHO AND MAKAZIWE. THE PRISON AUTHORITIES REFUSED HIM PERMISSION TO BURY HER...
BUT THE PAIN OF BEING SEPARATED FROM FAMILY REACHED NEW LEVELS WHEN HIS ELDEST SON, MADIBA THEMBEKILE, DIED IN A CAR ACCIDENT. MANDELA HAD NOT SEEN HIS GROWN SON IN YEARS, AND WAS NOT ALLOWED TO ATTEND HIS FUNERAL.
I CHOSE THE STRUGGLE ABOVE MY OWN FAMILY... I REMEMBER HOW THEMBI USED TO DRESS IN MY CLOTHES AS A CHILD... NOW I WILL HAVE TO LIVE WITH THE GUILT OF NOT BEING THERE FOR HIM OR MY MOTHER...

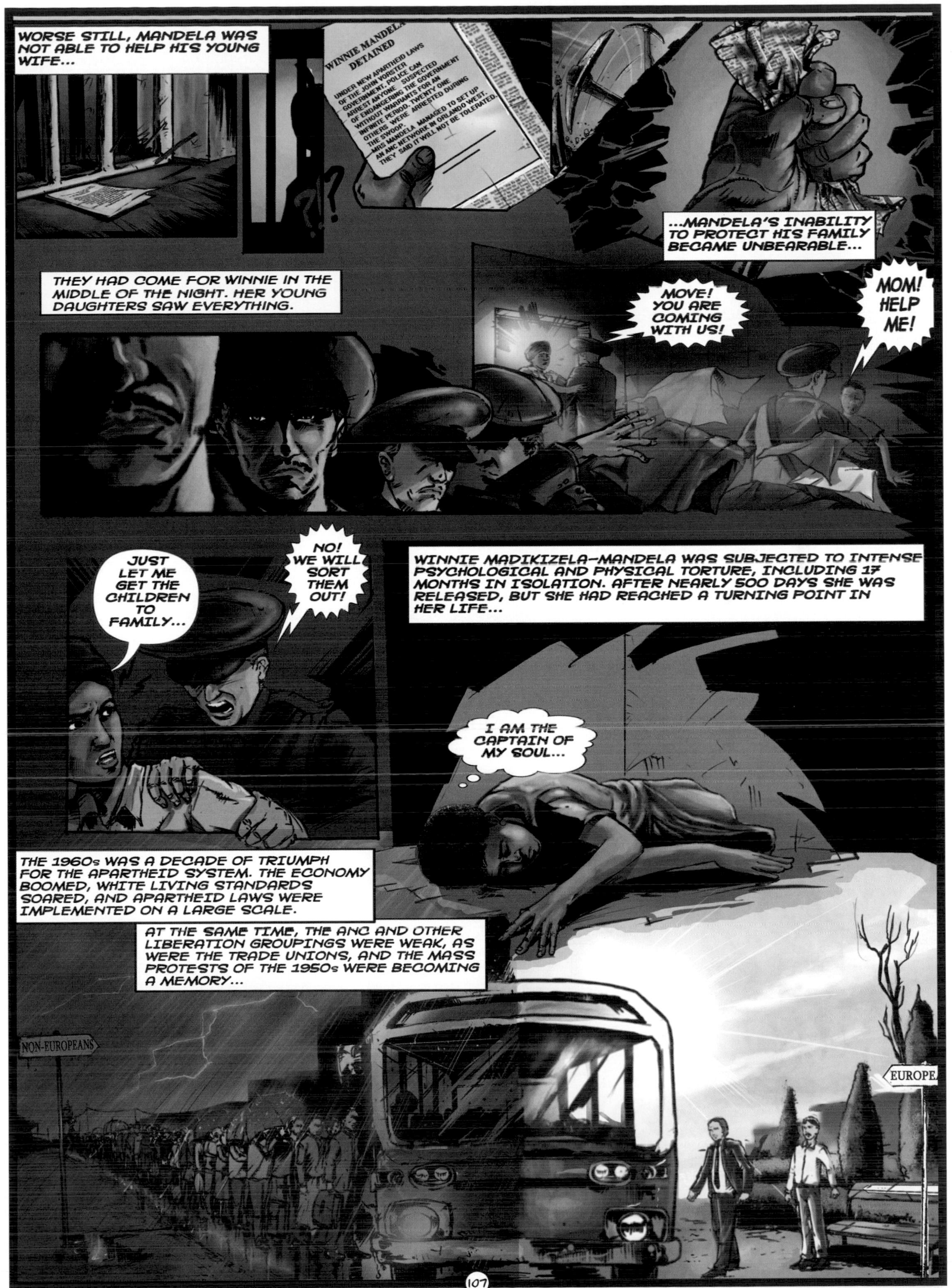
WORSE STILL, MANDELA WAS NOT ABLE TO HELP HIS YOUNG WIFE...
WINNIE MANDELA DETAINED
UNDER NEW APARTHEID LAWS OF THE JOHN VORSTER GOVERNMENT, POLICE CAN ARREST ANYONE SUSPECTED OF ENDANGERING THE GOVERNMENT WITHOUT WARRANTS FOR AN INFINITE PERIOD. TWENTY ONE OTHERS WERE ARRESTED DURING THE SWOOP.
MRS MANDELA MANAGED TO SET UP AN ANC NETWORK IN ORLANDO WEST. THEY SAID IT WILL NOT BE TOLERATED.
?!?
...MANDELA'S INABILITY TO PROTECT HIS FAMILY BECAME UNBEARABLE...
THEY HAD COME FOR WINNIE IN THE MIDDLE OF THE NIGHT. HER YOUNG DAUGHTERS SAW EVERYTHING.
MOVE! YOU ARE COMING WITH US!
MOM! HELP ME!
JUST LET ME GET THE CHILDREN TO FAMILY...
NO! WE WILL SORT THEM OUT!
WINNIE MADIKIZELA-MANDELA WAS SUBJECTED TO INTENSE PSYCHOLOGICAL AND PHYSICAL TORTURE, INCLUDING 17 MONTHS IN ISOLATION. AFTER NEARLY 500 DAYS SHE WAS RELEASED, BUT SHE HAD REACHED A TURNING POINT IN HER LIFE...
I AM THE CAPTAIN OF MY SOUL...
THE 1960s WAS A DECADE OF TRIUMPH FOR THE APARTHEID SYSTEM. THE ECONOMY BOOMED, WHITE LIVING STANDARDS SOARED, AND APARTHEID LAWS WERE IMPLEMENTED ON A LARGE SCALE.
AT THE SAME TIME, THE ANC AND OTHER LIBERATION GROUPINGS WERE WEAK, AS WERE THE TRADE UNIONS, AND THE MASS PROTESTS OF THE 1950s WERE BECOMING A MEMORY...
NON-EUROPEANS
EUROPE

AGAIN TWO YEARS PASSED BEFORE WINNIE RECEIVED PERMISSION FROM THE MINISTER OF JUSTICE TO VISIT MANDELA. HER HEALTH WAS POOR AFTER HER ORDEAL AND MANDELA APPLIED TO HAVE HER BANNING ORDER LIFTED. HIS REQUEST WAS IGNORED...
OUR CAUSE IS JUST... BE STRONG...
THANKS TO THE PRISONERS' TENACITY AND PRESSURE FROM OUTSIDE, CONDITIONS ON THE ISLAND IMPROVED...
...BY THE LATE 1960s THE ANC LEADERSHIP ON ROBBEN ISLAND WAS COMMUNICATING WITH THE LEADERSHIP OUTSIDE THE COUNTRY THROUGH CODED MESSAGES...
SO WHAT DO YOU THINK?
WHATEVER DECISION IS TAKEN ON ANC MEMBERSHIP, THE PRINCIPLE OF NON-RACIALISM MUST BE RESPECTED!
OLIVER TAMBO'S LEADERSHIP OF THE ANC IS UNQUESTIONED. HE IS THE LEADER...
WHAT IS OUR POSITION ON THE NEW STRUCTURE IN THE GENERAL SECTION?
THE ORGANISATION WILL BRING ALL PRISONERS TOGETHER TO ORGANISE AND TO MAINTAIN DISCIPLINE...
1969
THE HIGH ORGAN DISCUSSED ISSUES WITHIN THE PRISON AND ISSUES RELATING TO THE BROADER STRUGGLE FOR LIBERATION. THERE WERE OFTEN INTENSE DEBATES BETWEEN THEM.

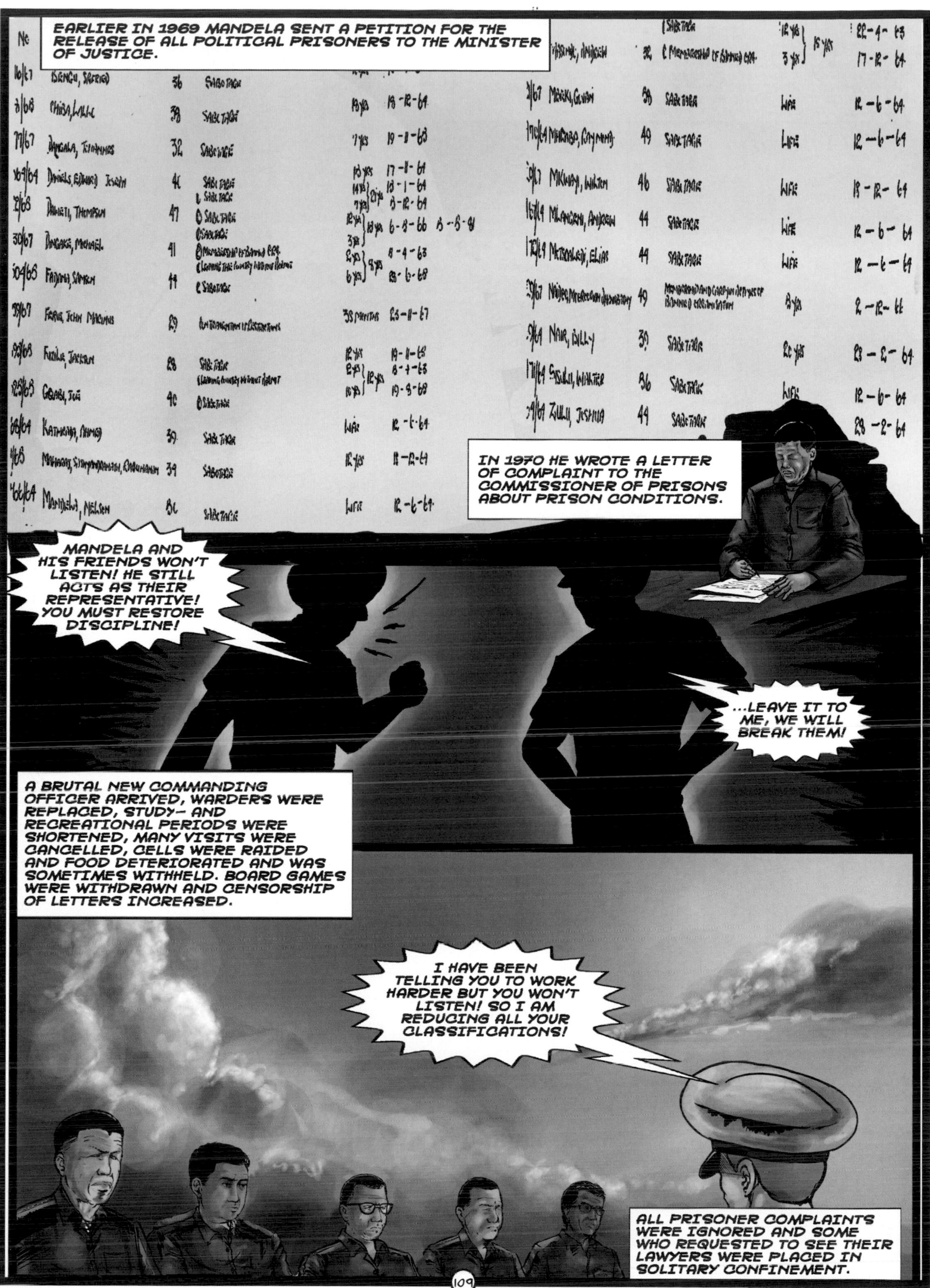
EARLIER IN 1969 MANDELA SENT A PETITION FOR THE RELEASE OF ALL POLITICAL PRISONERS TO THE MINISTER OF JUSTICE.
IN 1970 HE WROTE A LETTER OF COMPLAINT TO THE COMMISSIONER OF PRISONS ABOUT PRISON CONDITIONS.
MANDELA AND HIS FRIENDS WON'T LISTEN! HE STILL ACTS AS THEIR REPRESENTATIVE! YOU MUST RESTORE DISCIPLINE!
...LEAVE IT TO ME, WE WILL BREAK THEM!
A BRUTAL NEW COMMANDING OFFICER ARRIVED, WARDERS WERE REPLACED, STUDY- AND RECREATIONAL PERIODS WERE SHORTENED, MANY VISITS WERE CANCELLED, CELLS WERE RAIDED AND FOOD DETERIORATED AND WAS SOMETIMES WITHHELD. BOARD GAMES WERE WITHDRAWN AND CENSORSHIP OF LETTERS INCREASED.
I HAVE BEEN TELLING YOU TO WORK HARDER BUT YOU WON'T LISTEN! SO I AM REDUCING ALL YOUR CLASSIFICATIONS!
ALL PRISONER COMPLAINTS WERE IGNORED AND SOME WHO REQUESTED TO SEE THEIR LAWYERS WERE PLACED IN SOLITARY CONFINEMENT.

IN 1971 NAMIBIAN FREEDOM FIGHTERS FROM THE SOUTH WEST AFRICAN PEOPLE'S ORGANISATION (SWAPO) WERE BROUGHT TO A SEPARATE WING IN B SECTION, WHERE THEY HAD NO CONTACT WITH THE SOUTH AFRICAN PRISONERS.
THEIR LEADER, ANDIMBA TOIVO JA TOIVO, WAS PLACED IN ISOLATION AFTER A RUN-IN WITH WARDERS. THE NAMIBIANS STARTED A HUNGER STRIKE WHICH THE SOUTH AFRICAN PRISONERS JOINED.
THE AUTHORITIES WERE FURIOUS AND ON A COLD NIGHT INVADED THE POLITICAL PRISONERS' CELLS...
STRIP AND STAND AGAINST THE WALL!
IT'S THE MIDDLE OF THE NIGHT!
IT IS FREEZING.
THE DRUNK COWARDS ARE DESTROYING OUR CELLS!
1971
THE COLD, STRESS AND LACK OF FOOD, CAUSED GOVAN MBEKI TO COLLAPSE.
IN TOIVO JA TOIVO'S CELL THERE WAS AN ARGUMENT. HE KNOCKED A WARDER DOWN...
AAAAAA!...
TOIVO! YOU WILL LEARN TO SHOW RESPECT!!!
HE WAS PLACED IN SOLITARY CONFINEMENT AFTER BEING ASSAULTED. HIS COMRADES WERE SENT TO THE COMMUNAL CELLS.
IT TOOK NINE MONTHS BEFORE TOIVO JA TOIVO WAS REMOVED FROM SOLITARY CONFINEMENT. FROM THEN ON HE WAS KEPT IN B SECTION.

THE PRISONERS WERE SETTING THEIR OWN PACE AT THE QUARRY. THEY USED THEIR TIME TO DEBATE AND TO EDUCATE EACH OTHER...
NO MY FRIEND! THERE IS A SPECIFIC WORD FOR TIGER IN ISIXHOSA...
...SO AT SOME POINT THERE MUST HAVE BEEN TIGERS IN AFRICA!
INDIANS HAD A HINDI WORD FOR FLYING MACHINE THOUSANDS OF YEARS AGO! THAT DOES NOT MEAN THERE HAD BEEN AIRCRAFT AT THE TIME!
POPULAR DEBATES THAT RAGED FOR YEARS CENTRED AROUND THE FREEDOM CHARTER, CIRCUMCISION AND OPERATION MAYIBUYE.
COME ON, IT HAS BEEN YEARS! TIGERS! AND MORE TIGERS!
THE NEW COMMANDING OFFICER TURNED TO MANDELA TO HELP MAINTAIN DISCIPLINE...
HE ASKED ME TO HOLD A MEETING...HE NEEDS US TO HELP MAINTAIN DISCIPLINE ON THE ISLAND...
WE MUST AT LEAST APPEAR TO BE WORKING WHILE WE TEACH, LEARN AND DEBATE.
I HAVE SOME NEW STUDY MATERIAL THAT WE CAN GO OVER TOMORROW.
ROBBEN ISLAND BECAME KNOWN AS 'THE UNIVERSITY' BECAUSE OF THE CONSTANT FORMAL ACADEMIC STUDY AND INFORMAL TEACHING THAT PREVAILED ON THE ISLAND. THE MEN GRASPED THE OPPORTUNITY TO EDUCATE THEMSELVES AND EACH OTHER...
NOT A SINGLE POLITICAL PRISONER WHO WAS ILLITERATE LEFT THE ISLAND UNABLE TO READ AND WRITE, WHILE CAREFULLY WORKED OUT COURSES ON TOPICS SUCH AS ANC HISTORY, THE INDIAN STRUGGLE, MARXISM AND POLITICAL ECONOMY WERE TAUGHT AT THE QUARRY AND ELSEWHERE.

IN 1979 MANDELA WAS DEEPLY TROUBLED WHEN WINNIE WAS ARRESTED FOR BREAKING HER STRICT BANNING ORDER.
SHE SPENT SIX MONTHS IN JAIL. MANDELA WAS FEELING HIS FAMILY SLIPPING AWAY FROM HIM...
I MUST SEE ZINDZI... SHE WAS ONLY THREE WHEN I LEFT! I CANNOT WAIT FOR HER SIXTEENTH BIRTHDAY. WINNIE MUST MAKE A PLAN...
WILL SHE RESENT ME FOR NOT BEING THERE FOR HER AS A CHILD?
1975
WINNIE ALTERED ZINDZI'S BIRTH CERTIFICATE AND IN 1975 THE MANDELAS BRIEFLY MANAGED TO BE TOGETHER AS A FAMILY FOR THE FIRST TIME IN 12 YEARS...
HAVE YOU MET MY GUARD OF HONOUR?!
UNFORTUNATELY WINNIE HAD TO BRING BAD NEWS...
BRAM HAS DIED...
I HAVE SACRIFICED BUT BRAM'S SACRIFICE WAS THE GREATEST... HE HAD TO FIGHT AGAINST HIS OWN PEOPLE FOR THE FREEDOM OF OTHERS...
IT IS IMPOSSIBLE NOT TO THINK OF ESCAPE...
SHORTLY AFTER THE RIVONIA TRIAL BRAM FISCHER WAS ARRESTED. AFTER BEING RELEASED ON BAIL HE WENT UNDERGROUND TO CONTINUE THE STRUGGLE FOR FREEDOM. HE WAS CAPTURED IN 1965 AND RECEIVED A LIFE SENTENCE FOR CONSPIRACY TO COMMIT SABOTAGE. HE HAD BEEN RELEASED AFTER 10 YEARS, FOR HEALTH REASONS, A FEW WEEKS BEFORE HIS DEATH.

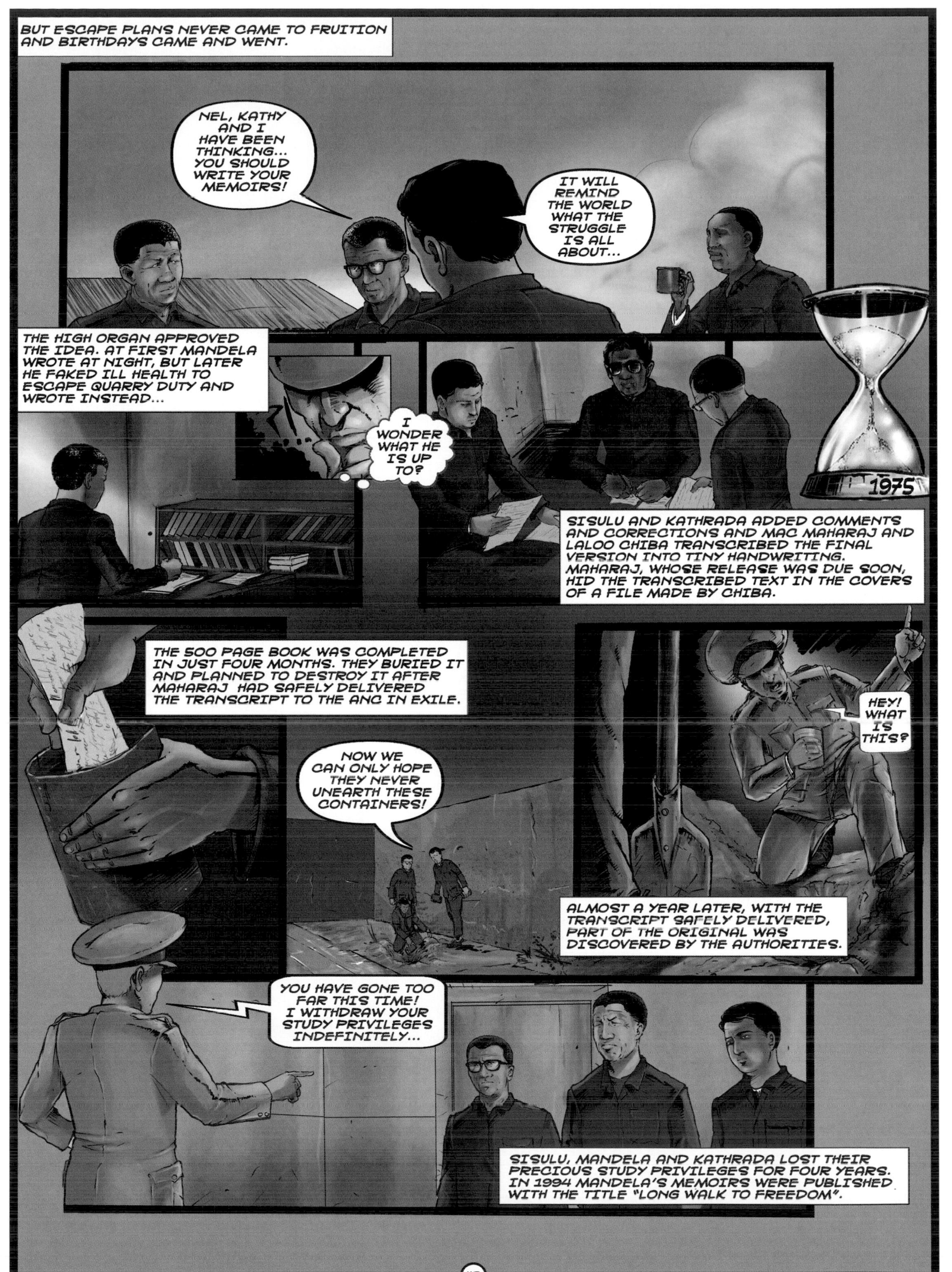
BUT ESCAPE PLANS NEVER CAME TO FRUITION AND BIRTHDAYS CAME AND WENT.
NEL, KATHY AND I HAVE BEEN THINKING... YOU SHOULD WRITE YOUR MEMOIRS!
IT WILL REMIND THE WORLD WHAT THE STRUGGLE IS ALL ABOUT...
THE HIGH ORGAN APPROVED THE IDEA. AT FIRST MANDELA WROTE AT NIGHT, BUT LATER HE FAKED ILL HEALTH TO ESCAPE QUARRY DUTY AND WROTE INSTEAD...
I WONDER WHAT HE IS UP TO?
1975
SISULU AND KATHRADA ADDED COMMENTS AND CORRECTIONS AND MAC MAHARAJ AND LALOO CHIBA TRANSCRIBED THE FINAL VERSION INTO TINY HANDWRITING. MAHARAJ, WHOSE RELEASE WAS DUE SOON, HID THE TRANSCRIBED TEXT IN THE COVERS OF A FILE MADE BY CHIBA.
THE 500 PAGE BOOK WAS COMPLETED IN JUST FOUR MONTHS. THEY BURIED IT AND PLANNED TO DESTROY IT AFTER MAHARAJ HAD SAFELY DELIVERED THE TRANSCRIPT TO THE ANC IN EXILE.
NOW WE CAN ONLY HOPE THEY NEVER UNEARTH THESE CONTAINERS!
HEY! WHAT IS THIS?
ALMOST A YEAR LATER, WITH THE TRANSCRIPT SAFELY DELIVERED, PART OF THE ORIGINAL WAS DISCOVERED BY THE AUTHORITIES.
YOU HAVE GONE TOO FAR THIS TIME! I WITHDRAW YOUR STUDY PRIVILEGES INDEFINITELY...
SISULU, MANDELA AND KATHRADA LOST THEIR PRECIOUS STUDY PRIVILEGES FOR FOUR YEARS. IN 1994 MANDELA'S MEMOIRS WERE PUBLISHED WITH THE TITLE "LONG WALK TO FREEDOM".

AFTER YEARS OF REPEATED REQUESTS, THE POLITICAL PRISONERS WERE ALLOWED TO CULTIVATE A SMALL GARDEN IN THE COURTYARD. MANDELA MADE A PROPER STUDY OF IT AND ASKED EVERYONE TO HAMMER THEIR BONES TO MEAL FOR THE SOIL.
IT IS LIBERATING TO WORK THE SOIL...
1976
...LIKE A GARDENER A LEADER TENDS HIS GARDEN, SOWS SEEDS, CULTIVATES AND HARVESTS THE RESULT...
... BUT OH, SO MANY RELATIONSHIPS THAT I COULD NOT NOURISH WHILE I AM HERE IN PRISON... SOMETIMES THERE IS NOTHING YOU CAN DO...
Dear Zami
A seed that had grown into a fragile seedling...
A robust plant with deep red fruit...
but by mistake or lack of care it withered.
Nothing could bring it back to health...
It died
and I washed the roots and buried it...
... OUTSIDE THE PRISON WALLS A NEW PHASE OF RESISTANCE TO APARTHEID WAS BEGINNING... THE BLACK CONSCOUSNESS MOVEMENT (BCM) UNDER THE LEADERSHIP OF STEVE BIKO EMERGED FROM THE SOUTH AFRICAN STUDENTS' ORGANISATION (SASO)...SOON ITS LEADERS WERE CHARGED UNDER THE TERRORISM ACT AND STARTED ARRIVING ON ROBBEN ISLAND. THEY WERE APPALLED BY CONDITIONS...MANDELA TALKED TO STRINI MOODLEY, A NEW ARRIVAL...
HOW DO YOU TOLERATE LIFE HERE?
I HAVE LEARNT ALL THAT I COULD ABOUT MY CAPTORS. I LEARNT THEIR LANGUAGE AND READ THEIR BOOKS. NOW I WOULD LIKE TO LEARN ABOUT YOUR PHILOSOPHY.

WE STAND FOR BLACK EMPOWERMENT! FOR THE DEVELOPMENT OF PRIDE, SELF-ESTEEM, CONFIDENCE AND SOLIDARITY OF THE BLACK OPPRESSED!
THIS PHILOSOPHY INSPIRED A NEW GENERATION. ON 16 JUNE 1976 SCHOOL CHILDREN IN SOWETO MARCHED IN PROTEST AGAINST BEING TAUGHT IN AFRIKAANS AT SCHOOL... SOON THE FIRST SHOTS WERE FIRED...
AWAY WITH AFRIKAANS
THE PEOPLE'S SPIRIT IS ALIVE! THE GOVERNMENT'S BANTU EDUCATION HAS COME BACK TO HAUNT THEM...
JUNE-16
1976
AMANDLA
POWER TO THE PEOPLE!!!
PLEASE! STAND UP! TAKE OFF YOUR CAP!!!
NO! WHAT FOR?
SOON ANGRY AND DEFIANT YOUTHS BEGAN ARRIVING AT ROBBEN ISLAND. THEY QUESTIONED THE ANC LEADERSHIP.
THE ARRIVAL OF THE YOUNG LIONS STIRRED UP POLITICAL DEBATES. ONE RELATED TO THE ROLE OF COMMUNISM.
IT WILL BE THE COMMUNIST PARTY THAT WILL LEAD THE OVERWHELMING MAJORITY OF THE POPULATION...
THE ANC IS A BROAD ALLIANCE OF DIFFERENT CLASS INTERESTS... IT CAN WORK WITH ALL OPPONENTS OF APARTHEID AND FASCISM...
DISCUSSION AND DEBATE RAGED FOR YEARS. LATER KATHRADA WAS ASKED TO SUMMARISE THE LENGTHY DISCUSSION IN A DOCUMENT ENTITLED "MARXISM AND INQINDI".
I AM GLAD WE HAVE RESOLVED OUR PROBLEMS. WE SHOULD TEACH THE YOUTH HERE ABOUT UNITY...

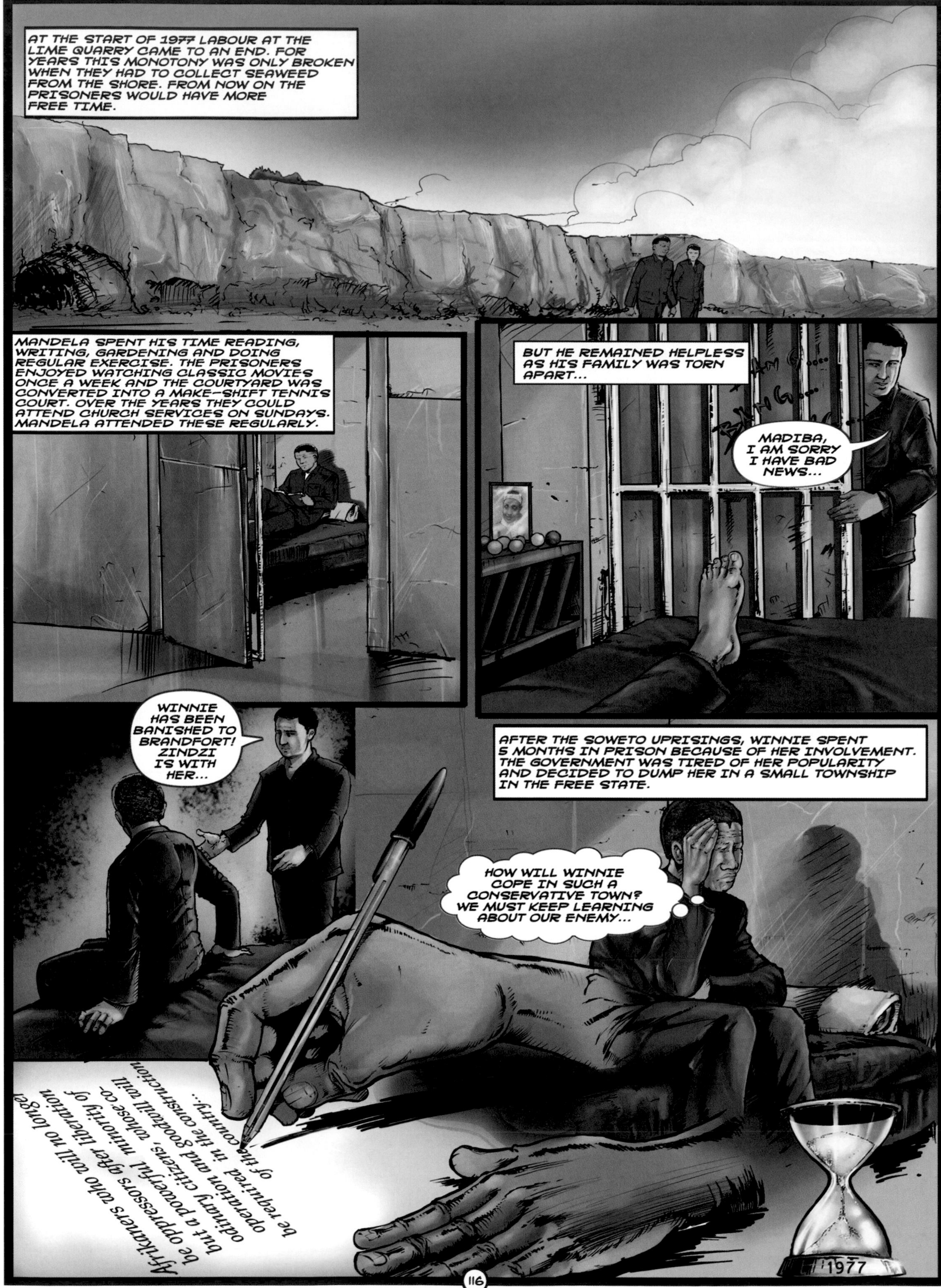
AT THE START OF 1977 LABOUR AT THE LIME QUARRY CAME TO AN END. FOR YEARS THIS MONOTONY WAS ONLY BROKEN WHEN THEY HAD TO COLLECT SEAWEED FROM THE SHORE. FROM NOW ON THE PRISONERS WOULD HAVE MORE FREE TIME.
MANDELA SPENT HIS TIME READING, WRITING, GARDENING AND DOING REGULAR EXERCISE. THE PRISONERS ENJOYED WATCHING CLASSIC MOVIES ONCE A WEEK AND THE COURTYARD WAS CONVERTED INTO A MAKE-SHIFT TENNIS COURT. OVER THE YEARS THEY COULD ATTEND CHURCH SERVICES ON SUNDAYS. MANDELA ATTENDED THESE REGULARLY.
BUT HE REMAINED HELPLESS AS HIS FAMILY WAS TORN APART...
MADIBA, I AM SORRY I HAVE BAD NEWS...
WINNIE HAS BEEN BANISHED TO BRANDFORT! ZINDZI IS WITH HER...
AFTER THE SOWETO UPRISINGS, WINNIE SPENT 5 MONTHS IN PRISON BECAUSE OF HER INVOLVEMENT. THE GOVERNMENT WAS TIRED OF HER POPULARITY AND DECIDED TO DUMP HER IN A SMALL TOWNSHIP IN THE FREE STATE.
HOW WILL WINNIE COPE IN SUCH A CONSERVATIVE TOWN? WE MUST KEEP LEARNING ABOUT OUR ENEMY...
Afrikaners who will no longer be oppressors after liberation but a powerful minority of ordinary citizens, whose co-operation and goodwill will be required in the construction of the country...
1977

PRISON CONDITIONS MIGHT HAVE IMPROVED, BUT IN 1977 AUTHORITIES OUTRAGED THE POLITICAL PRISONERS...
OK, LET'S GET GOING! YOU WILL WORK OUTSIDE TODAY...
THEY ARE UP TO SOMETHING... WHY ELSE WOULD WE GET NEW BEDS AND PILLOWS?
...THEY HAD INVITED A LARGE PRESS CORPS TO OBSERVE THE CONDITIONS ON THE ISLAND.
AGAIN THEY LIE TO THE WORLD! THEY HAVE CREATED A FALSE IMAGE OF LIFE HERE!
1977
WELL THAT WENT WELL! CONDITIONS HERE SEEM REASONABLE.
IN 1976 THE MINISTER OF JUSTICE, JIMMY KRUGER, HAD OFFERED TO RELEASE MANDELA IF HE AGREED TO SETTLE IN THE TRANSKEI. LATER KAISER MATANZIMA REQUESTED TO VISIT MANDELA. HE WAS THE FIRST PRIME MINISTER OF THE TRANSKEI, WHICH HAD BECOME A SO-CALLED INDEPENDENT REPUBLIC.
...DALIWONGA SOLD OUT HIMSELF AND HIS PEOPLE! I CAN NEVER AGREE TO BE RELEASED TO A HOMELAND.
... BUT I HAVE NO OBJECTION TO MEETING HIM.
THE HIGH ORGAN CANNOT AGREE THAT YOU SEE YOUR NEPHEW!
THE COMMUNAL CELLS ARE ALSO OPPOSING THE VISIT. THEY WORRY THAT IT MIGHT SEEM AS IF YOU ARE SUPPORTING THE HOMELAND SYSTEM.
I UNDERSTAND, BUT I WOULD HAVE LIKED TO TRY AND CHANGE HIS MIND!
I WONDER...
IN 1980 MATANZIMA DEPOSED THE THEMBU KING, SABATA, FOR WHOM MANDELA HAD BEEN GROOMED AS A YOUTH TO SERVE AS COUNSELLOR. SABATA ESCAPED TO LUSAKA WHERE HE JOINED THE ANC AND BECAME KNOWN AS THE COMRADE KING.

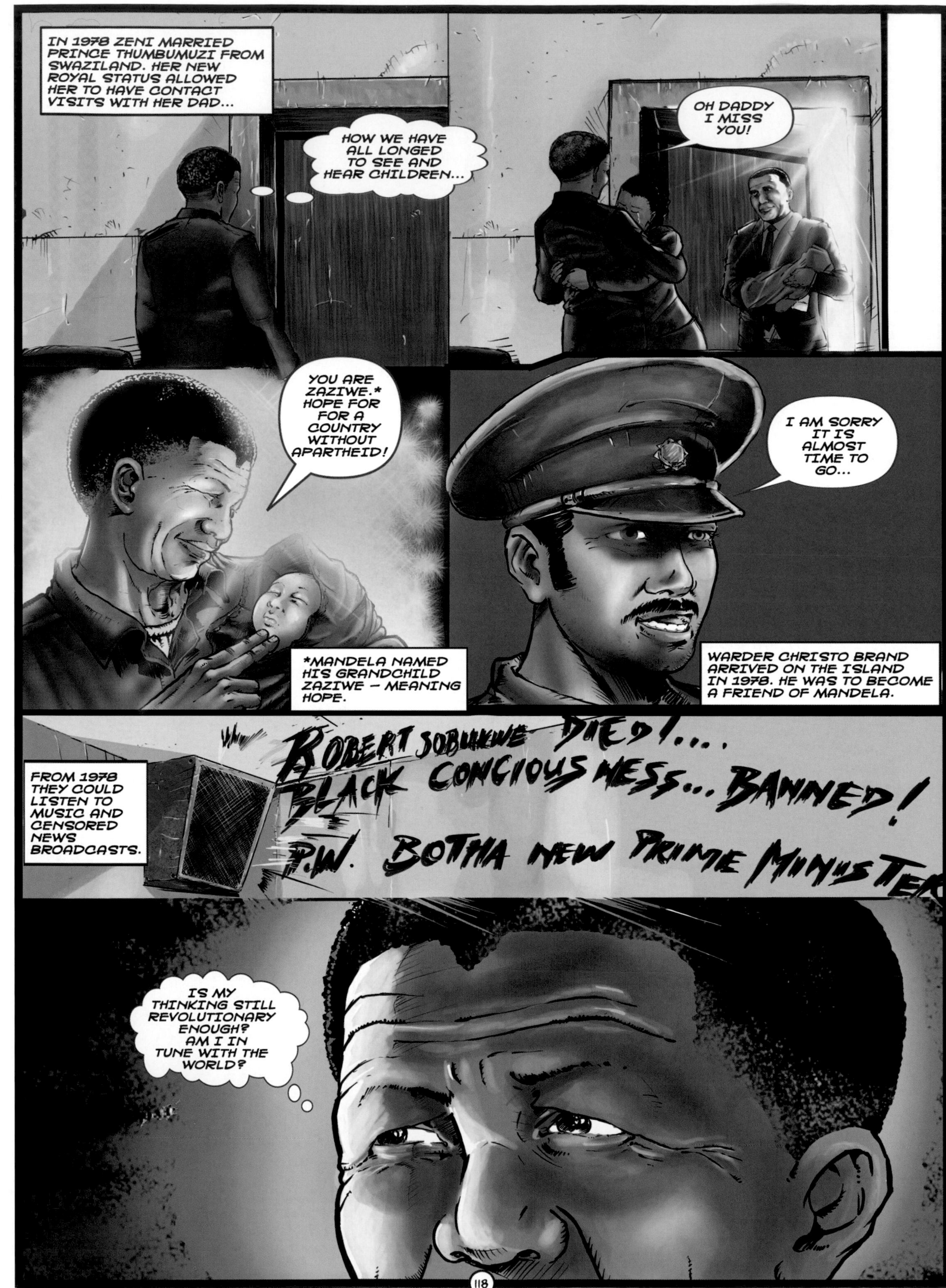
IN 1978 ZENI MARRIED PRINCE THUMBUMUZI FROM SWAZILAND. HER NEW ROYAL STATUS ALLOWED HER TO HAVE CONTACT VISITS WITH HER DAD...
HOW WE HAVE ALL LONGED TO SEE AND HEAR CHILDREN...
OH DADDY I MISS YOU!
YOU ARE ZAZIWE.* HOPE FOR FOR A COUNTRY WITHOUT APARTHEID!
*MANDELA NAMED HIS GRANDCHILD ZAZIWE – MEANING HOPE.
I AM SORRY IT IS ALMOST TIME TO GO...
WARDER CHRISTO BRAND ARRIVED ON THE ISLAND IN 1978. HE WAS TO BECOME A FRIEND OF MANDELA.
FROM 1978 THEY COULD LISTEN TO MUSIC AND CENSORED NEWS BROADCASTS.
ROBERT SOBUKWE DIED!...
BLACK CONCIOUSNESS... BANNED!
P.W. BOTHA NEW PRIME MINISTER
IS MY THINKING STILL REVOLUTIONARY ENOUGH? AM I IN TUNE WITH THE WORLD?

1980
EACH YEAR CHRISTMAS WAS MARKED WITH THE PRISONERS BEING ALLOWED TO BUY SOME SWEETS AND AN EXTRA MUG OF COFFEE AT NIGHT. THE PRISONERS MADE THE DAY SPECIAL BY PUTTING ON A PLAY, ORGANISING COMPETIONS AND GIVING A CHOIR PERFORMANCE TO THE WARDERS...
AND AT LAST, FROM 1980, THEY WERE ALLOWED TO BUY HEAVILY CENSORED NEWSPAPERS.
IN 1980 MK LAUNCHED A MILITARY CAMPAIGN, WHICH INCLUDED THE SABOTAGING OF STORAGE TANKS AT THE COUNTRY'S OIL REFINERY IN SECUNDA...
SUNDAY POST
'Free Mand
...AND PERCY QOBOZA OF THE SUNDAY POST LAUNCHED A FREE MANDELA PETITION, WHICH LATER REVERBATED AROUND THE WORLD AS THE FREE MANDELA CAMPAIGN.
IT IS TIME FOR A PROGRAMME OF TOTAL ONSLAUGHT AGAINST COMMUNIST POWERS!
DEFENCE MINISTER MAGNUS MALAN TOOK A HARD LINE AGAINST THE ANTI-APARTHEID MOVEMENT. ON ROBBEN ISLAND THE PRISONERS DISCUSSED HOW TO RESPOND TO THE REGIME'S CAMPAIGN OF "TOTAL ONSLAUGHT".
MANDELA IMPRESSED THE YOUNGER MEN WITH HIS AUTHORITY AND HIS WILLINGNESS TO LISTEN.

THE GOVERNMENT KEPT A CLOSE EYE ON MANDELA. REGULAR CHARACTER ASSESSMENTS AND PSYCHOLOGICAL ANALYSES WERE UNDERTAKEN.
MANDELA IS EXCEPTIONALLY MOTIVATED...NO VISIBLE SIGNS OF BITTERNESS TOWARDS WHITES...HE IS A PRACTICAL AND PRAGMATIC THINKER... AND HAS AN UNFLINCHING BELIEF IN HIS CAUSE!
...IT WOULD SEEM HIS TIME IN PRISON HAS CAUSED HIS PSYCHO-POLITICAL POSTURE TO INCREASE...
...MANDELA COMMANDS ALL THE QUALITIES OF THE NUMBER ONE BLACK LEADER IN SOUTH AFRICA!
BACK IN PRISON MANDELA RECEIVED BAD NEWS...
YOUR WIFE HAS BEEN IN A CAR ACCIDENT...
HOW IS SHE?
WE DON'T KNOW!
I DEMAND TO KNOW HOW SHE IS!
1982
THEY ARE CLEVER! WITHHOLDING INFORMATION IS A POWERFUL WEAPON!
MANDELA ARRANGED TO SEE DULLAH OMAR, WINNIE'S ATTORNEY, WHO REASSURED HIM THAT WINNIE'S INJURIES WERE MINOR.
PACK UP. YOU ARE LEAVING THE ISLAND LATER TODAY!
WHERE ARE YOU TAKING ME?
CAN'T SAY! INSTRUCTIONS FROM PRETORIA...
466/64
N. MANDELA
AFTER 18 YEARS ON ROBBEN ISLAND, WHERE WAS HE BEING TAKEN?

6

THE NEGOTIATOR

THIS IS THE ENTRANCE TO THE VICTOR VERSTER PRISON FROM WHERE THE MOST FAMOUS PRISONER IN THE WORLD WAS RELEASED.

VICTOR VERSTER

MARCH 1982 – NELSON MANDELA, WALTER SISULU, RAYMOND MHLABA AND ANDREW MLANGENI WERE TRANSFERRED FROM ROBBEN ISLAND. MANDELA HAD BEEN ON THE ISLAND FOR OVER 18 YEARS...
WHERE ARE THEY TAKING US?
THERE WAS NOT ENOUGH TIME FOR GOODBYES...
THE PRISONERS WERE PUT INTO A CLOSED TRUCK AND HAD TO STAND IN THE DARK FOR THE HOUR-LONG DRIVE.
THEY ARRIVED AT POLLSMOOR MAXIMUM SECURITY PRISON AND WERE TAKEN TO A CELL ON THE TOP FLOOR. IT HAD FOUR BEDS WITH SHEETS, A BATHROOM WITH TOWELS, AND A HUGE WALLED-IN COURTYARD ON THE ROOF.
A FIVE-STAR HOTEL FOR PRISONERS...

IN OCTOBER THEY WERE JOINED BY THEIR OLD FRIEND AHMED KATHRADA.
IT IS GOOD TO SEE YOU MADALA! I MISSED YOUR 70TH BIRTHDAY!
DO YOU KNOW WHY YOU WERE MOVED?
I THINK THEY ARE TRYING TO ISOLATE US. WE HAVE TOO MUCH INFLUENCE OVER OTHER PRISONERS...
THEY WERE JOINED BY PATRICK MAQUBELA, AN ANC MEMBER WHO HAD BEEN MOVED FROM DIEPKLOOF PRISON IN JOHANNESBURG. THEY HAD NO CONTACT WITH ANY OTHER PRISONERS AND HAD TO SPEND ALL THEIR TIME TOGETHER.
KRIII!
THIS CRICKET IS MAKING IT IMPOSSIBLE TO SLEEP!
KRIIII...
KRIIII...
KRIIII...
KRIIII...
OFF YOU GO... MAKE NOISE SOMEWHERE ELSE.
TYPICAL! MADIBA WON'T EVEN KILL A CRICKET...

LIVING SO CLOSELY TOGETHER WAS NOT ALWAYS EASY...
IT'S FIVE IN THE MORNING! I CAN'T BELIEVE YOU STILL EXERCISE! WE HARDLY SLEPT LAST NIGHT...
I HAVE TO KEEP FIT. WE ARE NOT AS ACTIVE HERE AS WE USED TO BE ON ROBBEN ISLAND...WE ONLY HAVE TIME IN THE COURTYARD... I MISS THE ISLAND'S NATURAL BEAUTY...
YES! AND THE CELLS ARE DAMP. BUT AT LEAST WE DON'T HAVE SEA WATER SHOWERS AND THE FOOD IS MUCH BETTER...
...I SUPPOSE IT IS EASIER FOR OUR FAMILIES TO VISIT US.
BY NOW MANDELA COULD RECEIVE 30 VISITS AND 52 LETTERS A YEAR. HE COULD GET PUBLICATIONS LIKE TIME MAGAZINE AND THE GUARDIAN WEEKLY AND COULD LISTEN TO FM RADIO... THE FOOD HAD IMPROVED AND HE WAS ALLOWED TO BUY EXTRA FOOD AND TOILETRIES.
WINNIE WAS STILL HIS LIFELINE. SHE TRIED TO VISIT WHENEVER SHE COULD LEAVE BRANDFORT, TO WHERE SHE HAD BEEN BANISHED.

IN SPIRIT I LIVE FAR BEYOND THESE WALLS, AND MY THOUGHTS ARE RARELY EVER IN THIS CELL...
MOZAMBIQUE
THE GOVERNMENT CONTINUED ITS CAMPAIGN, WHICH IT STARTED IN 1981, OF ATTACKING ANC OFFICES IN NEIGHBOURING COUNTRIES. THEN, IT RAIDED MAPUTO, MOZAMBIQUE, KILLING 13 ANC PEOPLE – INCLUDING WOMEN AND CHILDREN.
LESOTHO
IN DECEMBER 1982, 42 PEOPLE – INCLUDING TWELVE WOMEN AND CHILDREN – WERE KILLED IN MASERU, LESOTHO.
RUTH FIRST, AN ACTIVIST IN EXILE IN MAPUTO, WAS MURDERED BY A LETTER BOMB... PALLO JORDAN WAS INJURED. PETRUS AND JABU NZIMA WERE ASSASSINATED BY A CAR BOMB...
BOTSWANA
IN MAY 1983 MK RETALIATED BY ATTACKING TARGETS ACROSS SOUTH AFRICA. IT EXPLODED A CAR BOMB OUTSIDE THE AIR FORCE HEADQUARTERS IN PRETORIA, KILLING 19 PEOPLE AND INJURING 217...

IT WAS A TURBULENT TIME. IN 1982 PRESIDENT PW BOTHA PROPOSED A SIGNIFICANT CHANGE TO THE COUNTRY'S CONSTITUTION...
THERE WILL BE A PARLIAMENT WITH THREE HOUSES: ONE FOR WHITES, ONE FOR INDIANS AND ONE FOR COLOUREDS...THEY WILL BE ALLOWED TO VOTE ABOUT EDUCATION, HOUSING AND WELFARE...
HE IS AIMING TO LURE INDIANS AND COLOUREDS INTO BELIEVING HE IS MAKING REFORMS! BUT HE IS ISOLATING AFRICANS EVEN MORE...
MANDELA ASKED FOR 16 FORTY-FOUR GALLON OIL DRUMS TO BE SLICED IN HALF. IN THEM HE GREW A GARDEN IN THE COURT-YARD. HE LIKED SPENDING TWO HOURS A DAY TENDING HIS PLANTS AND ON SUNDAYS SUPPLIED VEGETABLES FOR COMMON LAW PRISONERS.
TAMBO WAS RIGHT IN CALLING 1983 THE YEAR FOR UNITED ACTION! AND BOESAK* HAS CALLED FOR A UNITED FRONT!
THE SOIL HAS BEEN PREPARED, NOW THEY CAN TAKE FORWARD THIS UNITED ACTION.
* ALLAN BOESAK WAS THE PRESIDENT OF THE WORLD ALLIANCE OF REFORMED CHURCHES.
THE UNITED DEMOCRATIC FRONT (UDF) WAS LAUNCHED IN MITCHELLS PLAIN NEAR CAPE TOWN ON 20 AUGUST 1983. IT AIMED TO BRING HUNDREDS OF RESISTANCE GROUPS TOGETHER UNDER ONE UMBRELLA. ITS FIRST TASK WAS TO RALLY OPPOSITION TO THE TRICAMERAL PARLIAMENT.
EQUAL RIGHTS FOR ALL
FORWARD TO A NON-RACIAL AND DEMOCRATIC SOUTH AFRICA. FORWARD!
UDF SAYS NO TO NEW DEAL!
UDF
UDF UNITES
THE PRISONERS HEARD OF THE LAUNCH FROM SISULU'S SON. THEY WERE CONCERNED FOR MA SISULU, WHO WAS IN DIEPKLOOF PRISON, AS SHE WAS ELECTED A UDF PRESIDENT.

YES
BOTHA'S GOVERMENT ARRANGED A REFERENDUM. VOTE "YES" FOR A TRICAMERAL PARLIAMENT OR VOTE "NO"...
NO
INDIANS, AFRICANS, COLOUREDS AND WHITES MUST UNITE AGAINST APARTHEID!!
76% OF THE VOTERS IN THE ALL-WHITE REFERENDUM VOTED "YES" FOR THE TRICAMERAL PARLIAMENT. IT WAS A TRUIMPH FOR BOTHA AND A DEFEAT FOR THE UDF...
My Dear friend,
A minister once said: Glory lies not in falling but rising every time you fall
A TRICAMERAL PARLIAMENT WILL BE LIKE HANDING THE INDIANS AND COLOUREDS TOY TELEPHONES! LIKE THE NATIVE REPRESENTATIVE COUNCILS OF 40 YEARS AGO!
MAY 1984 BROUGHT UNEXPECTED JOY WHEN MANDELA WAS ALLOWED A CONTACT VISIT WITH WINNIE WHO VISITED WITH ZENANI AND HER DAUGHTER. MANDELA AND HIS WIFE HAD NOT TOUCHED IN 21 YEARS.
ON HER RETURN TO BRANDFORT WINNIE WAS HAPPY TO SEE THE METHODIST CHURCH HAD ADDED SOME ROOMS TO HER HOUSE FOR HER COMMUNITY CLINIC. SHE ALSO RAN A CRECHE WITH MONEY FROM SUPPORTERS. BUT LOCAL POLITICIANS DID NOT WANT HER IN THE AREA, SAYING SHE ENCOURAGED RESISTANCE.

THE WOMEN OF SOUTH AFRICA FOUGHT SIDE-BY-SIDE WITH THE MEN. RELEASED ON BAIL, MA SISULU CONTINUED TO SPEAK OUT AGAINST APARTHEID. AT A 1984 UDF RALLY IN JOHANNESBURG SHE SAID:
SONS AND DAUGHTERS OF AFRICA, TO ME TODAY I'M A GREAT BIG MOTHER, FOR TODAY OUR MULTIRACIAL BABY IS BORN, FOR TODAY OUR BABY THAT WILL RULE THIS SOUTH AFRICA IN FUTURE IS BORN, THE MULTIRACIAL BABY, THE UNITED DEMOCRATIC FRONT, WHICH IS UNITING PEOPLE TO SPEAK WITH ONE VOICE!
BY NOW THE UDF HAD OVER 600 AFFILIATES. ITS BOYCOTT CAMPAIGN AGAINST THE TRICAMERAL ELECTIONS WAS A SUCCESS. ONLY 30% OF COLOUREDS AND 19% OF INDIANS WHO WERE REGISTERED, VOTED IN THE FIRST TRICAMERAL ELECTIONS. BUT THE GOVERNMENT STILL OPENED THE NEW PARLIAMENT ON 9 SEPTEMBER 1984.
THE SAME DAY VIOLENCE ERUPTED AT SHARPEVILLE WHEN RESIDENTS MARCHED AGAINST RENT HIKES...
...THE UNREST SPREAD TO OTHER TOWNSHIPS LEAVING 30 PEOPLE DEAD AND OVER 300 INJURED.
THE ARMY OCCUPIED TOWNSHIPS, STUDENTS BOYCOTTED SCHOOL AND WORKERS STAYED AT HOME...

FREE MANDELA
MANDELA WROTE TO BISHOP DESMOND TUTU IN OCTOBER 1984 CONGRATULATING HIM ON HIS NOBEL PEACE PRIZE. BUT THE LETTER WAS NEVER DELIVERED. TUTU CALLED FOR EQUAL RIGHTS FOR ALL, THE ABOLITION OF PASS LAWS, ONE EDUCATION SYSTEM AND THE END OF FORCED REMOVALS TO THE SO-CALLED HOMELANDS...
...MANDELA WAS OFFENDED THAT HIS COUSIN, MATANZIMA, STILL WANTED HIM RELEASED INTO THE TRANSKEI. HE MADE IT CLEAR THAT HE WOULD NEVER ACCEPT A CONDITIONAL RELEASE...
...MANDELA REPRESENTED FREEDOM AND DEMOCRACY. PEOPLE AROUND THE WORLD PUSHED FOR HIS RELEASE. IN 1984 THE UNITED NATIONS RECEIVED A 34 000 SIGNATURE PETITION CALLING FOR HIS FREEDOM.
PROTESTS SPREAD. IN JANUARY 1985 ANC PRESIDENT OLIVER TAMBO CALLED ON THE PEOPLE TO MAKE THE COUNTRY "UNGOVERNABLE".
OLIVER IS RIGHT. WE HAVE NO OTHER CHOICE...
CONTINUING PROTESTS IS OUR STRONGEST BARGAINING CHIP!
PW BOTHA WAS UNDER INCREASING PRESSURE TO RELEASE MANDELA...
PLEASE COME WITH ME TO BRIGADIER MUNRO'S OFFICE.
ON 31 JANUARY 1985 BOTHA OFFERED CONDITIONAL RELEASE TO MANDELA, HIS COLLEAGUES AND OTHER POLITICAL PRISONERS...
THE PRESIDENT IS OFFERING TO RELEASE YOU...
HERE IS A COPY OF THE ANNOUNCEMENT HE MADE IN PARLIAMENT...
WE CAN HAVE OUR FREEDOM PROVIDED WE UNCONDITIONALLY REJECT VIOLENCE AS A POLITICAL INSTRUMENT!

UNBELIEVABLE THAT BOTHA CAN SAY IT IS NOT THE GOVERNMENT STANDING IN THE WAY OF YOUR FREEDOM. BUT THAT IT IS YOU!
BECAUSE YOU WILL NOT RENOUNCE THE ARMED STRUGGLE!
WE ONLY TURNED TO ARMED STRUGGLE AFTER THEY CLOSED THE DOOR TO PEACEFUL PROTEST. IT IS BOTHA WHO SHOULD RENOUNCE VIOLENCE!
MANDELA, SISULU, KATHRADA, MLANGENI AND MHLABA ALL REJECTED THE OFFER IN A LETTER TO PRESIDENT BOTHA.
HE HAS MADE A PUBLIC CHALLENGE AND I WILL MAKE A PUBLIC RESPONSE.
MANDELA PREPARED A STATEMENT TO BE READ BY ZINDZI AT A RALLY AT SOWETO'S JABULANI STADIUM ON 10 FEBRUARY. HE GAVE IT TO WINNIE DURING A VISIT.
YOU MUST STOP TALKING ABOUT POLITICS!
THIS IS A MATTER OF NATIONAL IMPORTANCE! IF YOU WANT ME TO STOP, YOU'D BETTER GET DIRECT ORDERS FROM THE PRESIDENT...
My father says...
What freedom am I being offered while the organisation of the people remains banned?
What freedom am I being offered when I may be arrested on a pass offence?
What freedom am I being offered to live my life as a family with my dear wife who remains in banishment in Brandfort?
What freedom am I being offered when I must ask for permission to live in an urban area... when my very South African citizenship is not respected?
Only free men can negotiate. Prisoners cannot enter into contracts...
I cannot and will not give any undertaking at a time when I and you, the people, are not free.
Your freedom and mine cannot be separated.
I will return!
IT WAS A POWERFUL MESSAGE. THE PEOPLE WERE MOVED...
BOTHA WAS IN TROUBLE...
WE HAVE PAINTED OURSELVES INTO A CORNER... A TOTAL DEADLOCK!

THE MINISTER OF JUSTICE, KOBIE COETSEE, EARLIER ALLOWED HIGH PROFILE VISITORS TO MEET MANDELA. THEY WANTED TO LEARN MORE ABOUT WHAT MOTIVATED HIM. FIRST HE MET WITH LORD BETHELL FROM THE BRITISH CONSERVATIVE PARTY...
IT IS VERY GOOD TO MEET YOU. YOU LOOK LIKE A RELATION OF CHURCHILL!
HA-HA! TELL ME ABOUT YOUR LIFE IN PRISON!
LATER THEY TALKED ABOUT THE ARMED STRUGGLE.
WE DEEPLY REGRET THE BOMB TWO YEARS AGO THAT KILLED INNOCENT PEOPLE...
THE ARMED STRUGGLE WAS FORCED UPON US... BUT THEY MUST LEGALISE THE ANC BEFORE WE CAN NEGOTIATE...
...UNTIL THEY DO THEY WILL HAVE TO LIVE WITH THE ARMED STRUGGLE...
SOON AFTERWARDS PROFESSOR SAMUEL DASH FROM AMERICA VISITED...
WHAT DO YOU NEED SO THAT A SETTLEMENT CAN BE REACHED?
...A UNIFIED SOUTH AFRICA, NO HOMELANDS, ONE PERSON ONE VOTE...
BUT ARE YOU NOT HAPPY THAT THE MIXED MARRIAGES ACT HAS BEEN REPEALED?
IT IS A PINPRICK! IT IS NOT MY AMBITION TO MARRY A WHITE WOMAN OR SWIM IN A WHITE POOL! IT IS POLITICAL EQUALITY WE WANT!
BETHELL AND DASH BOTH LEFT WITH NEW RESPECT FOR MANDELA. THEY COULD SEE HE WAS A MAN OF PRINCIPLE.

ABOUT 20 RADIO NEWS BULLETINS A DAY KEPT THE PRISONERS UP-TO- DATE WITH WORLD EVENTS...
...TODAY ON THE 25TH ANNIVERSARY OF SHARPEVILLE 19 PEOPLE DIED IN UITENHAGE DURING A CLASH BETWEEN THE POLICE AND PROTESTORS...
AMANDLA!
...WINNIE MANDELA WAS ON THE FRONTLINE OF THE STRUGGLE AND HAD BECOME A LEADER IN HER OWN RIGHT...
...THE UDF WAS BLAMED FOR THE UNREST, THOUSANDS WERE DETAINED, TORTURED AND ABDUCTED.
WE BID FAREWELL TO THESE COMRADES...
BEYERS NAUDE* SPOKE AT THE FUNERAL OF THE CRADOCK FOUR WHO HAD BEEN ABDUCTED AND MURDERED BY THE SECURITY POLICE.
* DR BEYERS NAUDE, AN AFRIKANER PREACHER, REJECTED APARTHEID AND BECAME A LEADING ANTI-APARTHEID ACTIVIST.

RESISTANCE WAS AT AN ALL–TIME HIGH. THE GOVERNMENT WAS LOSING CONTROL. IT HAD TO ACT. BOTHA WAS EXPECTED TO RELEASE MANDELA AND OTHER POLITICAL PRISONERS...
NO PEACE UNDER APARTHEID
...HE DID NOT. ON 15 AUGUST 1985 HE SAID:
I BLAME THE UNREST ON COMMUNIST AGITATORS!
DON'T PUSH US TOO FAR!
MANDELA IS A COMMUNIST! HE MUST PROMISE NOT TO PLAN, INITIATE OR COMMIT ACTS OF VIOLENCE BEFORE HE WILL BE RELEASED!
WILL THIS MADNESS EVER END?
POLICE ATTACKED PROTESTORS WHO TRIED TO MARCH TO POLLSMOOR TO DEMAND MANDELA'S RELEASE...
RAND PLUMMETS
Popular uprising
STATE REPRESSION!
ANC STRONGER
SANCTIONS DEMANDED
LIBERATION before education!
MANDELA more popular
multinational banks withdraw from SA
...AND ALTHOUGH A MASSIVE BUST OF MANDELA WAS UNVEILED IN LONDON BY OLIVER TAMBO – WITNESSED BY ZENANI – PRIME MINISTER THATCHER WOULD NOT MOVE. SHE TOLD THE COMMONWEALTH:
"THE STRUGGLE IS MY LIFE"
GAOLED 5th AUGUST 1962
SENTENCED TO LIFE IMPRISONMENT
12th JUNE 1964 FOR HIS ACTIONS
AGAINST APARTHEID
ERECTED BY THE GREATER LONDON COUNCIL
UNVEILED BY OLIVER TAMBO,
...I WILL NOT RUSH INTO IMPOSING ECONOMIC SANCTIONS!
BUT I AGREE A GROUP OF EMINENT PERSONS CAN VISIT SOUTH AFRICA TO SEARCH FOR A SETTLEMENT.

SOUTH AFRICA WAS HEADING FOR A 'BLACK CHRISTMAS': TOWNSHIP RESIDENTS WERE SET TO BOYCOTT WHITE BUSINESSES. MANDELA WAS ADMITTED TO THE VOLKS HOSPITAL.
WE HAVE TO OPERATE. YOUR PROSTATE GLAND IS ENLARGED.
THE PRESS GATHERED OUTSIDE ANXIOUS FOR NEWS ON MANDELA.
I WONDER IF IT'S TRUE?
THEY SAY MANDELA WILL BE RELEASED.
IF HE DIES ALL HELL WILL BREAK LOOSE!
MANDELA WAS RECOVERING WELL. HE HAD EARLIER WRITTEN TO MINISTER COETSEE REQUESTING A MEETING, BUT WAS SURPRISED WHEN HE PAID HIM AN UNSCHEDULED MEETING.
IT IS GOOD TO MEET YOU. YOU MUST HAVE RECEIVED MY LETTER?
YES, BUT TELL ME HOW YOU ARE DOING?
THEY DID NOT DISCUSS POLITICS, BUT MANDELA DID ASK COETSEE TO LIFT WINNIE'S BANISHMENT. HE PROMISED TO LOOK INTO IT.
A FEW WEEKS LATER HE WAS RETURNED TO POLLSMOOR, AND PUT INTO A DIFFERENT SECTION WHERE HE HAD THREE CELLS FOR HIS OWN USE.
AFTER ALL THESE YEARS THEY ARE ISOLATING ME...
HIS OLD FRIENDS WERE NOT HAPPY...
WE SHOULD PROTEST.
THIS REALLY MAKES US ANGRY!
WAIT. I THINK SOMETHING GOOD MIGHT COME OF THIS...
MAYBE I CAN USE THIS ISOLATION... IT WILL BE EASIER FOR THE GOVERNMENT TO APPROACH ME ON MY OWN...
...A MILITARY VICTORY IS IMPOSSIBLE...
IT IS TIME TO TALK, BUT BOTH SIDES THINK IT IS A SIGN OF WEAKNESS AND BETRAYAL!
MANDELA PUSHED AHEAD AND WROTE TO COETSEE AGAIN. HE REQUESTED "TALKS ABOUT TALKS". LATER HE ASKED GEORGE BIZOS TO SEND WORD TO OLIVER TAMBO IN LUSAKA.
THE ANC APPROVES THE PRINCIPLE OF PRELIMINARY TALKS...

COETSEE DID NOT ANSWER MANDELA'S LETTER, BUT IN MARCH BRIGADIER MUNRO CAME TO SEE HIM...
THE SEVEN EMINENT PERSONS FROM THE COMMONWEALTH ARE COMING IN TWO DAYS. YOU WILL NEED A SUIT!
MANDELA, YOU LOOK LIKE A PRIME MINISTER NOW, NOT A PRISONER.
IN MARCH AND MAY 1986 MANDELA MET THE GROUP. IT WAS LOOKING FOR SOLUTIONS FOR SOUTH AFRICA. MINISTER COETSEE WAS THERE DURING THE INTRODUCTIONS...
I AM SORRY YOU ARE LEAVING, MR COETSEE.
THE TIME FOR NEGOTIATIONS HAS COME!
...COETSEE DID NOT STAY AND MANDELA FOUND HIMSELF ANSWERING QUESTIONS ABOUT THE ANC'S IDEOLOGY AND THE MOUNTING VIOLENCE IN THE COUNTRY. THE GROUP LATER MET WITH SOME CABINET MINISTERS IN SOUTH AFRICA AND TAMBO IN ZAMBIA.
I BELIEVE THE FREEDOM CHARTER EMBODIES THE PRINCIPLES OF DEMOCRACY AND HUMAN RIGHTS...
...THE WHITE MINORITY SHOULD FEEL A SENSE OF SECURITY IN ANY NEW SOUTH AFRICA...
I AGREE THAT VIOLENCE CAN NEVER BE THE ULTIMATE SOLUTION...
I SEE A REAL CHANCE FOR PEACE AND THE ANC MIGHT AGREE TO SUSPEND THE ARMED STRUGGLE...
BUT WHILE THE EMINENT PERSONS GROUP WAS WRAPPED IN TALKS, MAGNUS MALAN, THE MINISTER OF DEFENCE, PROPOSED AIR STRIKES ON ANC BASES IN LUSAKA, HARARE AND GABORONE. BOTHA GAVE HIM THE GO-AHEAD.
I AM NOT INTERESTED IN NEGOTIATING ABOUT THE TRANSFER OF POWER!
THE GROUP OF SEVEN QUICKLY LEFT THE COUNTRY. TALKS WERE NOW IMPOSSIBLE. BOTHA IMPOSED ANOTHER STATE OF EMERGENCY ON 12 JUNE 1986. OVER THE NEXT EIGHT MONTHS, 26 000 ACTIVISTS WERE DETAINED.

WHY ARE WE ALLOWING THIS COUNTRY TO BE DESTROYED?
BY NOW THE ONLY PERMITTED GATHERINGS WERE IN CHURCHES. AFTER THE FAILURE OF THE COMMONWEALTH'S EMINENT PERSONS GROUP MISSION, THATCHER STILL RESISTED IMPOSING SANCTIONS ON SOUTH AFRICA.
INSTEAD SHE SENT THE BRITISH FOREIGN MINISTER GEOFFREY HOWE TO INTERVENE. BUT IT WAS A FAILURE. BOTH MANDELA AND BISHOP TUTU REFUSED TO MEET WITH HIM...
MANDELA DECIDED TO LAUNCH A NEW INITIATIVE AND ASKED TO SEE GENERAL WILLEMSE, THE COMMISSIONER OF PRISONS.
GENERAL, I NEED TO MEET WITH MR COETSEE...
ABOUT TALKS BETWEEN THE GOVERNMENT AND THE ANC!
WILLEMSE IMMEDIATELY CALLED COETSEE, WHO TOLD HIM TO SEND MANDELA TO HIS HOUSE. IT WAS A HIGHLY IRREGULAR WAY OF MEETING AND THEY SPENT THREE HOURS TALKING...
SO, MANDELA, WHAT IS THE NEXT STEP?
A MEETING WITH PRESIDENT BOTHA AND THE FOREIGN MINISTER...
MANDELA HAD TO PASS THROUGH 15 GATES, FROM HIS CELL TO THE OUTSIDE, EVERY TIME HE WENT FOR A MEETING...
MONTHS PASSED WITH NO WORD FROM COETSEE. MANDELA FELT THE AUTHORITIES MIGHT BE PREPARING HIM FOR RELEASE WHEN, IN DECEMBER, THEY TOOK HIM ON DRIVES AROUND THE CAPE.
THEY ARE GIVING ME LITTLE FREEDOMS... BUT STILL I CANNOT HELP BUT THINK OF WHAT I HAVE LOST...
THEMBI, MAKGATHO, MAKI, ZINDZI, ZENI, ZAMI... MY GRANDCHILDREN...

MANDELA AND THE OTHERS WERE ALLOWED TV AND VIDEO FROM 1986. MANDELA ENJOYED THE BOLSHOI BALLET, THE FOOTBALL WORLD CUP, AND THE 1975 WORLD HEAVYWEIGHT CHAMPIONSHIP BETWEEN MUHAMMAD ALI AND JOE FRAZIER...
...I MISS BOXING...
HE WAS ALLOWED TO JOIN HIS OLD FRIENDS FOR A CHRISTMAS MEAL IN 1986. THEY COULD ORDER FOOD FROM OUTSIDE THE PRISON...
AT LEAST THE PASS LAWS HAVE BEEN ABOLISHED!
...AND AMERICA AT LAST VOTED FOR COMPREHENSIVE SANCTIONS...
IN 1987, COETSEE CONTACTED MANDELA FOR SECRET MEETINGS AT HIS HOUSE IN CAPE TOWN...
WE ARE APPOINTING A COMMITTEE TO TAKE THE DISCUSSIONS FURTHER... IT WILL BE WITH THE KNOWLEDGE OF THE PRESIDENT.
I HAVE TO THINK ABOUT IT... AND CONSULT WITH THE OTHERS AT POLLSMOOR.
AT FIRST THE PRISON AUTHORITIES REFUSED TO LET HIM CONSULT WITH HIS FRIENDS, BUT HE PERSEVERED AND WAS EVENTUALLY ALLOWED TO MEET THEM ONE AT A TIME IN THE VISITORS' AREA...
NEL, I DON'T HAVE ANYTHING AGAINST NEGOTIATIONS IN PRINCIPLE, BUT I WOULD HAVE PREFERRED IT IF THE GOVERNMENT MADE THE FIRST MOVE...
WALTER YOU ARE A MAN OF REASON AND WISDOM, THERE IS NO-ONE'S OPINION THAT I TRUST OR VALUE MORE...
HE ALSO SENT A MESSAGE TO OLIVER TAMBO WITH GOVAN MBEKI, WHO WAS RELEASED IN NOVEMBER 1987, AGED 77. RUMOURS SPREAD THAT MANDELA HAD SOLD OUT TO THE GOVERNMENT.
OLIVER WANTS TO KNOW WHAT I AM DOING! SURELY HE DOES NOT BELIEVE THAT I AM SELLING OUT?
THE THOUGHT OF TAMBO MISTRUSTING HIM ANGERED MANDELA AND HE REPLIED CURTLY...
I am talking with the government about one thing and one thing only: A meeting between the National Executive of the AN and the South African Gover
BY OCTOBER 1987 THE ANC PRODUCED A DOCUMENT CALLED: POSSIBLE RESPONSE TO NEGOTIATIONS INITIATIVE, WITH THE AIM TO TRANSFER POWER TO ALL PEOPLE...

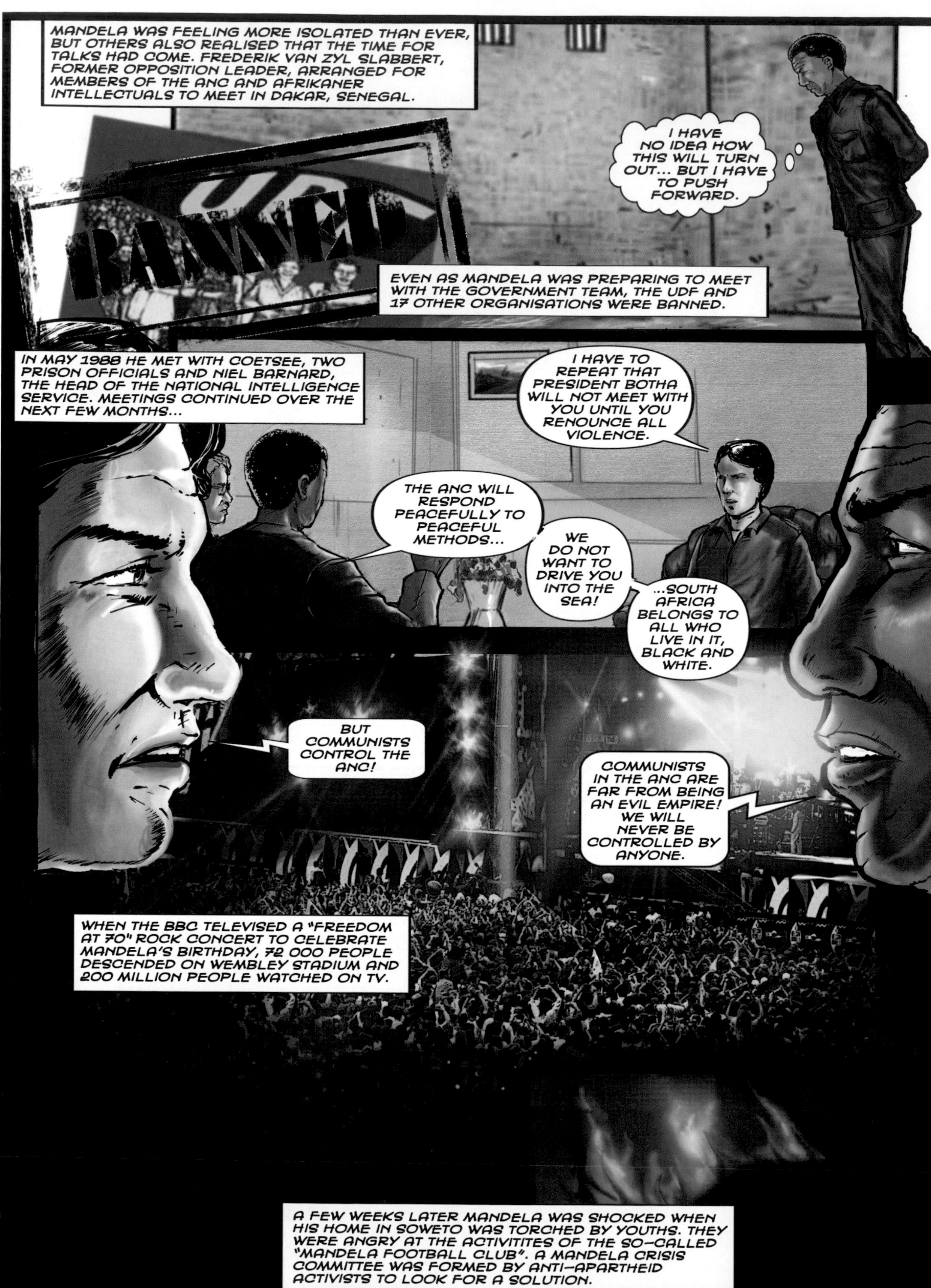
MANDELA WAS FEELING MORE ISOLATED THAN EVER, BUT OTHERS ALSO REALISED THAT THE TIME FOR TALKS HAD COME. FREDERIK VAN ZYL SLABBERT, FORMER OPPOSITION LEADER, ARRANGED FOR MEMBERS OF THE ANC AND AFRIKANER INTELLECTUALS TO MEET IN DAKAR, SENEGAL.
I HAVE NO IDEA HOW THIS WILL TURN OUT... BUT I HAVE TO PUSH FORWARD.
BANNED
EVEN AS MANDELA WAS PREPARING TO MEET WITH THE GOVERNMENT TEAM, THE UDF AND 17 OTHER ORGANISATIONS WERE BANNED.
IN MAY 1988 HE MET WITH COETSEE, TWO PRISON OFFICIALS AND NIEL BARNARD, THE HEAD OF THE NATIONAL INTELLIGENCE SERVICE. MEETINGS CONTINUED OVER THE NEXT FEW MONTHS...
I HAVE TO REPEAT THAT PRESIDENT BOTHA WILL NOT MEET WITH YOU UNTIL YOU RENOUNCE ALL VIOLENCE.
THE ANC WILL RESPOND PEACEFULLY TO PEACEFUL METHODS...
WE DO NOT WANT TO DRIVE YOU INTO THE SEA!
...SOUTH AFRICA BELONGS TO ALL WHO LIVE IN IT, BLACK AND WHITE.
BUT COMMUNISTS CONTROL THE ANC!
COMMUNISTS IN THE ANC ARE FAR FROM BEING AN EVIL EMPIRE! WE WILL NEVER BE CONTROLLED BY ANYONE.
WHEN THE BBC TELEVISED A "FREEDOM AT 70" ROCK CONCERT TO CELEBRATE MANDELA'S BIRTHDAY, 72 000 PEOPLE DESCENDED ON WEMBLEY STADIUM AND 200 MILLION PEOPLE WATCHED ON TV.
A FEW WEEKS LATER MANDELA WAS SHOCKED WHEN HIS HOME IN SOWETO WAS TORCHED BY YOUTHS. THEY WERE ANGRY AT THE ACTIVITITES OF THE SO-CALLED "MANDELA FOOTBALL CLUB". A MANDELA CRISIS COMMITTEE WAS FORMED BY ANTI-APARTHEID ACTIVISTS TO LOOK FOR A SOLUTION.

MANDELA BECAME VERY ILL...
I FEEL REALLY SICK!
I CAN'T STOP COUGHING.
I NEED HELP...
HE WAS TAKEN TO TYGERBERG HOSPITAL, WHERE AN ENTIRE FLOOR HAD BEEN CLEARED FOR HIM.
I AM SURE IT IS BECAUSE OF MY DAMP CELL.
YOU HAVE A GREAT DEAL OF WATER ON YOUR LUNG. WE HAVE TO DRAIN IT.
MANDELA SPENT SIX WEEKS RECUPERATING FROM TUBERCULOSIS. HE WAS MOVED TO THE CONSTANTIABERG CLINIC WHERE TALKS WITH THE TEAM CONTINUED.
MINISTER COETSEE AND MAJOR MARAIS ARE HERE TO SEE YOU.
WE WANT TO MOVE YOU HALFWAY BETWEEN CONFINEMENT AND FREEDOM...
SO I WILL NOT BE RELEASED, BUT IT IS A STEP IN THAT DIRECTION.
DURING THE MEETING MAJOR MARAIS TRIED TO TAKE MANDELA'S PLATE...
NO MANDELA! YOU ARE SUPPOSED TO BE ON A LOW-CHOLESTEROL DIET.
MAJOR, I AM SORRY. IF THIS BREAKFAST WILL KILL ME, THEN TODAY I AM PREPARED TO DIE!

ON 9 DECEMBER 1988 MANDELA ARRIVED AT HIS HALFWAY HOUSE – THE VICTOR VERSTER PRISON IN PAARL, A WINE REGION CLOSE TO CAPE TOWN.
THEY ARE GIVING ME THE ILLUSION OF FREEDOM...
WOULD YOU LIKE SOMETHING TO DRINK?
NO THANK YOU. I ONLY OCCASIONALLY HAVE SWEET WINE.
HE WAS NO LONGER INCARCERATED IN A CELL, BUT LIVED IN A HOUSE ON THE PRISON GROUNDS WITH OFFICER JACK SWART AS HIS PERSONAL COOK AND CLEANER.
I WILL DO THE DISHES! YOU HAVE COOKED. IT IS ONLY FAIR THAT I HELP.
NO. IT IS MY DUTY TO DO IT!
MANDELA ALSO CONTINUED MAKING HIS OWN BED DESPITE SWART'S PROTESTATIONS. FOR THE FIRST TIME IN YEARS MANDELA COULD SET HIS OWN ROUTINE OF SLEEPING, EATING, SWIMMING OR SIMPLY WALKING IN THE GARDEN...
BUT HE WAS ALSO FACING PERSONAL PROBLEMS. WINNIE WAS IMPLICATED IN VIOLENCE LINKED TO THE MANDELA FOOTBALL CLUB...
LET IT NOT BE TRUE!
WHAT IS OUR COURSE OF ACTION?
STANLEY MOGOBA, A METHODIST MINISTER, VISITED MANDELA TO DISCUSS THE SITUATION.

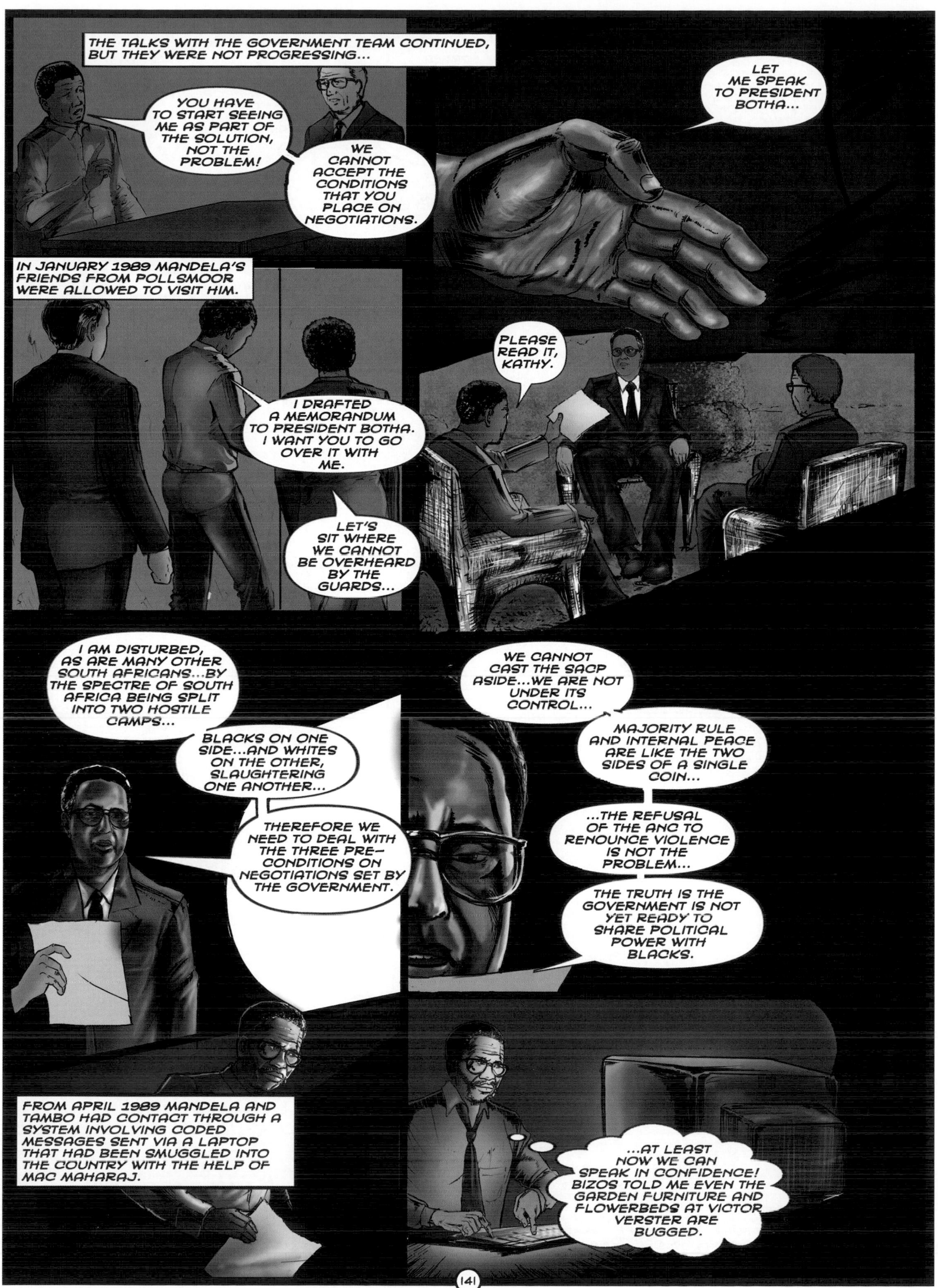
THE TALKS WITH THE GOVERNMENT TEAM CONTINUED, BUT THEY WERE NOT PROGRESSING...
YOU HAVE TO START SEEING ME AS PART OF THE SOLUTION, NOT THE PROBLEM!
WE CANNOT ACCEPT THE CONDITIONS THAT YOU PLACE ON NEGOTIATIONS.
LET ME SPEAK TO PRESIDENT BOTHA...
IN JANUARY 1989 MANDELA'S FRIENDS FROM POLLSMOOR WERE ALLOWED TO VISIT HIM.
I DRAFTED A MEMORANDUM TO PRESIDENT BOTHA. I WANT YOU TO GO OVER IT WITH ME.
LET'S SIT WHERE WE CANNOT BE OVERHEARD BY THE GUARDS...
PLEASE READ IT, KATHY.
I AM DISTURBED, AS ARE MANY OTHER SOUTH AFRICANS...BY THE SPECTRE OF SOUTH AFRICA BEING SPLIT INTO TWO HOSTILE CAMPS...
BLACKS ON ONE SIDE...AND WHITES ON THE OTHER, SLAUGHTERING ONE ANOTHER...
THEREFORE WE NEED TO DEAL WITH THE THREE PRE-CONDITIONS ON NEGOTIATIONS SET BY THE GOVERNMENT.
WE CANNOT CAST THE SACP ASIDE...WE ARE NOT UNDER ITS CONTROL...
MAJORITY RULE AND INTERNAL PEACE ARE LIKE THE TWO SIDES OF A SINGLE COIN...
...THE REFUSAL OF THE ANC TO RENOUNCE VIOLENCE IS NOT THE PROBLEM...
THE TRUTH IS THE GOVERNMENT IS NOT YET READY TO SHARE POLITICAL POWER WITH BLACKS.
FROM APRIL 1989 MANDELA AND TAMBO HAD CONTACT THROUGH A SYSTEM INVOLVING CODED MESSAGES SENT VIA A LAPTOP THAT HAD BEEN SMUGGLED INTO THE COUNTRY WITH THE HELP OF MAC MAHARAJ.
...AT LEAST NOW WE CAN SPEAK IN CONFIDENCE! BIZOS TOLD ME EVEN THE GARDEN FURNITURE AND FLOWERBEDS AT VICTOR VERSTER ARE BUGGED.

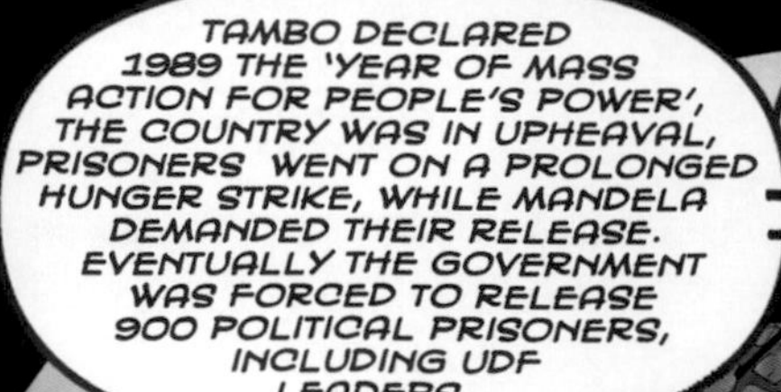
TAMBO DECLARED 1989 THE 'YEAR OF MASS ACTION FOR PEOPLE'S POWER', THE COUNTRY WAS IN UPHEAVAL, PRISONERS WENT ON A PROLONGED HUNGER STRIKE, WHILE MANDELA DEMANDED THEIR RELEASE. EVENTUALLY THE GOVERNMENT WAS FORCED TO RELEASE 900 POLITICAL PRISONERS, INCLUDING UDF LEADERS...

THE UDF FORMED AN ALLIANCE WITH TRADE UNIONS LIKE COSATU, AND STARTED THE "MASS DEMOCRATIC MOVEMENT" WHICH LAUNCHED A DEFIANCE CAMPAIGN AGAINST APARTHEID INSTITUTIONS SUCH AS HOSPITALS FOR WHITES ONLY...

HOSPITAL

whites only

UMKHONTO WE SIZWE INTENSIFIED ATTACKS ON GOVERNMENT PROPERTY. IT USED MORTARS TO DESTROY A MILITARY RADAR STATION...

MANDELA AND TAMBO KEPT PUSHING FOR SANCTIONS AGAINST SOUTH AFRICA AS AN ALTERNATIVE TO BLOODSHED.

IN JULY, SIX MONTHS AFTER HE SUFFERED A STROKE, PRESIDENT BOTHA ASKED TO SEE MANDELA...

I THINK THE AFRIKANERS WERE THE FIRST REAL FREEDOM FIGHTERS IN SOUTH AFRICA.

WELL, I THINK YOU CAN CONTRIBUTE TO A PEACEFUL SOLUTION AND SO CAN THE AFRIKANERS...

WE NEED THE GOVERNMENT TO RELEASE ALL POLITICAL PRISONERS...

I AM SORRY, BUT I CANNOT DO THAT.

SIX WEEKS LATER BOTHA RESIGNED AS PRESIDENT.

IN AUGUST THE GOVERNMENT TEAM RESPONDED TO THE MEMORANDUM SENT TO BOTHA. SOME AGREEMENT ABOUT PRE-NEGOTIATIONS WITH THE GOVERNMENT HAD BEEN REACHED...

THE OAU ENDORSED TAMBO'S HARARE DECLARATION. IT DID NOT ABANDON THE ARMED STRUGGLE BUT STRESSED THAT THE ANC PREFERRED PEACE-FUL METHODS....

THABO MBEKI MET NATIONAL INTELLIGENCE AGENT MIKE LOUW IN SWITZERLAND AND SAID THE ANC WAS READY TO NEGOTIATE...

FW DE KLERK BECAME SOUTH AFRICA'S NEW PRESIDENT. WHEN LOUW TOLD HIM ABOUT THE MBEKI BREAKTHROUGH HE DECIDED TO "TAKE THE BALL AND RUN WITH IT"....

...HE ANNOUNCED HIS WILLINGNESS TO TALK TO GROUPS COMMITTED TO PEACE AND STARTED DISMANTLING APARTHEID RESTRICTIONS SUCH AS SEGREGATED BEACHES, PARKS, TOILETS AND THE NATIONAL SECURITY MANAGEMENT SYSTEM THAT CONTROLLED THE TOWNSHIPS.
WHITES ONLY
STRAND SEE
NET BLANKES

MANDELA WROTE TO DE KLERK REQUESTING A MEETING. HE ALSO DEMANDED THE RELEASE OF TEN POLITICAL PRISONERS, INCLUDING HIS OLD FRIENDS AT POLLSMOOR. THEY CAME TO VISIT HIM AT VICTOR VERSTER PRISON...

CHAPS, THIS IS A GOODBYE VISIT.

YOU ARE GOING TO BE RELEASED.

US! RELEASED? I DON'T BELIEVE IT...

THAT EVENING, AFTER THEY HAD SAID GOODBYE TO MANDELA, THE MEN HAD DINNER WITH HIGH-RANKING PRISON OFFICIALS. A TELEVISION WAS BROUGHT IN...

...EIGHT POLITICAL PRISONERS WILL BE RELEASED... SISULU, KATHRADA, MHLABA, MKWAYI, MLANGENI, MOTSOALEDI, MASEMOLA AND MPETHA...

!?

IT IS TRUE!

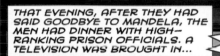

FIVE DAYS LATER, ON SUNDAY MORNING, 15 OCTOBER 1989, THE MEN WERE RELEASED...

MANDELA WAS THE LAST MAJOR OPPOSITION LEADER LEFT IN PRISON. POLITICIANS, FRIENDS, CLERGY, TRADE UNIONISTS AND YOUTH LEADERS CONVERGED ON VICTOR VERSTER. IN DECEMBER DE KLERK AND MANDELA MET AT TUYNHUIS.

...I HOPE WE WILL BE ABLE TO WORK TOGETHER...

IT WAS A TRICKY TIME. MANDELA LOST A VALUABLE LINK TO THE OUTSIDE WHEN TAMBO SUFFERED A STROKE. HE MADE SURE A COPY OF THE MEMORANDUM THAT HE HANDED TO DE KLERK REACHED THE ANC IN LUSAKA.

MANDELA HAD TO TACKLE THE GOVERNMENT'S NEW IDEA OF GROUP RIGHTS, WHERE NO RACIAL GROUP WOULD TAKE PRECEDENCE OVER ANY OTHER...

THE NP'S IDEA OF GROUP RIGHTS SEEMS LIKE A WAY TO MODERNISE APARTHEID...

...THE ANC HAS NOT STRUGGLED AGAINST APARTHEID FOR 75 YEARS, TO YIELD TO A DISGUISED FORM OF IT...

YOU KNOW, WE ARE TRYING TO DEAL WITH WHITE FEARS OF BLACK DOMINATION... YOU TOLD BOTHA WE HAD TO FIND A WAY TO DEAL WITH IT!

UNFORTUNATELY, MR DE KLERK, THE IDEA OF GROUP RIGHTS IS DOING MORE TO INCREASE BLACK FEARS THAN TO ALLAY WHITE ONES!

ON FEBRUARY 2, 1990, DE KLERK MADE A DRAMATIC ANNOUNCEMENT IN PARLIAMENT...

ALL POLITICAL PARTIES WILL BE UNBANNED... NELSON MANDELA WILL BE RELEASED WITH NO CONDITIONS...

A WEEK LATER... AFTER WORKING THROUGH THE NIGHT ON A SPEECH WITH COLLEAGUES SUCH AS CYRIL RAMAPHOSA AND TREVOR MANUEL, MANDELA PREPARED FOR HIS RELEASE THE NEXT MORNING... AFTER MORE THAN 10 000 DAYS IN PRISON.
HIS BAGS PACKED, MANDELA BID FAREWELL TO THE WARDERS AND LEFT TO GREET A WORLD THAT HAD GROWN UP WITHOUT HIM... AND ONE WHICH HAD LITTLE IDEA OF WHAT WAS GOING TO HAPPEN NEXT...
AS HE TOOK HIS FIRST STEPS TO FREEDOM MANDELA WAS GREETED BY JOURNALISTS FROM ALL OVER THE WORLD, AND THOUSANDS OF SUPPORTERS. THEY DANCED, CHEERED AND CRIED WITH HAPPINESS. THEIR CHANCE FOR A NEW FUTURE HAD COME...

7

PRESIDENT-IN-WAITING

11 FEBRUARY 1990, MANDELA IS FREE AFTER 27 YEARS IN PRISON. MILLIONS WATCHED FOR A GLIMPSE OF HIM.
MANDELA AND WINNIE STRUGGLED TO GET TO THE CAPE TOWN CITY HALL. THOUSANDS HAD GATHERED AT THE GRAND PARADE TO SEE HIM. THE DRIVER TOOK A WRONG TURN AND THEIR CAR WAS SURROUNDED BY A THRONG OF EXCITED PEOPLE.
LET THEM PASS! GET OUT OF THE WAY!
THE PEOPLE WILL KILL US WITH THEIR LOVE!
THEY EVENTUALLY ARRIVED AT THE CITY HALL, WHERE MANDELA DELIVERED HIS FIRST SPEECH SINCE HIS RELEASE. SOME PEOPLE TRIED TO CLIMB UP THE BALCONY TO GET CLOSE TO HIM.
...I STAND HERE BEFORE YOU, NOT AS A PROPHET BUT AS A HUMBLE SERVANT OF YOU, THE PEOPLE...
...YOUR TIRELESS AND HEROIC SACRIFICES HAVE MADE IT POSSIBLE FOR ME TO BE HERE TODAY. I THEREFORE PLACE THE REMAINING YEARS OF MY LIFE IN YOUR HANDS...

MANDELA WAS WHISKED OFF TO THE HOME OF ARCHBISHOP DESMOND TUTU, IN THE TRADITIONALLY WHITE SUBURB OF BISHOPSCOURT, TO SPEND THE NIGHT.
...TO DRIVE TO THE TRANSKEI, VISIT THE PLACES OF MY CHILDHOOD... MY MOTHER'S GRAVE... IT WILL HAVE TO WAIT...
THE NEXT MORNING HE FACED HUNDREDS OF JOURNALISTS AT HIS FIRST PRESS CONFERENCE.
MR MANDELA WHY ARE YOU STILL SUPPORTING THE ARMED STRUGGLE AND SANCTIONS?
THE ABSENCE OF RIGHTS FOR BLACKS IS STILL THE STATUS QUO. I MIGHT BE OUT OF JAIL, BUT I AM NOT YET FREE...
WHITES ARE FELLOW SOUTH AFRICANS ...ANY MAN OR WOMAN WHO ABANDONS APARTHEID WILL BE EMBRACED IN OUR STRUGGLE FOR A DEMOCRATIC, NON-RACIAL SOUTH AFRICA.
HE TRIED TO ALLEVIATE WHITE FEARS AND SURPRISED THE WORLD WITH HIS COMPLETE LACK OF BITTERNESS...
THERE WAS NO TIME TO REST AND REFLECT. MANDELA WAS URGED TO RETURN TO JOHANNESBURG WHERE SUPPORTERS WERE WAITING. HE SPENT HIS SECOND NIGHT OF FREEDOM AT THE HOME OF A SUPPORTER IN JOHANNESBURG.
ON 13 FEBRUARY 1990, A CROWD OF 100 000 CONVERGED AT SOCCER CITY IN SOWETO TO WELCOME MANDELA. HE URGED LEARNERS TO GO TO SCHOOL AND CONDEMNED CRIME. HE LEFT BY HELICOPTER AT THE END OF THE RALLY.

AT LAST HE RETURNED TO HIS HUMBLE HOME IN ORLANDO WEST...
"TODAY MY RETURN TO SOWETO FILLS MY HEART WITH JOY. AT THE SAME TIME I ALSO RETURN WITH A DEEP SENSE OF SADNESS: SADNESS TO LEARN THAT YOU ARE STILL SUFFERING UNDER AN INHUMAN SYSTEM..."
AT LONG LAST MANDELA AT HOME!!!
MANDELA, WHO HAD BECOME USED TO SOLITUDE, WAS SURROUNDED BY ADMIRERS, POLITICIANS, THE MEDIA, FAMILY AND FRIENDS.
YOU HAVE TO UNDERSTAND, I AM JUST A SERVANT OF THE ANC...
HE WAS AT HOME AFTER 27 YEARS, BUT WAS DENIED THE ORDINARY FAMILY LIFE HE HAD LONGED FOR. MANDELA BELONGED TO THE PEOPLE. HIS TIME WAS NOT HIS OWN.
FOR MANY NIGHTS PEOPLE GATHERED OUTSIDE AND SANG FREEDOM SONGS...
THIS IS WHERE I BELONG... AMONG MY PEOPLE...

ON 27 FEBRUARY, MANDELA AND HIS COLLEAGUES FLEW TO LUSAKA TO REPORT TO THE ANC'S NATIONAL EXECUTIVE COMMITTEE.
THEY WILL WANT TO SEE IF I HAD BEEN BROKEN...
MANDELA WAS ELECTED AS DEPUTY PRESIDENT OF THE ANC, ALFRED NZO BECAME ACTING PRESIDENT WHILE OLIVER TAMBO RECUPERATED FROM A STROKE.
WELCOME MANDELA
VIVA! ANC MANDELA
WELL DONE, COMRADE.
MANDELA HAD TO SHOW THAT HE WAS STILL A STRONG LEADER. SOME STILL BELIEVED HE HAD SOLD OUT. HE RECOMMITTED HIMSELF TO THE ARMED STRUGGLE.
WE HAVE NOT YET ACHIEVED THE GOAL FOR WHICH WE HAVE TAKEN UP ARMS...
HE WAS APPALLED BY THE VIOLENCE THAT HAD BEEN BEEN RAGING IN KWAZULU-NATAL BETWEEN SUPPORTERS OF INKATHA AND THE ANC...
HE SPOKE TO 100 000 PEOPLE AT A RALLY IN DURBAN JUST TWO WEEKS AFTER HIS RELEASE:
TAKE YOUR GUNS, YOUR KNIVES AND YOUR PANGAS, AND THROW THEM INTO THE SEA!
BUT THE KILLINGS CONTINUED... VILLAGES WERE SET ALIGHT AND THOUSANDS WERE DISPLACED... MANDELA VISITED VIOLENCE-STRICKEN COMMUNITIES.
DE KLERK AND THE GOVERNMENT ARE DOING NOTHING TO STOP THIS! WHY?
WHY IS CHIEF BUTHELEZI NOT TELLING HIS PEOPLE TO STOP?!
MANDELA DID NOT MANAGE TO MEET WITH CHIEF BUTHELEZI AND KING ZWELETHINI, WITH WHOM HE TRIED TO MAINTAIN GOOD RELATIONSHIPS.

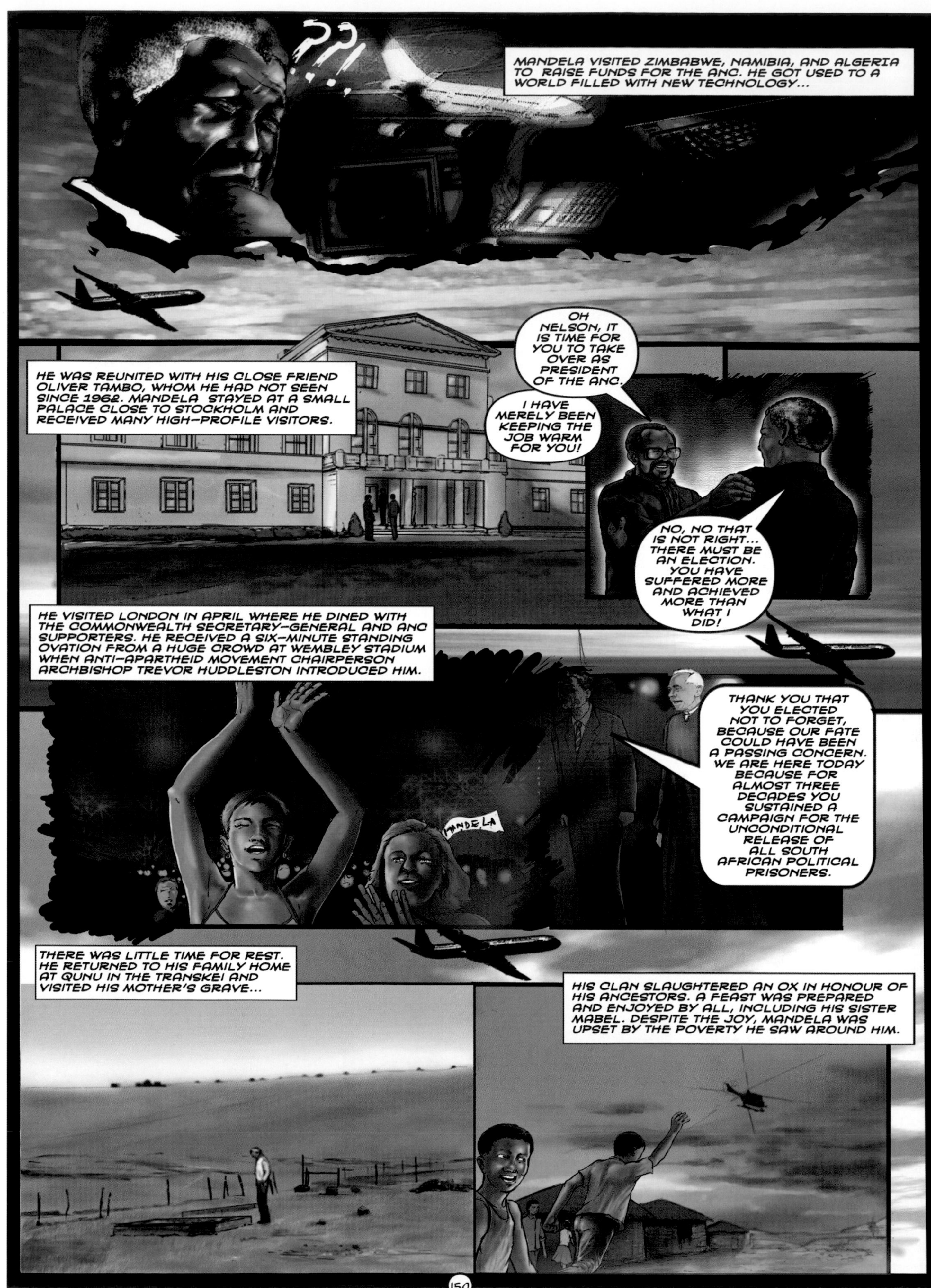
MANDELA VISITED ZIMBABWE, NAMIBIA, AND ALGERIA TO RAISE FUNDS FOR THE ANC. HE GOT USED TO A WORLD FILLED WITH NEW TECHNOLOGY...
HE WAS REUNITED WITH HIS CLOSE FRIEND OLIVER TAMBO, WHOM HE HAD NOT SEEN SINCE 1962. MANDELA STAYED AT A SMALL PALACE CLOSE TO STOCKHOLM AND RECEIVED MANY HIGH-PROFILE VISITORS.
OH NELSON, IT IS TIME FOR YOU TO TAKE OVER AS PRESIDENT OF THE ANC.
I HAVE MERELY BEEN KEEPING THE JOB WARM FOR YOU!
NO, NO THAT IS NOT RIGHT... THERE MUST BE AN ELECTION. YOU HAVE SUFFERED MORE AND ACHIEVED MORE THAN WHAT I DID!
HE VISITED LONDON IN APRIL WHERE HE DINED WITH THE COMMONWEALTH SECRETARY-GENERAL AND ANC SUPPORTERS. HE RECEIVED A SIX-MINUTE STANDING OVATION FROM A HUGE CROWD AT WEMBLEY STADIUM WHEN ANTI-APARTHEID MOVEMENT CHAIRPERSON ARCHBISHOP TREVOR HUDDLESTON INTRODUCED HIM.
MANDELA
THANK YOU THAT YOU ELECTED NOT TO FORGET, BECAUSE OUR FATE COULD HAVE BEEN A PASSING CONCERN. WE ARE HERE TODAY BECAUSE FOR ALMOST THREE DECADES YOU SUSTAINED A CAMPAIGN FOR THE UNCONDITIONAL RELEASE OF ALL SOUTH AFRICAN POLITICAL PRISONERS.
THERE WAS LITTLE TIME FOR REST. HE RETURNED TO HIS FAMILY HOME AT QUNU IN THE TRANSKEI AND VISITED HIS MOTHER'S GRAVE...
HIS CLAN SLAUGHTERED AN OX IN HONOUR OF HIS ANCESTORS. A FEAST WAS PREPARED AND ENJOYED BY ALL, INCLUDING HIS SISTER MABEL. DESPITE THE JOY, MANDELA WAS UPSET BY THE POVERTY HE SAW AROUND HIM.

MANDELA HAD TO HELP LEAD THE ANC TO POLITICAL POWER. BUT FIRST A NEGOTIATED SETTLEMENT HAD TO BE FOUND.
DISASTER STRUCK JUST BEFORE THE ANC AND GOVERNMENT WERE DUE TO SET A DATE FOR "TALKS ABOUT TALKS".
SEVERAL ANC SUPPORTERS WERE KILLED AND HUNDREDS INJURED WHEN THE POLICE FIRED ON DEMONSTRATORS IN SEBOKENG ON 26 MARCH 1990.
EVERY WHITE POLICEMAN IN SOUTH AFRICA REGARDS EVERY BLACK PERSON AS A MILITARY TARGET!
THE ANC IS SUSPENDING TALKS... DE KLERK HAS TO UNDERSTAND, YOU CANNOT TALK ABOUT NEGOTIATIONS ON THE ONE HAND AND MURDER OUR PEOPLE ON THE OTHER!
AT LAST, ON 2 MAY 1990, AT GROOTE SCHUUR, THE PRESIDENTIAL RESIDENCE IN CAPE TOWN, THE ANC AND GOVERNMENT MET...
MANDELA, SISULU, NZO, THABO MBEKI, KATHRADA, JOE MODISE, RUTH MOMPATI, ARCHIE GUMEDE, BEYERS NAUDE, CHERYL CAROLUS AND JOE SLOVO REPRESENTED THE ANC IN THE THREE DAYS OF TALKS.
THE TWO PARTIES REACHED AN AGREEMENT CALLED "THE GROOTE SCHUUR MINUTE". IT WAS ABOUT THE RELEASE OF POLITICAL PRISONERS, THE RETURN OF EXILES AND AMENDING SECURITY LEGISLATION. THE ANC AND THE GOVERNMENT ALSO PROMISED TO CONTINUE PEACEFUL NEGOTIATIONS AND WORK TOWARDS LIFTING THE STATE OF EMERGENCY.
WE WENT INTO THESE DISCUSSIONS IN THE SPIRIT THAT THERE SHOULD BE NEITHER WINNERS NOR LOSERS...
NOT ONLY ARE WE CLOSER TO ONE ANOTHER, THE ANC AND THE GOVERNMENT, BUT WE ARE ALL VICTORS. SOUTH AFRICA IS A VICTOR.

ONE OF MANDELA'S CLOSEST FRIENDS, WALTER SISULU, HAD HIS FAMILY BACK TOGETHER FOR THE FIRST TIME IN DECADES.
HIS DAUGHTER LINDIWE RETURNED AFTER 14 YEARS IN EXILE...
HIS SON MAX RETURNED A FEW MONTHS LATER AFTER 24 YEARS IN EXILE...
HIS SON ZWELAKHE, WHO WAS IN DETENTION BETWEEN 1986 AND 1988, WAS WORKING AS MANDELA'S PRESS AIDE...
HIS FREEDOM FIGHTER SON JONGI, WHOM HE HAD LAST SEEN WHEN HE WAS FIVE YEARS OLD, WAS RELEASED FROM PRISON AND WAITED FOR HIS FATHER AT THE AIRPORT...
TATA THIS IS JONGI!
I DID NOT RECOGNISE YOU! I JUST DID NOT RECOGNISE YOU...
IN THE MEANTIME, MANDELA MOVED TO A BIGGER HOUSE IN SOWETO, BUT HIS WORK LEFT HIM LITTLE TIME FOR HIS FAMILY.
BY NOW, WINNIE WAS CAUGHT UP IN THE CONTROVERSY SURROUNDING THE DEATH OF ACTIVIST STOMPIE SEIPEI. MANDELA STUCK BY HER.
YOU KNOW THE GIRLS WERE SAYING THAT YOU WERE MORE ACCESSIBLE TO THEM WHEN YOU WERE IN PRISON...
IN JUNE, JUST BEFORE MANDELA WENT ON AN INTERNATIONAL TOUR, DE KLERK IMPLORED HIM NOT TO KEEP PUSHING FOR SANCTIONS. BUT MANDELA DID NOT AGREE.

MANDELA VISITED COUNTRIES IN AFRICA, EUROPE, AND NORTH AMERICA. HE RECEIVED A HERO'S WELCOME WHEREVER HE WENT. IN NEW YORK A TICKER TAPE PARADE WAS HELD IN HIS HONOUR.
THE EMPIRE STATE BUILDING WAS LIT UP IN THE ANC COLOURS.
IN NEW YORK HE STAYED AT THE OPULENT GRACIE MANSION. A FAR CRY FROM THE DAMP CELL HE HAD BECOME USED TO.
JUST A QUICK JOG AND I WILL BE READY FOR THE DAY...
BUT HE SOON REALISED THAT EVEN HERE HIS FREEDOM WAS NOT COMPLETE...
STOP! IT IS TOO DANGEROUS. WE HAVE TO SEND A GUARD WITH YOU.
IN ENGLAND, HE MET WITH MARGARET THATCHER, THE BRITISH PRIME MINISTER WHO HAD OPPOSED SANCTIONS AGAINST SOUTH AFRICA.
HOW CAN YOU TALK TO SOMEONE WHO HAS DENOUNCED YOU AS A TERRORIST?
I AM WORKING WITH SOUTH AFRICANS WHO HAVE DONE MUCH WORSE THINGS...
SHE EVEN WARNED ME TO TAKE BETTER CARE OF MYSELF!
WHEN MANDELA RETURNED TO SOUTH AFRICA IN JULY VIOLENCE IN THE TOWNSHIPS AROUND JOHANNESBURG HAD INCREASED DRAMATICALLY. HUNDREDS OF PEOPLE WERE KILLED IN SIX MONTHS.
THEY ARE PLANNING SOMETHING! WE HAVE NOTIFIED THE MINISTER OF LAW AND ORDER...WE HAVE ASKED HIM TO PROTECT THE PEOPLE!
MR. DE KLERK, 30 PEOPLE WERE KILLED, HUNDREDS WERE INJURED! YOU WERE WARNED IN ADVANCE... AND YET YOU DID NOTHING! WHY IS THAT? WHY HAVE THE POLICE SAT ON THEIR HANDS?
ON 22 JULY, COMBI-LOADS OF MEN ARMED WITH TRADITIONAL WEAPONS WERE BUSSED TO SEBOKENG, WHERE THEY ATTACKED FAMILIES AS THEY SLEPT.
JUST AS MANDELA CONFRONTED DE KLERK ABOUT VIOLENCE, DE KLERK LATER CONFRONTED MANDELA ABOUT OPERATION VULA.

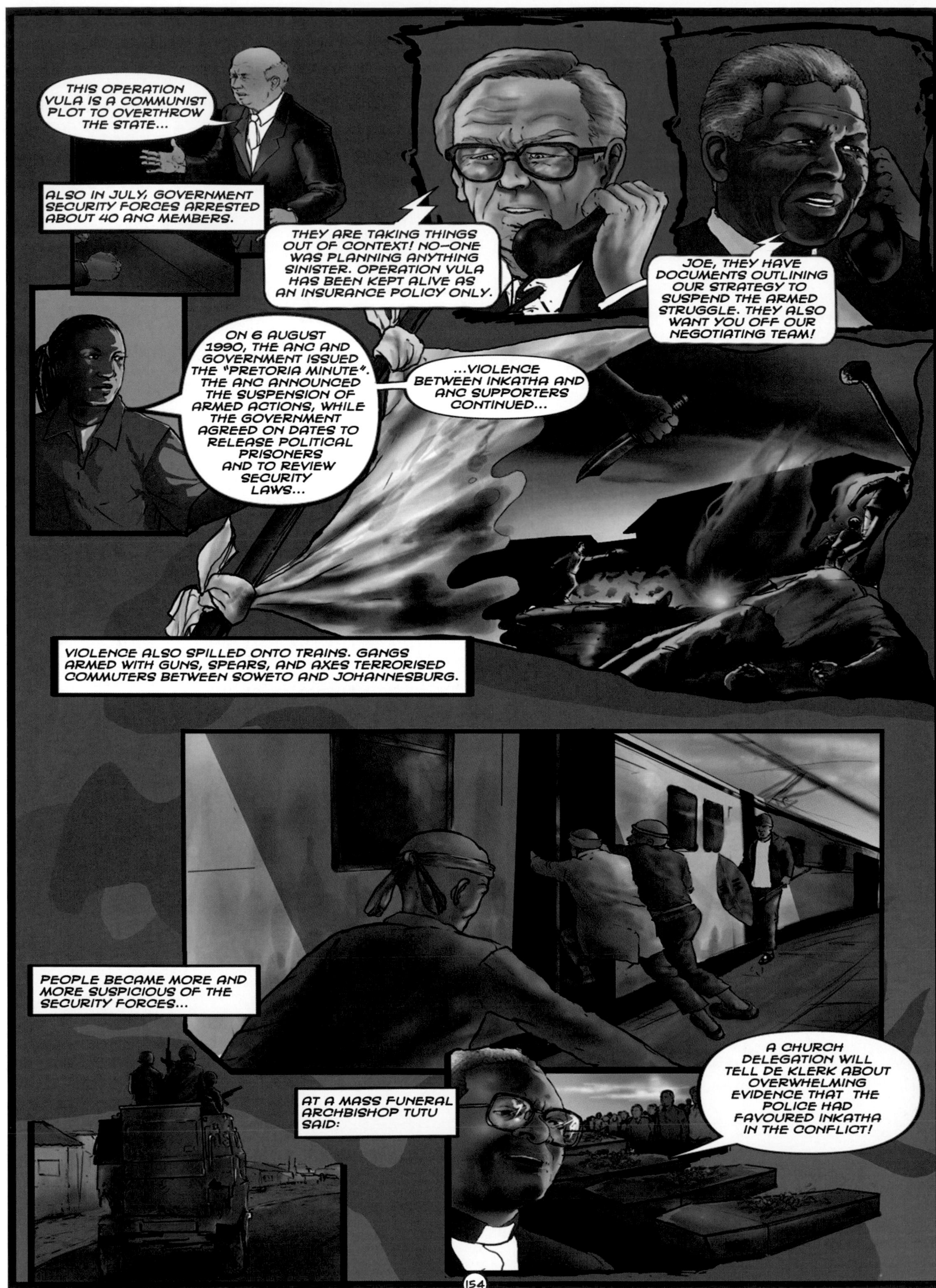
THIS OPERATION VULA IS A COMMUNIST PLOT TO OVERTHROW THE STATE...
ALSO IN JULY, GOVERNMENT SECURITY FORCES ARRESTED ABOUT 40 ANC MEMBERS.
THEY ARE TAKING THINGS OUT OF CONTEXT! NO-ONE WAS PLANNING ANYTHING SINISTER. OPERATION VULA HAS BEEN KEPT ALIVE AS AN INSURANCE POLICY ONLY.
JOE, THEY HAVE DOCUMENTS OUTLINING OUR STRATEGY TO SUSPEND THE ARMED STRUGGLE. THEY ALSO WANT YOU OFF OUR NEGOTIATING TEAM!
ON 6 AUGUST 1990, THE ANC AND GOVERNMENT ISSUED THE "PRETORIA MINUTE". THE ANC ANNOUNCED THE SUSPENSION OF ARMED ACTIONS, WHILE THE GOVERNMENT AGREED ON DATES TO RELEASE POLITICAL PRISONERS AND TO REVIEW SECURITY LAWS...
...VIOLENCE BETWEEN INKATHA AND ANC SUPPORTERS CONTINUED...
VIOLENCE ALSO SPILLED ONTO TRAINS. GANGS ARMED WITH GUNS, SPEARS, AND AXES TERRORISED COMMUTERS BETWEEN SOWETO AND JOHANNESBURG.
PEOPLE BECAME MORE AND MORE SUSPICIOUS OF THE SECURITY FORCES...
AT A MASS FUNERAL ARCHBISHOP TUTU SAID:
A CHURCH DELEGATION WILL TELL DE KLERK ABOUT OVERWHELMING EVIDENCE THAT THE POLICE HAD FAVOURED INKATHA IN THE CONFLICT!

THE ANC SET UP ARMED SELF-DEFENCE UNITS TO PROTECT THE PEOPLE IN THE VIOLENCE-RAVAGED TOWNSHIPS. MANDELA VISITED THE BATTLEFIELDS AND KEPT BEING TOLD THE POLICE SUPPORTED INKATHA...
THE POLICE WERE ON INKATHA'S SIDE... I SAW THEM HANDING OUT GUNS!
THERE ARE FORCES CLOSE TO YOU, MR PRESIDENT, WITH A DOUBLE AGENDA!
DE KLERK HAD SOUGHT AN ALLIANCE WITH INKATHA BUT IT WAS NOT TO BE. BUTHELEZI WAS ALSO COURTED BY CONSERVATIVES IN THE WEST WHO SAW INKATHA AS AN ANTI-COMMUNIST OPPOSITION TO THE ANC.
I WILL HAVE TO INVESTIGATE THESE ALLEGATIONS!
MANDELA DESPERATELY WANTED THE SENSELESS VIOLENCE TO END. AT LAST, IN JANUARY 1991, HE MET WITH BUTHELEZI. IT WAS THEIR FIRST MEETING IN 30 YEARS.
IT IS GOOD TO MEET AFTER SUCH A LONG TIME...
THANK YOU FOR ALL YOUR EFFORTS OVER THE YEARS TO SECURE MY RELEASE FROM PRISON...
THE MEN AGREED TO PROMOTE PEACE AND TO URGE THEIR PEOPLE TO STOP THE KILLINGS, BUT WORSE WAS TO COME. IN MARCH 45 PEOPLE WERE KILLED IN ALEXANDRA TOWNSHIP, WHERE MANDELA ONCE LIVED. MORE THAN 400 PEOPLE WERE KILLED IN THE FIRST THREE MONTHS OF THE YEAR. MANDELA MET WITH BUTHELEZI FOR A SECOND TIME.
MANDELA SAID: "I AM NOW CONVINCED THE GOVERNMENT HAS A HAND IN THIS VIOLENCE"
THE ANC DECLARED IT BELIEVED THE GOVERNMENT WAS BEHIND THE VIOLENCE. IT WROTE AN OPEN LETTER TO THE GOVERNMENT WITH THE BACKING OF THE SACP AND COSATU.
...WE CALL FOR THE DISMISSAL OF MINISTERS MALAN AND VLOK BEFORE MAY OR WE WILL SUSPEND ALL TALKS WITH THE GOVERNMENT!
NO MORE TALK!
THE GOVERNMENT REFUSED TO CO-OPERATE AND THE ANC, AGAIN, BROKE OFF TALKS. THE PEOPLE THEN EMBARKED ON A CAMPAIGN OF MASS ACTION, TO DEMONSTRATE THEIR STRENGTH.

ON 2 JULY 1991, THE ANC HELD A NATIONAL CONFERENCE IN SOUTH AFRICA FOR THE FIRST TIME IN 30 YEARS.
OLIVER TAMBO HAD RETURNED TO THE COUNTRY, BUT STEPPED DOWN AS ANC PRESIDENT. NELSON ROLIHLAHLA MANDELA WAS ELECTED IN HIS PLACE.
THE OLD GUARD WAS STILL STRONG IN THE ANC, BUT YOUNGER LEADERS CAME TO THE FORE. CYRIL RAMAPHOSA WAS ELECTED AS SECRETARY-GENERAL.
MANDELA FACED OPEN CRITICISM FROM MILITANTS IN THE ANC...
WE NEED A YOUNGER MORE MILITANT MAN TO LEAD US IN THE STRUGGLE...
AT HOME HE ALSO FACED CRITICISM WHEN HIS DAUGHTER MAKAZIWE RETURNED FROM AMERICA IN 1990.
MAKI...
YOU ARE A FATHER TO ALL OUR PEOPLE BUT YOU HAVE NEVER HAD THE TIME TO BE A FATHER TO ME...
SHE HAS NOT FORGIVEN ME...
MANDELA ADORED CHILDREN. HE HAD MISSED THEIR COMPANY FOR 27 YEARS.
MADIBA! WHY DID YOU GO TO PRISON FOR SOOOO LONG?
WELL I HAD TO STAY THERE TO FIGHT FOR DEMOCRACY...
YOU MUST BE VERY STUPID TO STAY THERE SO LONG...
HA! I THINK YOU MIGHT BE RIGHT!

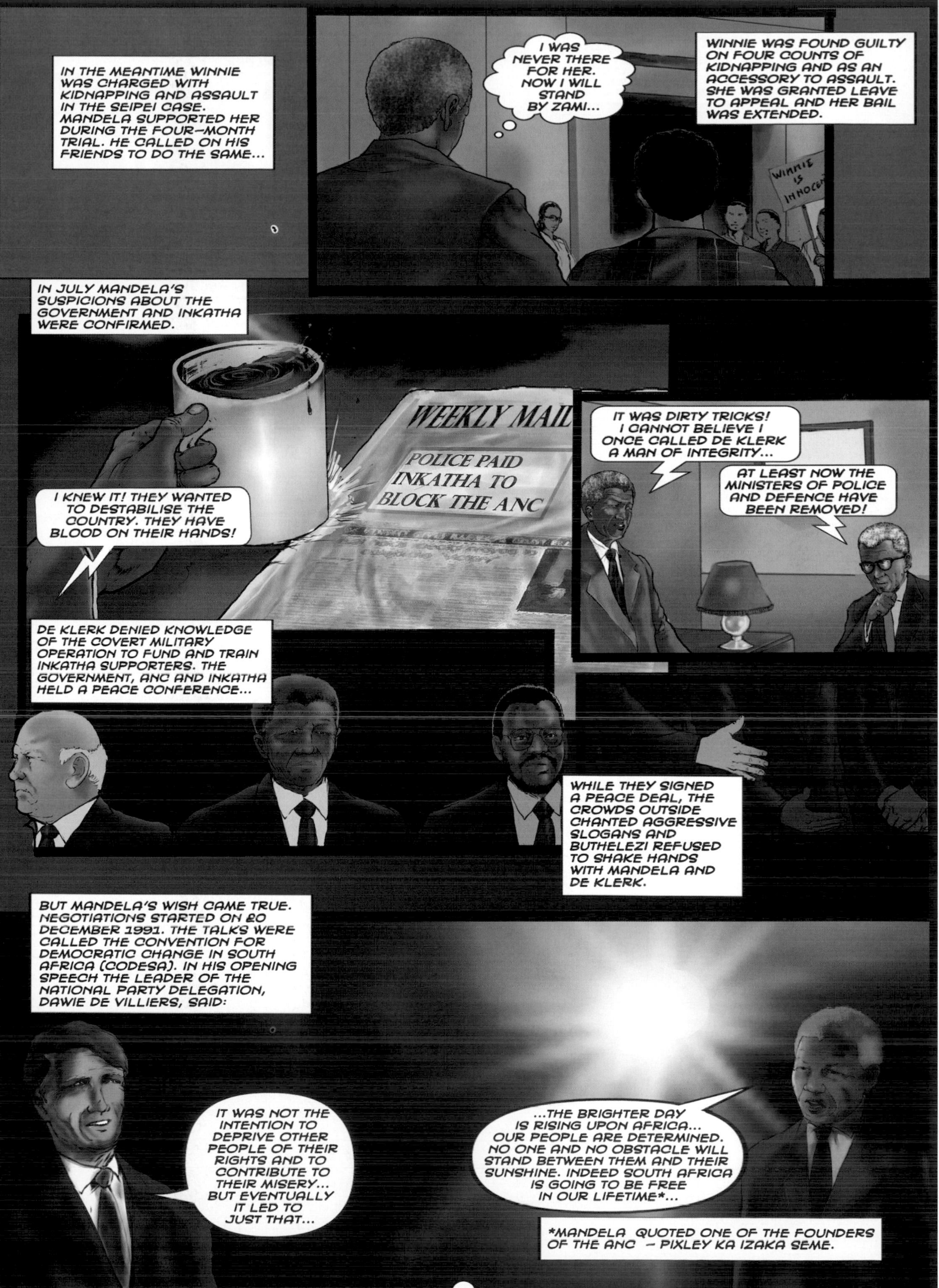

IN THE MEANTIME WINNIE WAS CHARGED WITH KIDNAPPING AND ASSAULT IN THE SEIPEI CASE. MANDELA SUPPORTED HER DURING THE FOUR-MONTH TRIAL. HE CALLED ON HIS FRIENDS TO DO THE SAME...
I WAS NEVER THERE FOR HER. NOW I WILL STAND BY ZAMI...
WINNIE WAS FOUND GUILTY ON FOUR COUNTS OF KIDNAPPING AND AS AN ACCESSORY TO ASSAULT. SHE WAS GRANTED LEAVE TO APPEAL AND HER BAIL WAS EXTENDED.
WINNIE IS INNOCE
IN JULY MANDELA'S SUSPICIONS ABOUT THE GOVERNMENT AND INKATHA WERE CONFIRMED.
WEEKLY MAIL
POLICE PAID INKATHA TO BLOCK THE ANC
I KNEW IT! THEY WANTED TO DESTABILISE THE COUNTRY. THEY HAVE BLOOD ON THEIR HANDS!
IT WAS DIRTY TRICKS! I CANNOT BELIEVE I ONCE CALLED DE KLERK A MAN OF INTEGRITY...
AT LEAST NOW THE MINISTERS OF POLICE AND DEFENCE HAVE BEEN REMOVED!
DE KLERK DENIED KNOWLEDGE OF THE COVERT MILITARY OPERATION TO FUND AND TRAIN INKATHA SUPPORTERS. THE GOVERNMENT, ANC AND INKATHA HELD A PEACE CONFERENCE...
WHILE THEY SIGNED A PEACE DEAL, THE CROWDS OUTSIDE CHANTED AGGRESSIVE SLOGANS AND BUTHELEZI REFUSED TO SHAKE HANDS WITH MANDELA AND DE KLERK.
BUT MANDELA'S WISH CAME TRUE. NEGOTIATIONS STARTED ON 20 DECEMBER 1991. THE TALKS WERE CALLED THE CONVENTION FOR DEMOCRATIC CHANGE IN SOUTH AFRICA (CODESA). IN HIS OPENING SPEECH THE LEADER OF THE NATIONAL PARTY DELEGATION, DAWIE DE VILLIERS, SAID:
IT WAS NOT THE INTENTION TO DEPRIVE OTHER PEOPLE OF THEIR RIGHTS AND TO CONTRIBUTE TO THEIR MISERY... BUT EVENTUALLY IT LED TO JUST THAT...
...THE BRIGHTER DAY IS RISING UPON AFRICA... OUR PEOPLE ARE DETERMINED. NO ONE AND NO OBSTACLE WILL STAND BETWEEN THEM AND THEIR SUNSHINE. INDEED SOUTH AFRICA IS GOING TO BE FREE IN OUR LIFETIME*...
*MANDELA QUOTED ONE OF THE FOUNDERS OF THE ANC – PIXLEY KA IZAKA SEME.

INKATHA AND RIGHT–WING AFRIKANER PARTIES DID NOT PARTICIPATE IN CODESA. DELEGATES SIGNED A DECLARATION OF INTENT, TO BRING ABOUT AN UNDIVIDED SOUTH AFRICA, BUT AT THE END OF HIS SPEECH DE KLERK BEGAN ATTACKING THE ANC...
...THE ANC IS HIDING ARMS! IT IS KEEPING MK AS A PRIVATE ARMY...
SO THAT IS WHY HE WANTED TO BE THE LAST SPEAKER! HE IS ADMONISHING US LIKE WE ARE SCHOOL CHILDREN!
MANDELA BROKE THE RULES AND LAUNCHED A COUNTER–ATTACK ON DE KLERK.
EVEN THE HEAD OF AN ILLEGITIMATE, DISCREDITED MINORITY REGIME, SUCH AS HIS, HAS CERTAIN STANDARDS TO UPHOLD!
MIRACULOUSLY NEGOTIATIONS DID NOT BREAK DOWN AGAIN. FIVE TEAMS WERE LEFT TO WORK OUT DETAILED AGREEMENTS BEFORE THE NEXT FULL CODESA MEETING IN MAY 1992. CYRIL RAMAPHOSA HEADED THE ANC'S NEGOTIATION TEAM, AND ROELF MEYER THE NP'S.
BUT IN HIS PERSONAL LIFE MANDELA WAS EXPERIENCING BREAKDOWN. AT A PRESS CONFERENCE ON 13 APRIL 1992 HE ANNOUNCED THE END OF HIS MARRIAGE TO WINNIE.
I PART WITH MY WIFE WITH NO RECRIMINATIONS... I HOPE YOU APPRECIATE THE PAIN I HAVE GONE THROUGH.
MANDELA'S SADNESS WAS VISIBLE. IN HIS SPEECH AT ZINDZI'S WEDDING HE SAID...
TO BE THE FATHER OF A NATION IS A GREAT HONOUR, BUT TO BE THE FATHER OF A FAMILY IS A GREATER JOY...
BUT IT WAS A JOY I HAD FAR TOO LITTLE OF...

DE KLERK CALLED AN ALL–WHITE REFERENDUM TO DETERMINE IF WHITES SUPPORTED HIS REFORMS. 69% SAID THEY DID.
BUT CODESA 2 BROKE DOWN BECAUSE THE WORKING GROUPS COULD NOT AGREE ON ISSUES AROUND A NEW CONSTITUTION AND THE SHAPE OF AN INTERIM GOVERNMENT.
MANDELA FELT THE STALEMATE WAS CAUSED BY THE NP'S RELUCTANCE TO SUBMIT TO MAJORITY RULE. BILATERAL TALKS BETWEEN THE ANC AND NP CONTINUED.
ON 16 JUNE 1992 THE ANC LAUNCHED A MASS ACTION CAMPAIGN TO SHOW ITS STRENGTH, BUT THE NEXT DAY THE PEOPLE OF BOIPATONG WERE ATTACKED...
MOVE! IT'S TIME!
SOME OF THEM HAVE WHITE FACES! HIDE!
FORTY–FIVE PEOPLE, INCLUDING WOMEN AND CHILDREN, WERE KILLED...
MANDELA WENT TO THE SITE OF THE MASSACRE.
MANDELA GIVE US GUNS!!!
THE ONLY WAY TO OVERTHROW APARTHEID IS WITH GUNS!
KILL THE BOER...
DE KLERK ALSO WENT TO PAY HIS RESPECTS TO THE PEOPLE OF BOIPATONG, BUT HAD TO FLEE...
MANDELA STOPPED TALKS WITH DE KLERK AND TURNED TO THE UNITED NATIONS FOR SUPPORT. A SPECIAL MEETING OF THE SECURITY COUNCIL WAS HELD AND UN SPECIAL ENVOY, CYRUS VANCE, WAS SENT TO GET TALKS BACK ON TRACK.
I CAN NO LONGER EXPLAIN TO OUR PEOPLE WHY WE CONTINUE TO TALK TO A REGIME THAT IS MURDERING OUR PEOPLE!
THE MASS ACTION CULMINATED IN THE BIGGEST STRIKE IN THE COUNTRY'S HISTORY. MANDELA LED A MASSIVE MARCH TO THE UNION BUILDINGS ON 5 AUGUST. HE WARNED PEOPLE NOT TO LET THE MARCH SPILL OVER INTO VIOLENCE.

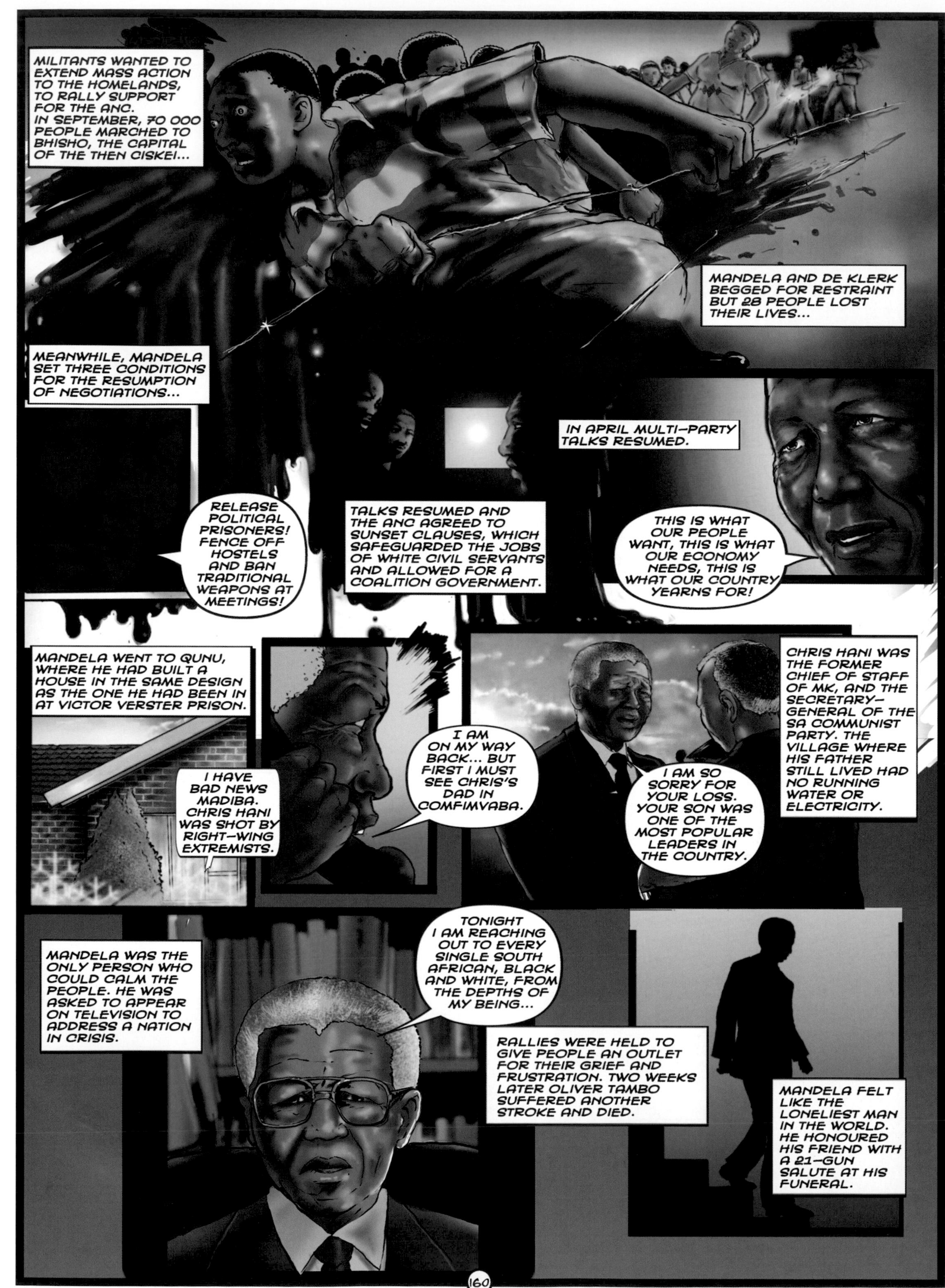
MILITANTS WANTED TO EXTEND MASS ACTION TO THE HOMELANDS, TO RALLY SUPPORT FOR THE ANC. IN SEPTEMBER, 70 000 PEOPLE MARCHED TO BHISHO, THE CAPITAL OF THE THEN CISKEI...
MANDELA AND DE KLERK BEGGED FOR RESTRAINT BUT 28 PEOPLE LOST THEIR LIVES...
MEANWHILE, MANDELA SET THREE CONDITIONS FOR THE RESUMPTION OF NEGOTIATIONS...
RELEASE POLITICAL PRISONERS! FENCE OFF HOSTELS AND BAN TRADITIONAL WEAPONS AT MEETINGS!
TALKS RESUMED AND THE ANC AGREED TO SUNSET CLAUSES, WHICH SAFEGUARDED THE JOBS OF WHITE CIVIL SERVANTS AND ALLOWED FOR A COALITION GOVERNMENT.
IN APRIL MULTI-PARTY TALKS RESUMED.
THIS IS WHAT OUR PEOPLE WANT, THIS IS WHAT OUR ECONOMY NEEDS, THIS IS WHAT OUR COUNTRY YEARNS FOR!
MANDELA WENT TO QUNU, WHERE HE HAD BUILT A HOUSE IN THE SAME DESIGN AS THE ONE HE HAD BEEN IN AT VICTOR VERSTER PRISON.
I HAVE BAD NEWS MADIBA. CHRIS HANI WAS SHOT BY RIGHT-WING EXTREMISTS.
I AM ON MY WAY BACK... BUT FIRST I MUST SEE CHRIS'S DAD IN COMFIMVABA.
I AM SO SORRY FOR YOUR LOSS. YOUR SON WAS ONE OF THE MOST POPULAR LEADERS IN THE COUNTRY.
CHRIS HANI WAS THE FORMER CHIEF OF STAFF OF MK, AND THE SECRETARY-GENERAL OF THE SA COMMUNIST PARTY. THE VILLAGE WHERE HIS FATHER STILL LIVED HAD NO RUNNING WATER OR ELECTRICITY.
MANDELA WAS THE ONLY PERSON WHO COULD CALM THE PEOPLE. HE WAS ASKED TO APPEAR ON TELEVISION TO ADDRESS A NATION IN CRISIS.
TONIGHT I AM REACHING OUT TO EVERY SINGLE SOUTH AFRICAN, BLACK AND WHITE, FROM THE DEPTHS OF MY BEING...
RALLIES WERE HELD TO GIVE PEOPLE AN OUTLET FOR THEIR GRIEF AND FRUSTRATION. TWO WEEKS LATER OLIVER TAMBO SUFFERED ANOTHER STROKE AND DIED.
MANDELA FELT LIKE THE LONELIEST MAN IN THE WORLD. HE HONOURED HIS FRIEND WITH A 21-GUN SALUTE AT HIS FUNERAL.

ON 2 JUNE 1999, THE APPEAL COURT UPHELD WINNIE'S CONVICTION FOR KIDNAPPING IN THE STOMPIE SEIPEI CASE, BUT RULED SHE HAD NOT BEEN AN ACCESSORY TO ASSAULT. SHE RECEIVED A TWO-YEAR SUSPENDED SENTENCE AND WAS FINED R15 000.
AMANDLA!!!
THE COUNTDOWN TO THE DEMOCRATIC TRANSFER OF POWER TO THE PEOPLE HAS BEGUN.
JUST A DAY LATER MANDELA TASTED VICTORY WHEN AGREEMENT WAS REACHED ON AN ELECTION DATE.
FIRST DEMOCRATIC ELECTIONS DATE 27 APRIL 1994
THE URGENCY TO NEGOTIATE A NEW CONSTITUTION BEFORE THE ELECTIONS INTENSIFIED, AND A CAMARADERIE DEVELOPED BETWEEN NEGOTIATORS.
BUT THERE WERE OTHERS WHO WOULD DO ANYTHING TO DISRUPT THE DEMOCRATIC PROCESS. ON 25 JUNE 1999, 3 000 THUGS FROM THE AWB, A SMALL RIGHT-WING MILITANT GROUP, DESCENDED ON THE WORLD TRADE CENTRE.
THEY CRASHED THROUGH THE GLASS DOORS, URINATED ON CARPETS AND HELD A BARBEQUE.
THE AZANIAN PEOPLE'S LIBERATION ARMY (APLA) ATTACKED WORSHIPPERS AT ST JAMES' CHURCH, IN CAPE TOWN, KILLING 11 PEOPLE AND INJURING 55 MORE.

BUT IN SEPTEMBER 1993, DE KLERK AGREED TO A TRANSITIONAL EXECUTIVE COUNCIL TO PREPARE FOR ELECTIONS. MANDELA FLEW TO THE UN IN NEW YORK TO ARGUE THAT THE TIME FOR ENDING SANCTIONS HAD COME.
THE ANC'S AND NP'S CHIEF NEGOTIATORS, RAMAPHOSA AND MEYER, SOMETIMES STRUGGLED TO CONVINCE THEIR PARTIES TO ACCEPT THEIR PROPOSALS. A BIG BREAKTHROUGH CAME ON 18 NOVEMBER WHEN AN INTERIM CONSTITUTION WAS AGREED TO.
I WILL NOT BUDGE! MAJORITY RULE WILL APPLY.
MINORITIES MUST BE SAFE-GUARDED!
WE DID IT! THEY ACCEPTED OUR COMPROMISE BETWEEN POWER-SHARING AND MAJORITY RULE!
YES! IT WAS TOUGH CONVINCING THEM, BUT THE NP NOW AGREES TO MAJORITY RULE...
AS SOON AS THE DEAL WAS STRUCK THE CELEBRATIONS STARTED.
NOT EVERYONE WAS HAPPY. INKATHA AND THE CONSERVATIVE PARTY DID NOT RECOGNISE THE AGREEMENT, AND MANY AFRIKANERS FELT THAT DE KLERK HAD SOLD THEM OUT.
IN DECEMBER, MANDELA AND DE KLERK JOINTLY RECEIVED THE NOBEL PEACE PRIZE. MANDELA WAS NOW IN THE COMPANY OF LEADERS LIKE CHIEF LUTHULI AND ARCH-BISHOP TUTU WHO HAD ALSO RECEIVED THE AWARD... SOME PEOPLE WERE OFFENDED THAT HE HAD TO SHARE THE PRIZE WITH DE KLERK.
AT THE NOBEL CEREMONY IN OSLO, MANDELA SAID:
...LET IT NEVER BE SAID BY FUTURE GENERATIONS THAT INDIFFERENCE, CYNICISM OR SELFISHNESS...
...MADE US FAIL TO LIVE UP TO THE IDEALS OF HUMANISM, WHICH THE NOBEL PEACE PRIZE ENCAPSULATES...

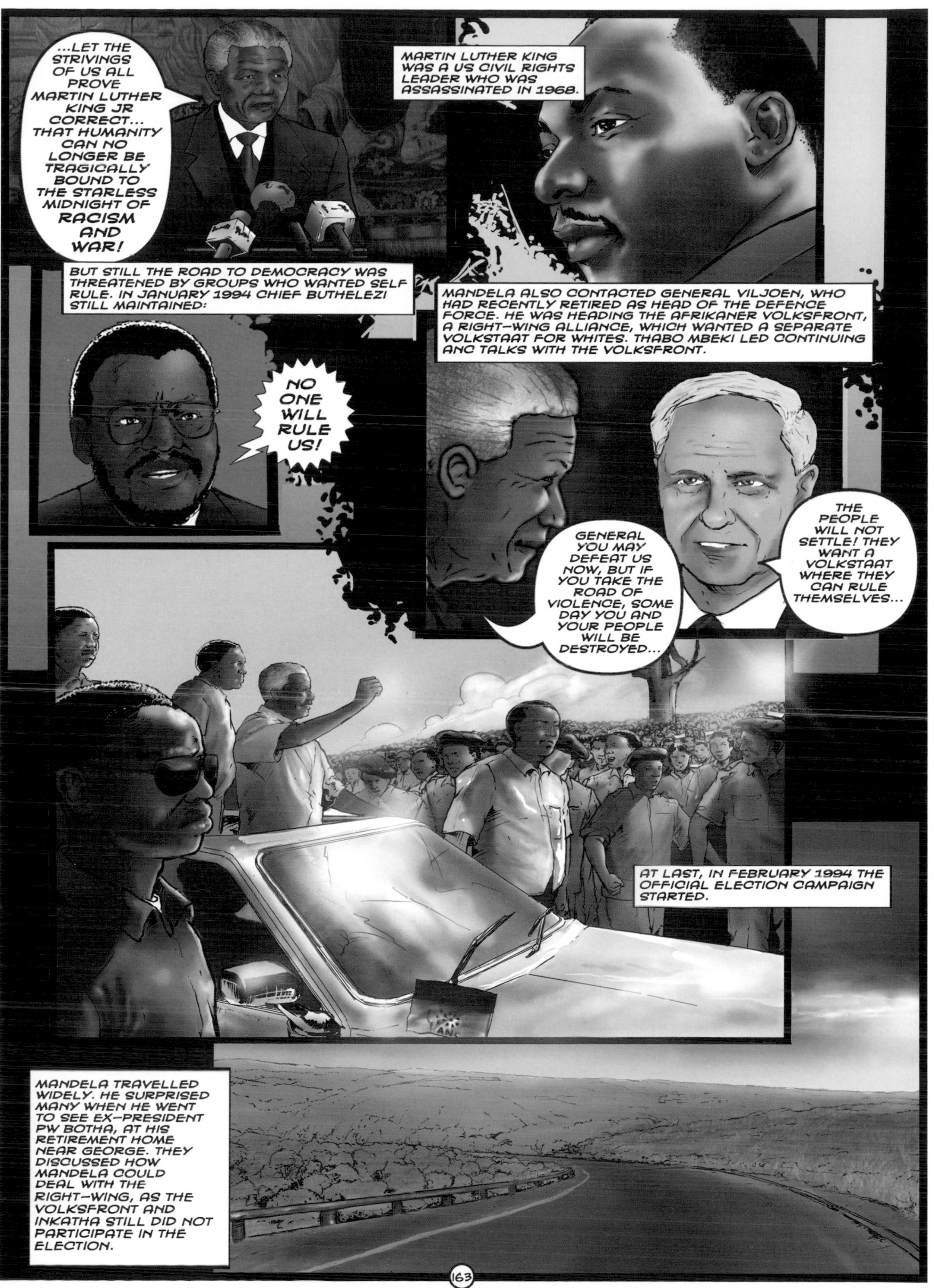
...LET THE STRIVINGS OF US ALL PROVE MARTIN LUTHER KING JR CORRECT... THAT HUMANITY CAN NO LONGER BE TRAGICALLY BOUND TO THE STARLESS MIDNIGHT OF RACISM AND WAR!
MARTIN LUTHER KING WAS A US CIVIL RIGHTS LEADER WHO WAS ASSASSINATED IN 1968.
BUT STILL THE ROAD TO DEMOCRACY WAS THREATENED BY GROUPS WHO WANTED SELF RULE. IN JANUARY 1994 CHIEF BUTHELEZI STILL MAINTAINED:
NO ONE WILL RULE US!
MANDELA ALSO CONTACTED GENERAL VILJOEN, WHO HAD RECENTLY RETIRED AS HEAD OF THE DEFENCE FORCE. HE WAS HEADING THE AFRIKANER VOLKSFRONT, A RIGHT-WING ALLIANCE, WHICH WANTED A SEPARATE VOLKSTAAT FOR WHITES. THABO MBEKI LED CONTINUING ANC TALKS WITH THE VOLKSFRONT.
THE PEOPLE WILL NOT SETTLE! THEY WANT A VOLKSTAAT WHERE THEY CAN RULE THEMSELVES...
GENERAL YOU MAY DEFEAT US NOW, BUT IF YOU TAKE THE ROAD OF VIOLENCE, SOME DAY YOU AND YOUR PEOPLE WILL BE DESTROYED...
AT LAST, IN FEBRUARY 1994 THE OFFICIAL ELECTION CAMPAIGN STARTED.
MANDELA TRAVELLED WIDELY. HE SURPRISED MANY WHEN HE WENT TO SEE EX-PRESIDENT PW BOTHA, AT HIS RETIREMENT HOME NEAR GEORGE. THEY DISCUSSED HOW MANDELA COULD DEAL WITH THE RIGHT-WING, AS THE VOLKSFRONT AND INKATHA STILL DID NOT PARTICIPATE IN THE ELECTION.

THE ANC SET UP A PROFESSIONAL ELECTION CAMPAIGN AND PEOPLE'S FORUMS TO HEAR PEOPLE AT GRASSROOTS LEVEL. BARBARA MASEKELA, JOEL NETSHITENZHE, CARL NIEHAUS AND JESSE DUARTE WERE AMONGST THOSE TRAVELLING WITH MANDELA ON HIS CAMPAIGN TOUR.
PRAISE SINGERS PERFORMED FOR HIM, JUST LIKE THEY DID OUTSIDE COURT, BEFORE MANDELA WENT TO PRISON...
IT REMINDS ME OF THE MEETINGS AT MQHEKEZWENI, THE GREAT PLACE, WITH THE REGENT JONGINTABA.
I CAN'T BELIEVE HE IS REALLY COMING TO TALK TO US!
TOGETHER WE HAVE WON THE RIGHT FOR ALL SOUTH AFRICANS TO VOTE! WE ARE PROUD OF OUR PAST AND CONFIDENT IN OUR FUTURE.
EXCUSE ME, BUT WHY DO YOU WEAR A SHIRT LIKE THAT?
YOU MUST REMEMBER THAT I WAS IN JAIL FOR 27 YEARS. I WANT TO FEEL FREEDOM!
MANDELA BECAME KNOWN FOR THE COLOURFUL SHIRTS HE WORE IN PREFERENCE TO COLLAR AND TIE.
I AM SEVENTY-FIVE, BUT AMONG YOU I FEEL LIKE A YOUNG MAN OF SIXTEEN...
...YOU ARE THE PEOPLE WHO INSPIRE ME EVERY DAY OF MY LIFE.
MANDELA ENJOYED SEEING YOUNG FACES AND EVEN TRIED TO GET THE VOTING AGE REDUCED TO 14 YEARS.

THE THREAT OF CIVIL WAR STILL HUNG IN THE AIR. RIGHT-WINGERS, INKATHA AND TWO HOMELANDS STILL RESISTED ELECTIONS.
THE PEOPLE OF BOPHUTHATSWANA WANTED TO VOTE, AGAINST THE WISHES OF THEIR DICTATOR LUCAS MANGOPE. HE ASKED VILJOEN'S VOLKSFRONT TO HELP HIM RESTORE ORDER...
WE WANT TO VOTE!..
THE AWB ALSO JOINED THE INVASION. THEY WENT ON THE RAMPAGE, KILLING 12 PEOPLE.
SOON MANGOPE'S ARMY TURNED ON THE WHITES WHO WERE SUPPOSED TO HELP THEM.
VILJOEN'S VOLKSFRONT WITHDREW... APPALLED BY THE AWB'S ACTIONS HE DECIDED TO PARTICIPATE IN THE ELECTION AND REGISTERED HIS PARTY AS THE FREEDOM FRONT.
A WEEK LATER, AFTER 24 PEOPLE WERE KILLED AND 900 WERE WOUNDED, MANGOPE WAS OVERTHROWN.
IT IS A TRAGEDY... YES, IT COULD HAVE BEEN MUCH WORSE!

A CROWD OF 50 000 PEOPLE GAVE MANDELA A HERO'S WELCOME AT BOPHUTHATSWANA'S INDEPENDENCE STADIUM. HE DESCRIBED AS "A PEOPLE'S UPRISING" THE REVOLT WHICH LED TO THE FALL OF LUCAS MANGOPE'S GOVERNMENT.
MANDELA FOR PRESIDENT
THE PEOPLE'S CHOICE
BUT BUTHELEZI STILL REFUSED TO PARTICIPATE IN THE ELECTION AND DID NOT REGISTER BY THE 11 MARCH DEADLINE.
THE MEDIA ARE NOT VERY OPTIMISTIC ABOUT BUTHELEZI... THEY ARE PREDICTING THE CONFLICT BETWEEN THE ANC AND IFP CAN ONLY END WITH A FIGHT RIGHT TO THE FINISH!
DE KLERK AND I WILL NOT ALLOW THE ELECTION DATE TO BE MOVED BECAUSE OF THEM.
TO MAKE THINGS WORSE THE GOLDSTONE COMMISSION IMPLICATED THREE SOUTH AFRICAN POLICE GENERALS IN SUPPLYING WEAPONS TO INKATHA.
ON 8 APRIL 1994 – MANDELA, DE KLERK, BUTHELEZI AND KING GOODWILL MET IN THE KRUGER PARK BUT COULD NOT RESOLVE THEIR DIFFERENCES. AN INTERNATIONAL MEDIATOR LATER SUCCEEDED IN PERSUADING BUTHELEZI TO RECONSIDER...
AT LAST INKATHA AGREED TO PARTICIPATE IN THE ELECTIONS AND THE PARTY'S NAME HAD TO BE STUCK ONTO THE BALLOT SHEETS. BUT THE SUCCESS OF THE ELECTIONS WAS THROWN INTO DOUBT AFTER A SERIES OF BOMBS SHOOK THE COUNTRY.

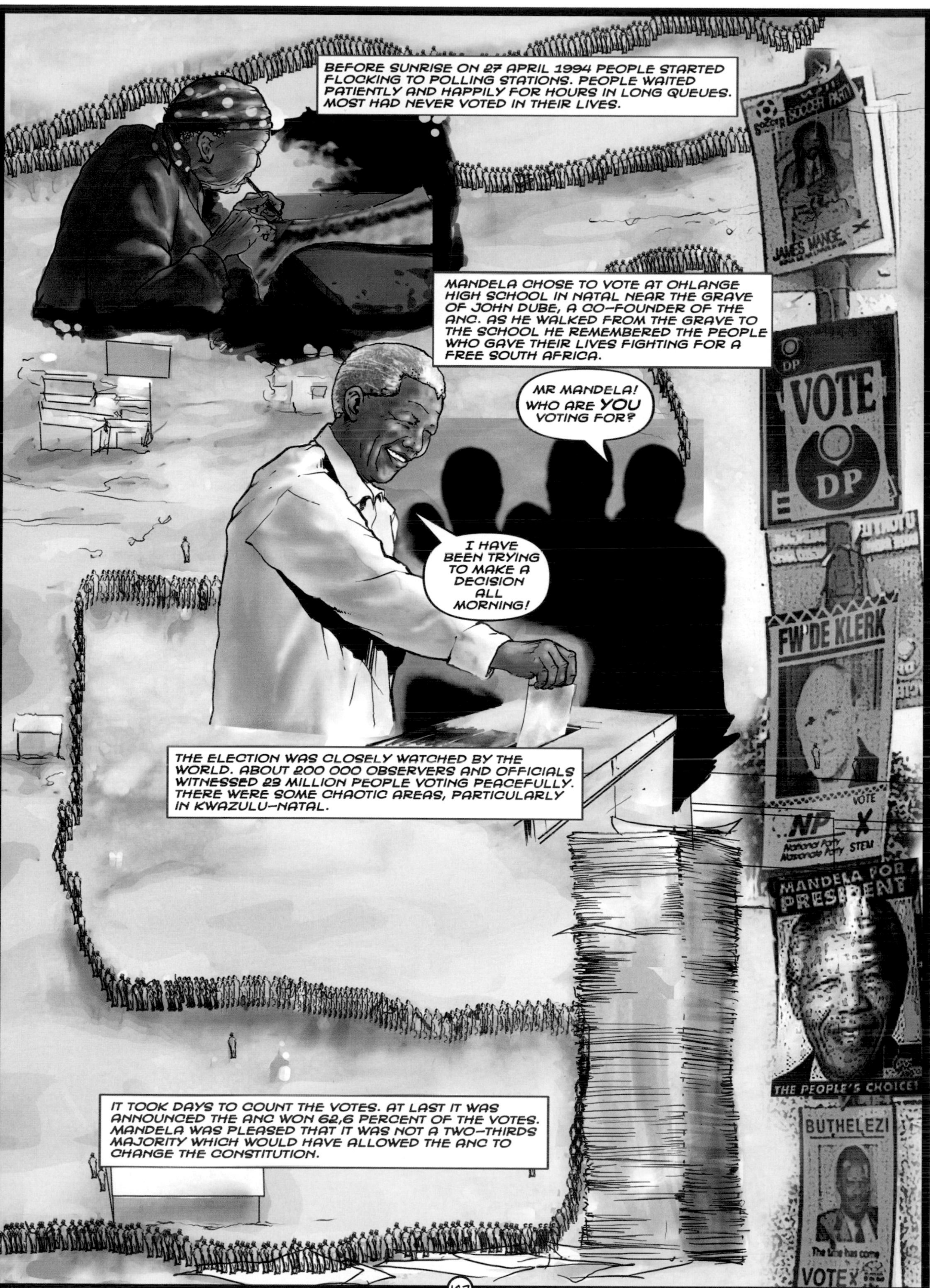
BEFORE SUNRISE ON 27 APRIL 1994 PEOPLE STARTED FLOCKING TO POLLING STATIONS. PEOPLE WAITED PATIENTLY AND HAPPILY FOR HOURS IN LONG QUEUES. MOST HAD NEVER VOTED IN THEIR LIVES.
JAMES MANGE
MANDELA CHOSE TO VOTE AT OHLANGE HIGH SCHOOL IN NATAL NEAR THE GRAVE OF JOHN DUBE, A CO-FOUNDER OF THE ANC. AS HE WALKED FROM THE GRAVE TO THE SCHOOL HE REMEMBERED THE PEOPLE WHO GAVE THEIR LIVES FIGHTING FOR A FREE SOUTH AFRICA.
MR MANDELA! WHO ARE YOU VOTING FOR?
I HAVE BEEN TRYING TO MAKE A DECISION ALL MORNING!
VOTE
DP
FW DE KLERK
THE ELECTION WAS CLOSELY WATCHED BY THE WORLD. ABOUT 200 000 OBSERVERS AND OFFICIALS WITNESSED 23 MILLION PEOPLE VOTING PEACEFULLY. THERE WERE SOME CHAOTIC AREAS, PARTICULARLY IN KWAZULU-NATAL.
NP
VOTE
STEM
MANDELA FOR PRESIDENT
THE PEOPLE'S CHOICE
IT TOOK DAYS TO COUNT THE VOTES. AT LAST IT WAS ANNOUNCED THE ANC WON 62,6 PERCENT OF THE VOTES. MANDELA WAS PLEASED THAT IT WAS NOT A TWO-THIRDS MAJORITY WHICH WOULD HAVE ALLOWED THE ANC TO CHANGE THE CONSTITUTION.
BUTHELEZI
The time has come
VOTE

THE PEOPLE OF SOUTH AFRICA HAD SPOKEN. ON 2 MAY DE KLERK MADE A CONCESSION SPEECH IN PRETORIA AND PRAISED MANDELA AS A MAN OF DESTINY.
IN JOHANNESBURG THE ANC HELD A VICTORY CELEBRATION IN THE CARLTON HOTEL. MANDELA WAS EXHAUSTED AND HAD COME DOWN WITH 'FLU, BUT ATTENDED THE IMPORTANT CELEBRATION.
FREE AT LAST! FREE AT LAST! I STAND BEFORE YOU HUMBLED BY YOUR COURAGE, WITH A HEART FULL OF LOVE FOR ALL OF YOU... THIS IS THE TIME TO HEAL OLD WOUNDS AND BUILD A NEW SOUTH AFRICA!
THE WORLD SAW MANDELA CELEBRATING WITH A DANCE THAT WAS SOON TO BECOME HIS TRADEMARK. BUT WHAT DID THE FUTURE HOLD FOR THE FLEDGELING DEMOCRACY AT THE TIP OF AFRICA?

8

MR PRESIDENT

WE'RE OUTSIDE THE HOUSES OF PARLIAMENT IN CAPE TOWN, WHERE NELSON MANDELA WAS NOMINATED AS PRESIDENT OF SOUTH AFRICA AND WAS UNANIMOUSLY ELECTED BY MEMBERS OF PARLIAMENT.

THE FIRST DEMOCRATICALLY ELECTED PARLIAMENT GATHERED IN CAPE TOWN ON 9 MAY 1994 TO GREAT EXCITEMENT.
MA ALBERTINA SISULU STOOD TO SPEAK.
I NOMINATE NELSON ROLIHLAHLA MANDELA AS PRESIDENT!
AN IMBONGI SANG THE PRAISES OF MANDELA...
TODAY AFRICA HAS RETURNED!!
IN A SHOW OF RECONCILIATION MANDELA HUGGED BUTHELEZI.
EVERYONE CHEERED AS CHIEF JUSTICE MICHAEL CORBETT DECLARED MANDELA SOUTH AFRICA'S PRESIDENT-ELECT, WHILE FRENE GINWALA WAS NOMINATED AS SPEAKER OF PARLIAMENT.
THE AFRICAN NATIONAL CONGRESS HAD WON 252 SEATS, THE NATIONAL PARTY 82, THE INKATHA FREEDOM PARTY 43, WHILE THE REMAINING SEATS WERE SHARED BY THE FREEDOM FRONT, DEMOCRATIC PARTY, PAN AFRICANIST CONGRESS AND THE AFRICAN CHRISTIAN DEMOCRATIC PARTY. SEVENTY OF THE 400 MEMBERS OF PARLIAMENT (MP'S) WERE WOMEN.
WALTER SISULU LATER SAID:
IT IS THE BIGGEST DAY OF ALL!
MANDELA AND HIS DEPUTIES, MBEKI AND DE KLERK, NOW HAD TO MOVE FORWARD IN THE GOVERNMENT OF NATIONAL UNITY.

10 MAY 1994. THE INAUGURATION OF NELSON MANDELA AS PRESIDENT. THOUSANDS OF ORDINARY PEOPLE GATHERED ON THE LAWNS IN FRONT OF THE UNION BUILDINGS IN PRETORIA WHILE LEADERS FROM SOUTH AFRICA AND AROUND THE WORLD GOT VIP SEATS.
I, NELSON ROLIHLAHLA MANDELA, DO HEREBY SWEAR TO BE FAITHFUL TO THE REPUBLIC OF SOUTH AFRICA...
...NEVER, NEVER AND NEVER AGAIN SHALL IT BE THAT THIS BEAUTIFUL LAND WILL AGAIN EXPERIENCE THE OPPRESSION OF ONE BY ANOTHER AND SUFFER THE INDIGNITY OF BEING THE SKUNK OF THE WORLD...
ON THE LAWNS BLACK AND WHITE CELEBRATED TOGETHER, UNITED IN THEIR LOVE AND RESPECT FOR A MAN WHO GAVE UP HIS FREEDOM SO THAT THEY COULD LIVE IN A DEMOCRACY.
AFTER THE POMP AND CEREMONY THE PRESIDENT WENT DOWN TO THE LAWNS WHERE HE GREETED THE CROWD AND DANCED IN CELEBRATION. LATER HE FLEW BY HELICOPTER TO ELLIS PARK STADIUM TO WATCH A FOOTBALL MATCH IN HIS HONOUR BETWEEN SOUTH AFRICA AND ZAMBIA.
LADUUMA!
AT HALF-TIME HE GREETED ALL THE PLAYERS. BY THE TIME HE WAS BACK IN HIS SEAT, SOUTH AFRICA'S BAFANA BAFANA HAD SCORED TWICE!

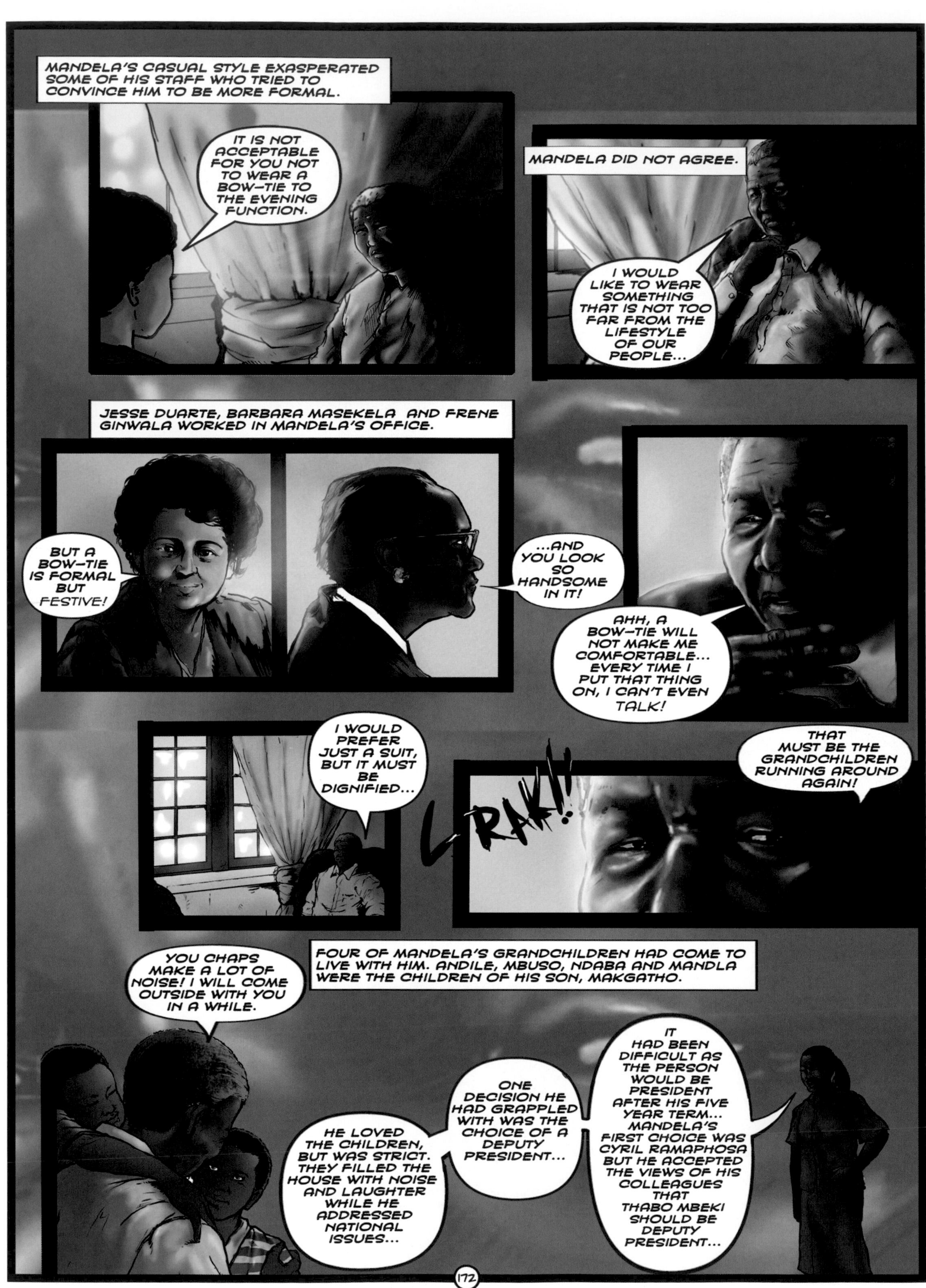
MANDELA'S CASUAL STYLE EXASPERATED SOME OF HIS STAFF WHO TRIED TO CONVINCE HIM TO BE MORE FORMAL.
IT IS NOT ACCEPTABLE FOR YOU NOT TO WEAR A BOW-TIE TO THE EVENING FUNCTION.
MANDELA DID NOT AGREE.
I WOULD LIKE TO WEAR SOMETHING THAT IS NOT TOO FAR FROM THE LIFESTYLE OF OUR PEOPLE...
JESSE DUARTE, BARBARA MASEKELA AND FRENE GINWALA WORKED IN MANDELA'S OFFICE.
BUT A BOW-TIE IS FORMAL BUT FESTIVE!
...AND YOU LOOK SO HANDSOME IN IT!
AHH, A BOW-TIE WILL NOT MAKE ME COMFORTABLE... EVERY TIME I PUT THAT THING ON, I CAN'T EVEN TALK!
I WOULD PREFER JUST A SUIT, BUT IT MUST BE DIGNIFIED...
CRAK!!
THAT MUST BE THE GRANDCHILDREN RUNNING AROUND AGAIN!
YOU CHAPS MAKE A LOT OF NOISE! I WILL COME OUTSIDE WITH YOU IN A WHILE.
FOUR OF MANDELA'S GRANDCHILDREN HAD COME TO LIVE WITH HIM. ANDILE, MBUSO, NDABA AND MANDLA WERE THE CHILDREN OF HIS SON, MAKGATHO.
HE LOVED THE CHILDREN, BUT WAS STRICT. THEY FILLED THE HOUSE WITH NOISE AND LAUGHTER WHILE HE ADDRESSED NATIONAL ISSUES...
ONE DECISION HE HAD GRAPPLED WITH WAS THE CHOICE OF A DEPUTY PRESIDENT...
IT HAD BEEN DIFFICULT AS THE PERSON WOULD BE PRESIDENT AFTER HIS FIVE YEAR TERM... MANDELA'S FIRST CHOICE WAS CYRIL RAMAPHOSA BUT HE ACCEPTED THE VIEWS OF HIS COLLEAGUES THAT THABO MBEKI SHOULD BE DEPUTY PRESIDENT...

WHEN PARLIAMENT WAS IN SESSION IN CAPE TOWN, MANDELA STAYED IN HIS OFFICIAL RESIDENCE – WESTBROOK – WHICH HE RENAMED GENADENDAL IN 1995. FW AND MARIKE DE KLERK LIVED ON THE SAME ESTATE IN A HOUSE CALLED GROOTE SCHUUR.
THE PRESIDENT IS HERE! I'D BETTER HIDE
THAT IS STRANGE... WHY IS THE GARDENER AVOIDING ME?
STAFF MEMBERS HAD TO GET USED TO THEIR NEW BOSS.
MR PRESIDENT, CAN YOU PLEASE POSE FOR A PHOTO WITH THE HOUSE STAFF?
YES, BUT CALL EVERYONE, THE GARDENERS AND SO ON...
UHH! THEY CAN'T ENTER THE HOUSE. IT WILL GET DIRTY...
HA! BUT THAT IS WHAT VACUUM CLEANERS AND BROOMS ARE FOR!
THE OUTSIDE STAFF WERE CALLED BUT STILL REFUSED TO COME INSIDE FOR THE PHOTO...
MANDELA DECIDED TO GET TO THE BOTTOM OF THE PROBLEM...
WHAT IS GOING ON? YOU ALL RUN AWAY WHEN YOU SEE ME!
IN THE PAST WE WERE TOLD TO HIDE WHEN WE SAW THE PRESIDENT. IF WE DID NOT, WE COULD LOSE OUR JOBS!
WELL, YOU HAVE A NEW PRESIDENT NOW! THINGS HAVE CHANGED...
CAN YOU BELIEVE IT?
WE EVEN HAD OUR PHOTO TAKEN WITH HIM...

MANDELA STUCK TO HIS EARLY MORNING EXERCISE ROUTINE. HE ROSE AT 4:30 AM AND WAS READY FOR HIS WALK BY FIVE...
MEET ME AT THE FRONT DOOR...
THIS MEANT HIS BODYGUARDS WOULD HAVE TO BE UP TOO AS THEY HAD TO PROTECT HIM AT ALL TIMES...
...AND I WILL GO OUT AT THE BACK! I STILL KNOW HOW TO DODGE THESE CHAPS!
A POLICEMAN PATROLLING THE AREA SPOTTED THE PRESIDENT.
BUILDING THIS DEMOCRACY WILL NOT BE AN EASY TASK...
ANC CADRES DO NOT YET HAVE THE DEPTH OF EXPERIENCE...
WE NEED TO KEEP EXISTING EXPERTISE...
YOUR PRESIDENT IS IN THE STREET!
HE IS A DANGER TO HIMSELF! DON'T LET HIM OUT OF YOUR SIGHT!
MANDELA GOT ON WELL WITH THE MEMBERS OF HIS PROTECTION TEAM, BUT HE DID NOT MAKE LIFE EASY FOR THEM. HE OFTEN BROKE AWAY FROM HIS SCHEDULE TO GO AND GREET WELL-WISHERS...
MANDELA PERSONALLY REASSURED ALL THE OLD REGIME'S WHITE PRESIDENTIAL STAFF THAT THEIR JOBS WERE SAFE. HE SPENT A DAY GOING FROM OFFICE TO OFFICE INTRODUCING HIMSELF.
SO WHERE ARE YOU FROM?
THE PREVIOUS PRESIDENT NEVER CAME INTO OUR OFFICE!
YOU KNOW, *JAKES, I WONDER WHAT THEY WILL SAY WHEN THEY SEE THIS IN TUYNHUYS!
*HE HAD CHOSEN AS HIS DIRECTOR-GENERAL, JAKES GERWEL, A FORMER RECTOR OF THE UNIVERSITY OF THE WESTERN CAPE.

ON THE FIFTH ANNIVERSARY OF HIS RELEASE FROM PRISON HE RETURNED TO ROBBEN ISLAND FOR A REUNION OF FORMER POLITICAL PRISONERS.
MOTHER... THEMBI... SO MANY PEOPLE WERE LOST TO ME WHILE I WAS HERE...
MANDELA AND OTHER FORMER POLITICAL PRISONERS WERE ASKED TO HAMMER MARKS INTO A LARGE LIMESTONE ROCK TO BE DISPLAYED LATER IN A MUSEUM. WHILE MANDELA MADE HIS MARK SOME OF THE OTHERS GOT CARRIED AWAY AND ENDED UP SMASHING IT TO PIECES.
A FEW DAYS LATER THE "OLD MAN", AS MANY YOUNGER MP'S REFERRED TO HIM, OPENED PARLIAMENT IN A RELAXED ATMOSPHERE UNHEARD OF IN EARLIER YEARS.
MANY NEW ANC MP'S HAD TO PINCH THEMSELVES TO ACCEPT THAT IT WAS TRUE... SO-CALLED FORMER "TERRORISTS" WERE NOW LAW-MAKERS.
FROM PRISON TO PARLIAMENT!
MANDELA'S SCHEDULE WAS RELENTLESS. HIS STAFF AND SECURITY GUARDS HAD THEIR HANDS FULL.

STOP THE CAR! I NEED TO GO TO THOSE STREET CHILDREN.
TATA, IT IS TOO DANGEROUS!
MANDELA LOVED CHILDREN AND COULD NOT STAND SEEING THEM SUFFER...
IT IS YOUR JOB TO PROTECT ME!
IT'S NELSON MANDELA!
MADIBA! IT IS YOU!
WHY DO YOU LOVE US?
WHY DO YOU ASK THAT?
BECAUSE YOU ALWAYS TRY TO HELP US!
OHH... I TRY TO HELP BUT IT IS NEVER ENOUGH...
LATER THAT NIGHT...
I WILL SET UP A CHILDREN'S FUND...
IT IS POSSIBLE FOR ME TO DONATE A THIRD OF MY SALARY EVERY MONTH...
THERE ARE CHILDREN IN NEED EVERYWHERE!
* THE NELSON MANDELA CHILDREN'S FUND BECAME AN IMPORTANT CHARITY FOCUSING ON THE NEEDS OF CHILDREN IN SOUTH AFRICA. HE ALSO ANNOUNCED THAT WOMEN AND CHILDREN WOULD GET FREE TREATMENT AT STATE HOSPITALS.

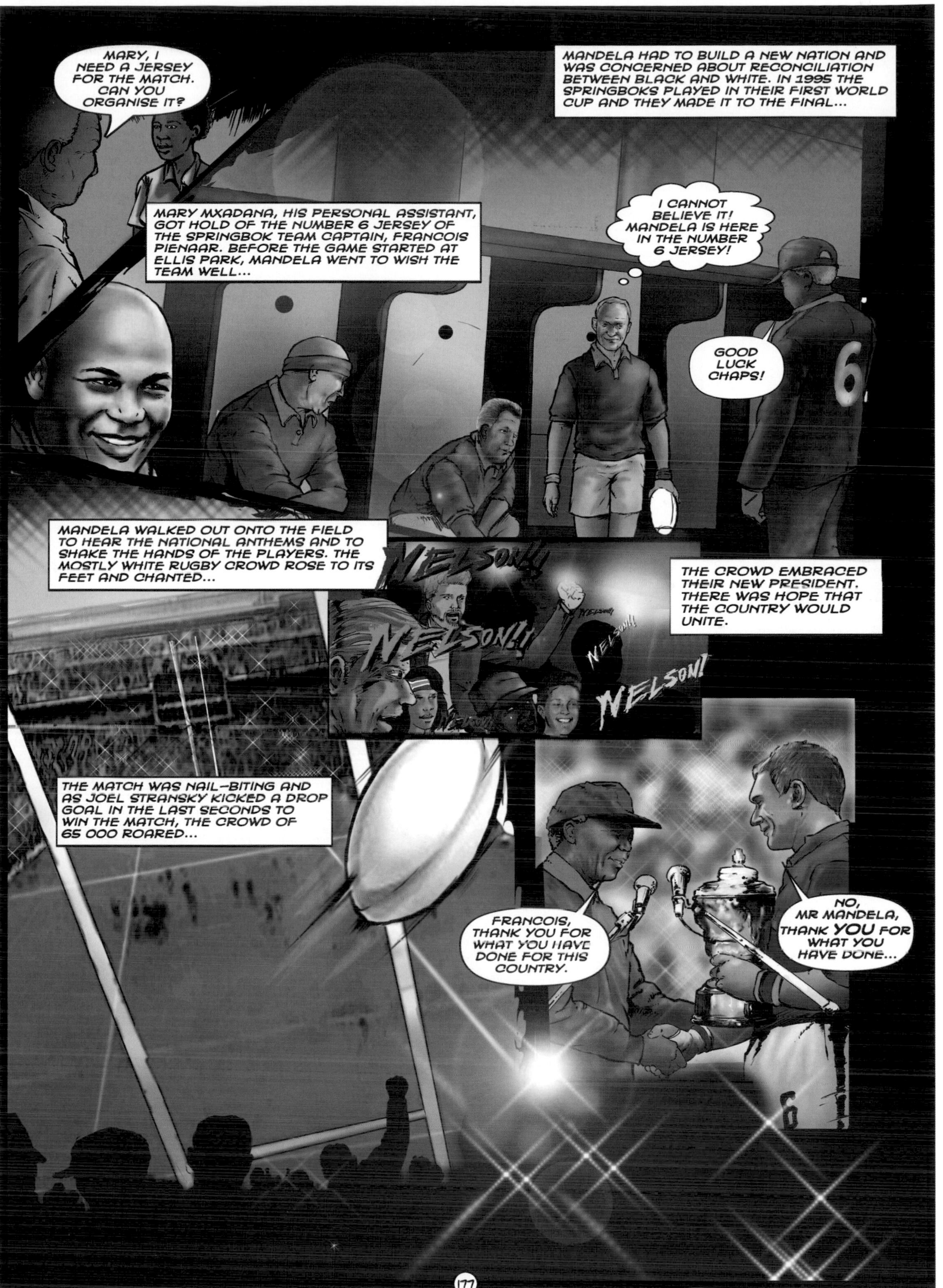
MARY, I NEED A JERSEY FOR THE MATCH. CAN YOU ORGANISE IT?
MANDELA HAD TO BUILD A NEW NATION AND WAS CONCERNED ABOUT RECONCILIATION BETWEEN BLACK AND WHITE. IN 1995 THE SPRINGBOKS PLAYED IN THEIR FIRST WORLD CUP AND THEY MADE IT TO THE FINAL...
MARY MXADANA, HIS PERSONAL ASSISTANT, GOT HOLD OF THE NUMBER 6 JERSEY OF THE SPRINGBOK TEAM CAPTAIN, FRANCOIS PIENAAR. BEFORE THE GAME STARTED AT ELLIS PARK, MANDELA WENT TO WISH THE TEAM WELL...
I CANNOT BELIEVE IT! MANDELA IS HERE IN THE NUMBER 6 JERSEY!
GOOD LUCK CHAPS!
MANDELA WALKED OUT ONTO THE FIELD TO HEAR THE NATIONAL ANTHEMS AND TO SHAKE THE HANDS OF THE PLAYERS. THE MOSTLY WHITE RUGBY CROWD ROSE TO ITS FEET AND CHANTED...
NELSON!
NELSON!
NELSON!
NELSON!
THE CROWD EMBRACED THEIR NEW PRESIDENT. THERE WAS HOPE THAT THE COUNTRY WOULD UNITE.
THE MATCH WAS NAIL-BITING AND AS JOEL STRANSKY KICKED A DROP GOAL IN THE LAST SECONDS TO WIN THE MATCH, THE CROWD OF 65 000 ROARED...
FRANCOIS, THANK YOU FOR WHAT YOU HAVE DONE FOR THIS COUNTRY.
NO, MR MANDELA, THANK YOU FOR WHAT YOU HAVE DONE...

CELEBRITIES, BUSINESS MOGULS, ROCK STARS AND POLITICIANS FLOCKED TO SEE HIM, BUT HE INSISTED ON SPENDING CHRISTMAS WITH HIS FAMILY IN THE TRANSKEI. IN 1995 HE WAS IN QUNU WITH TWO YOUNG GRANDSONS AND HIS NIECE ROCHELLE MTIRARA.
WALKING HERE IS A LINK TO THE PAST THAT I HAVE MISSED... THE VILLAGERS HAVE SUCH CONFIDENCE IN US...IT IS A GREAT RESPONSIBILITY...
ON CHRISTMAS DAY HE WENT FOR HIS USUAL EARLY MORNING WALK ON THE PATHS IN AND AROUND THE VILLAGES OF HIS CHILDHOOD.
HE THOUGHT BACK TO CHRISTMASSES PAST AND STOPPED TO TALK TO EVERYONE HE SAW.
HE GREETED EVERYONE AND ASKED EACH CHILD THEIR NAME, AGE AND WHERE THEY WENT TO SCHOOL.
I AM VUKILE, I AM SEVEN, AND I AM IN GRADE THREE.
THAT IS VERY GOOD! MY NAME IS MANDELA.
HE AGREED TO HAVE SOME JOURNALISTS JOIN HIM ON HIS WALK. SOME STRUGGLED TO KEEP UP WITH THE FIT 77-YEAR-OLD WHO WALKED FOR THREE HOURS.
WHEN I WAS A BOY HERDING CATTLE OR SHEEP MY DUTIES WOULD END EARLIER THAN USUAL ON CHRISTMAS.
ON THIS DAY WE CAME HOME FOR THE ONLY CUP OF TEA OF THE YEAR...
THEY GAVE US FOOD... WHAT ELDERLY PEOPLE DO, THEY EAT AND THEY KEEP ON GIVING YOU A PIECE. SOMETIMES IT IS ENOUGH TO FEED YOU...
MANDELA HOSTED A CHRISTMAS PARTY FOR CHILDREN EVERY YEAR. HE STARTED THE TRADITION IN QUNU, FOR THE POOR CHILDREN IN THE AREA. IT BECAME SO POPULAR THAT IN LATER YEARS THOUSANDS OF CHILDREN ARRIVED FROM DIFFERENT PARTS OF THE COUNTRY.
LATER THAT DAY FAMILY HELPED HIM TO HAND OUT CHUNKS OF FRESHLY COOKED MEAT TO WAITING CHILDREN. MANDELA MADE SURE THE CHILDREN WERE FED BEFORE THE REST OF THE FOOD WENT TO THE ADULTS.
SOME OF THESE CHILDREN HAVE BEEN WALKING FOR HOURS TO BE HERE...
IT IS A FORLORN ATTEMPT. THEY GO BACK TO THEIR SQUALOR, THEIR MISERY...

AS PRESIDENT, MANDELA VISITED MORE THAN 70 COUNTRIES AND HOSTED AS MANY LEADERS IN SOUTH AFRICA. IN JULY 1996 HE WENT ON A STATE VISIT TO THE UNITED KINGDOM AND STAYED IN BUCKINGHAM PALACE.
FOR MERIT
IN 1995 HE HAD RECEIVED THE ORDER OF MERIT FROM QUEEN ELIZABETH II. THIS PRESTIGIOUS AWARD WAS ALSO BESTOWED ON MOTHER TERESA AND FLORENCE NIGHTINGALE.
MANDELA WAS AT EASE IN THE OPULENT ENVIRONMENT AND GOT ON WELL WITH THE QUEEN.
OH, I AM JUST A BOY FROM THE COUNTRY!
THE 600 STAFF MEMBERS IMPRESSED HIM SO MUCH THAT HE BECAME THE FIRST HEAD OF STATE TO HAVE HIS PHOTO TAKEN WITH THEM.
HE ALSO HAD TEA WITH THE QUEEN MOTHER AT HER RESIDENCE, CLARENCE HOUSE...
MANDELA WAS MADE FREEMAN OF THE CITY OF LONDON. HE WAS THE FIRST SERVING HEAD OF STATE TO RECEIVE THIS HONOUR IN 350 YEARS.
THE BANQUET WAS A VERY FORMAL EVENT AND ALL THE MEN WERE WEARING SUITS AND BLACK BOW-TIES, BUT MANDELA WORE A 'MADIBA SHIRT'.
OUR CULTURES ARE TOTALLY DIFFERENT!

AFTER THE STATE VISIT MANDELA RETURNED TO QUNU...
KNOCK!!
KNOCK!!
I AM COMING!
I HAD A HUGE FAT CHICKEN! I FOLLOWED ITS PRINTS TO MY NEIGHBOUR... I AM SURE HE SLAUGHTERED IT AND ATE IT!
WELL HOW MUCH WAS THE CHICKEN WORTH TO YOU?
AT LEAST TEN RAND!
MANDELA WENT TO SEE THE NEIGHBOUR WHO DID NOT KNOW THE CHICKEN BELONGED TO SOMEONE ELSE, BUT HE AGREED TO GIVE MANDELA R10 COMPENSATION TO GIVE TO THE WOMAN.
THIS IS NO USE TO ME! A CHICKEN WAS STOLEN AND A CHICKEN MUST BE REPLACED!
??!
MANDELA WENT BACK AND CONVINCED THE MAN TO BUY A CHICKEN.
THIS IS A PITIFUL BIRD. IT IS NOWHERE NEAR AS FAT AS MINE WAS!
MANDELA WENT BACK TO THE NEIGHBOUR AND MANAGED TO CONVINCE HIM TO BUY A SECOND CHICKEN...
YES! TWO THIN CHICKENS IS JUST REWARD FOR THE LOSS OF ONE FAT BIRD! TONIGHT I WILL EAT ONE AND THE OTHER ONE WILL BE FATTENED UP AND MIGHT LAY EGGS!

SOMETIMES PROBLEMS KEPT MANDELA AWAKE AT NIGHT. HE AGONISED ABOUT REMOVING WINNIE FROM HER POSITION AS DEPUTY MINISTER OF ARTS AND CULTURE OVER VARIOUS PERFORMANCE ISSUES.
I HAVE NO OTHER CHOICE!
MANDELA DEVELOPED A HABIT OF PHONING PEOPLE AT ALL HOURS OF THE NIGHT WHEN HE HAD SOMETHING ON HIS MIND. HE STILL VALUED THE OPINION OF WALTER SISULU ABOVE ALL OTHERS.
DID I WAKE YOU?
YES! YOU ARE VERY STUBBORN! THIS COULD HAVE WAITED FOR THE MORNING...
MTHATHA
AIRPORT 10 KM
BEFORE DAWN THE NEXT DAY MANDELA WAS ON HIS WAY TO MTHATHA AIRPORT TO FLY TO THE CAPITAL CITY OF SOUTH AFRICA – PRETORIA.
MANDELA ARRIVED AT HIS OFFICE AT THE UNION BUILDINGS JUST AFTER SEVEN.
GOOD MORNING MR PRESIDENT! YOU STILL HAVE TIME TO READ YOUR PAPERS.
GOOD MORNING BOSS!
MANDELA ENJOYED GOING THROUGH AT LEAST FIVE NEWSPAPERS EACH DAY – INCLUDING AFRIKAANS ONES.
ONE OF THE ANC'S STRATEGIES TO ALLEVIATE POVERTY WAS THE RECONSTRUCTION AND DEVELOPMENT PROGRAMME (RDP). HE MET WITH JAY NAIDOO, THE MINISTER IN CHARGE OF THE PROJECT.
WE ARE PLANNING TO BUILD THOUSANDS OF NEW HOUSES, BUT RESULTS HAVE BEEN SLOW...
WE HAVE TO LOOK AT EXAMPLES OF DEVELOPMENT THAT HAVE WORKED ELSEWHERE.
THE RDP BECAME A WIDELY RESPECTED POLICY FRAMEWORK ADDRESSING HOUSING, UNEMPLOYMENT, EDUCATION AND HEALTH CARE. IT WAS LATER CONTROVERSIALLY REPLACED BY GEAR, THE GROWTH, EMPLOYMENT AND REDISTRIBUTION STRATEGY.

AFTER A FULL DAY OF MEETINGS, INCLUDING THE SWEARING-IN OF A NEW DEPUTY MINISTER TO REPLACE HIS ESTRANGED WIFE, MANDELA BOARDED A PLANE TO CAPE TOWN.
AT NEETHLINGSHOF WINE FARM HE ADDRESSED A MOSTLY WHITE AUDIENCE OF BUSINESS LEADERS ABOUT ECONOMIC RECONSTRUCTION.
MY WARDER AT VICTOR VERSTER TOLD ME THE BEST WINES WERE DRY. BUT I ALWAYS THOUGHT ALL WINE WAS WET!
HE RETURNED TO JOHANNESBURG THE SAME NIGHT. IT WAS CLOSE TO MIDNIGHT WHEN HE FINALLY WENT TO BED IN HIS HOUGHTON HOME.
HE PREFERRED TO STAY THERE AND MOSTLY USED HIS OFFICIAL RESIDENCE, LIBERTAS – IN PRETORIA – DURING THE DAY FOR OFFICIAL MEETINGS OR LUNCH.
IN 1995 HE CHANGED THE NAME OF LIBERTAS TO MAHLAMBA NDLOPFU. IT COMES FROM A SHANGAAN EXPRESSION MEANING "NEW DAWN".
ALTHOUGH MANDELA MADE MANY NEW RICH AND FAMOUS FRIENDS, HE KEPT CLOSE TO HIS OLD COMRADES LIKE AHMED KATHRADA. IN 1994 'KATHY' HAD BEEN APPOINTED AS MANDELA'S PARLIAMENTARY COUNSELLOR.
AHHH! LUNCH IS HERE! AND ON TIME!
OH, MADIBA – IT IS SAMP AND BEANS! JAIL FOOD IS STILL YOUR FAVOURITE!
YES! DO YOU REMEMBER HOW AFRICANS WERE NOT ALLOWED TO EAT BREAD FOR TEN YEARS?
MANDELA OFTEN SET HIS OWN MENU. IT WAS SIMPLE AND HEALTHY AND SOMETIMES INCLUDED INDIAN CURRIES.

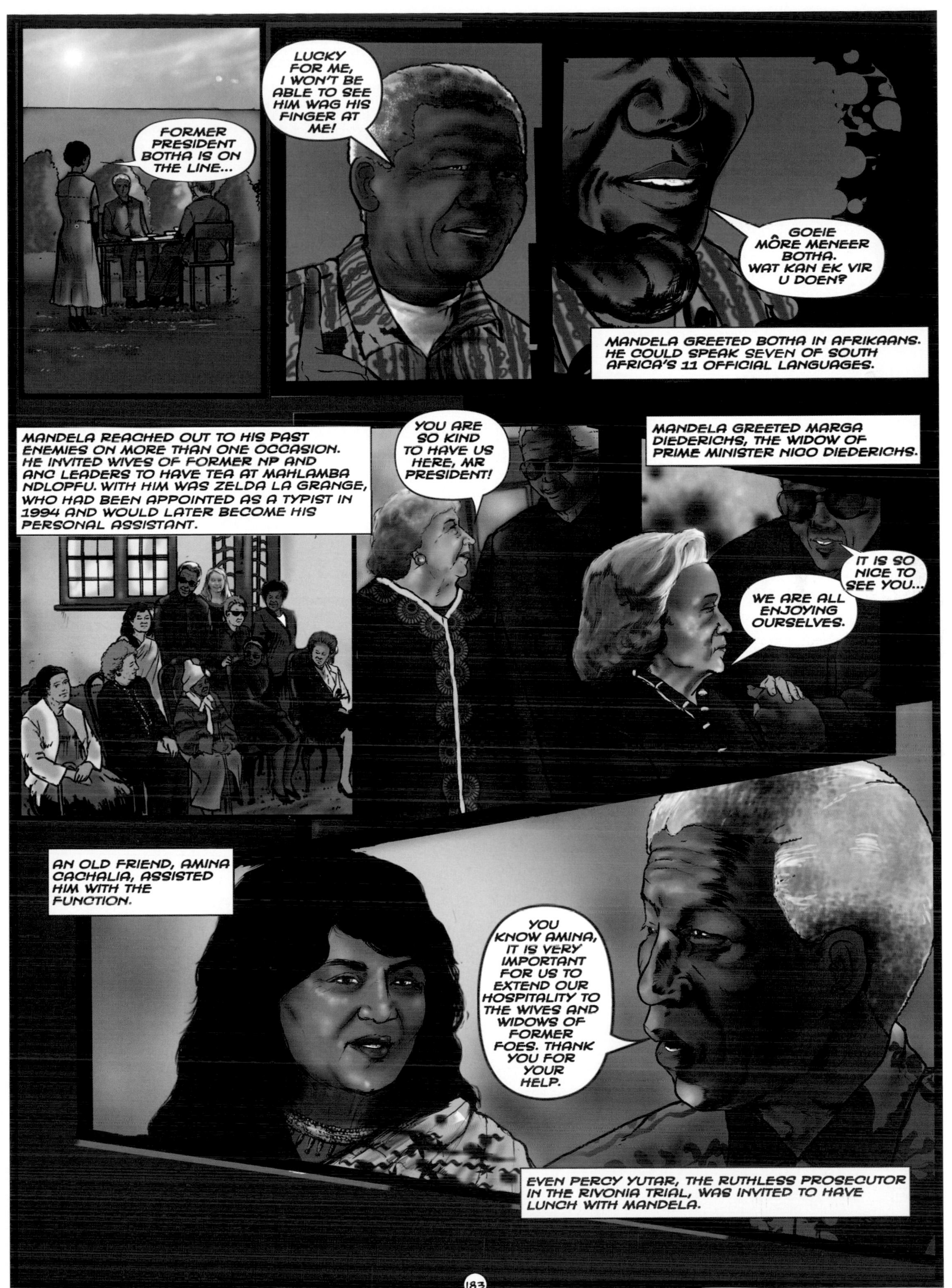
FORMER PRESIDENT BOTHA IS ON THE LINE...
LUCKY FOR ME, I WON'T BE ABLE TO SEE HIM WAG HIS FINGER AT ME!
GOEIE MÔRE MENEER BOTHA. WAT KAN EK VIR U DOEN?
MANDELA GREETED BOTHA IN AFRIKAANS. HE COULD SPEAK SEVEN OF SOUTH AFRICA'S 11 OFFICIAL LANGUAGES.
MANDELA REACHED OUT TO HIS PAST ENEMIES ON MORE THAN ONE OCCASION. HE INVITED WIVES OF FORMER NP AND ANC LEADERS TO HAVE TEA AT MAHLAMBA NDLOPFU. WITH HIM WAS ZELDA LA GRANGE, WHO HAD BEEN APPOINTED AS A TYPIST IN 1994 AND WOULD LATER BECOME HIS PERSONAL ASSISTANT.
YOU ARE SO KIND TO HAVE US HERE, MR PRESIDENT!
MANDELA GREETED MARGA DIEDERICHS, THE WIDOW OF PRIME MINISTER NICO DIEDERICHS.
IT IS SO NICE TO SEE YOU...
WE ARE ALL ENJOYING OURSELVES.
AN OLD FRIEND, AMINA CACHALIA, ASSISTED HIM WITH THE FUNCTION.
YOU KNOW AMINA, IT IS VERY IMPORTANT FOR US TO EXTEND OUR HOSPITALITY TO THE WIVES AND WIDOWS OF FORMER FOES. THANK YOU FOR YOUR HELP.
EVEN PERCY YUTAR, THE RUTHLESS PROSECUTOR IN THE RIVONIA TRIAL, WAS INVITED TO HAVE LUNCH WITH MANDELA.

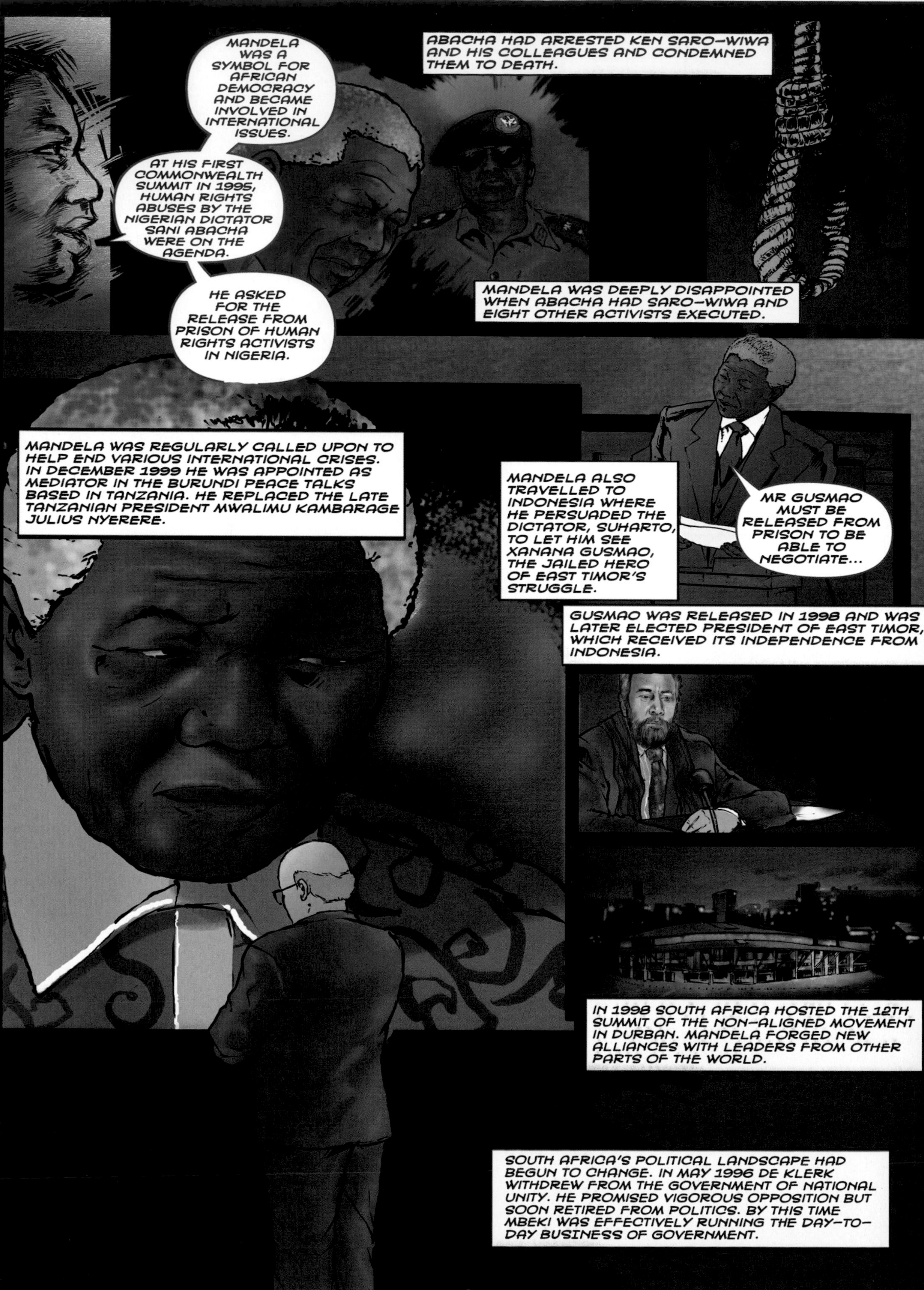
MANDELA WAS A SYMBOL FOR AFRICAN DEMOCRACY AND BECAME INVOLVED IN INTERNATIONAL ISSUES.
AT HIS FIRST COMMONWEALTH SUMMIT IN 1995, HUMAN RIGHTS ABUSES BY THE NIGERIAN DICTATOR SANI ABACHA WERE ON THE AGENDA.
HE ASKED FOR THE RELEASE FROM PRISON OF HUMAN RIGHTS ACTIVISTS IN NIGERIA.
ABACHA HAD ARRESTED KEN SARO-WIWA AND HIS COLLEAGUES AND CONDEMNED THEM TO DEATH.
MANDELA WAS DEEPLY DISAPPOINTED WHEN ABACHA HAD SARO-WIWA AND EIGHT OTHER ACTIVISTS EXECUTED.
MANDELA WAS REGULARLY CALLED UPON TO HELP END VARIOUS INTERNATIONAL CRISES. IN DECEMBER 1999 HE WAS APPOINTED AS MEDIATOR IN THE BURUNDI PEACE TALKS BASED IN TANZANIA. HE REPLACED THE LATE TANZANIAN PRESIDENT MWALIMU KAMBARAGE JULIUS NYERERE.
MANDELA ALSO TRAVELLED TO INDONESIA WHERE HE PERSUADED THE DICTATOR, SUHARTO, TO LET HIM SEE XANANA GUSMAO, THE JAILED HERO OF EAST TIMOR'S STRUGGLE.
MR GUSMAO MUST BE RELEASED FROM PRISON TO BE ABLE TO NEGOTIATE...
GUSMAO WAS RELEASED IN 1998 AND WAS LATER ELECTED PRESIDENT OF EAST TIMOR, WHICH RECEIVED ITS INDEPENDENCE FROM INDONESIA.
IN 1998 SOUTH AFRICA HOSTED THE 12TH SUMMIT OF THE NON-ALIGNED MOVEMENT IN DURBAN. MANDELA FORGED NEW ALLIANCES WITH LEADERS FROM OTHER PARTS OF THE WORLD.
SOUTH AFRICA'S POLITICAL LANDSCAPE HAD BEGUN TO CHANGE. IN MAY 1996 DE KLERK WITHDREW FROM THE GOVERNMENT OF NATIONAL UNITY. HE PROMISED VIGOROUS OPPOSITION BUT SOON RETIRED FROM POLITICS. BY THIS TIME MBEKI WAS EFFECTIVELY RUNNING THE DAY-TO-DAY BUSINESS OF GOVERNMENT.

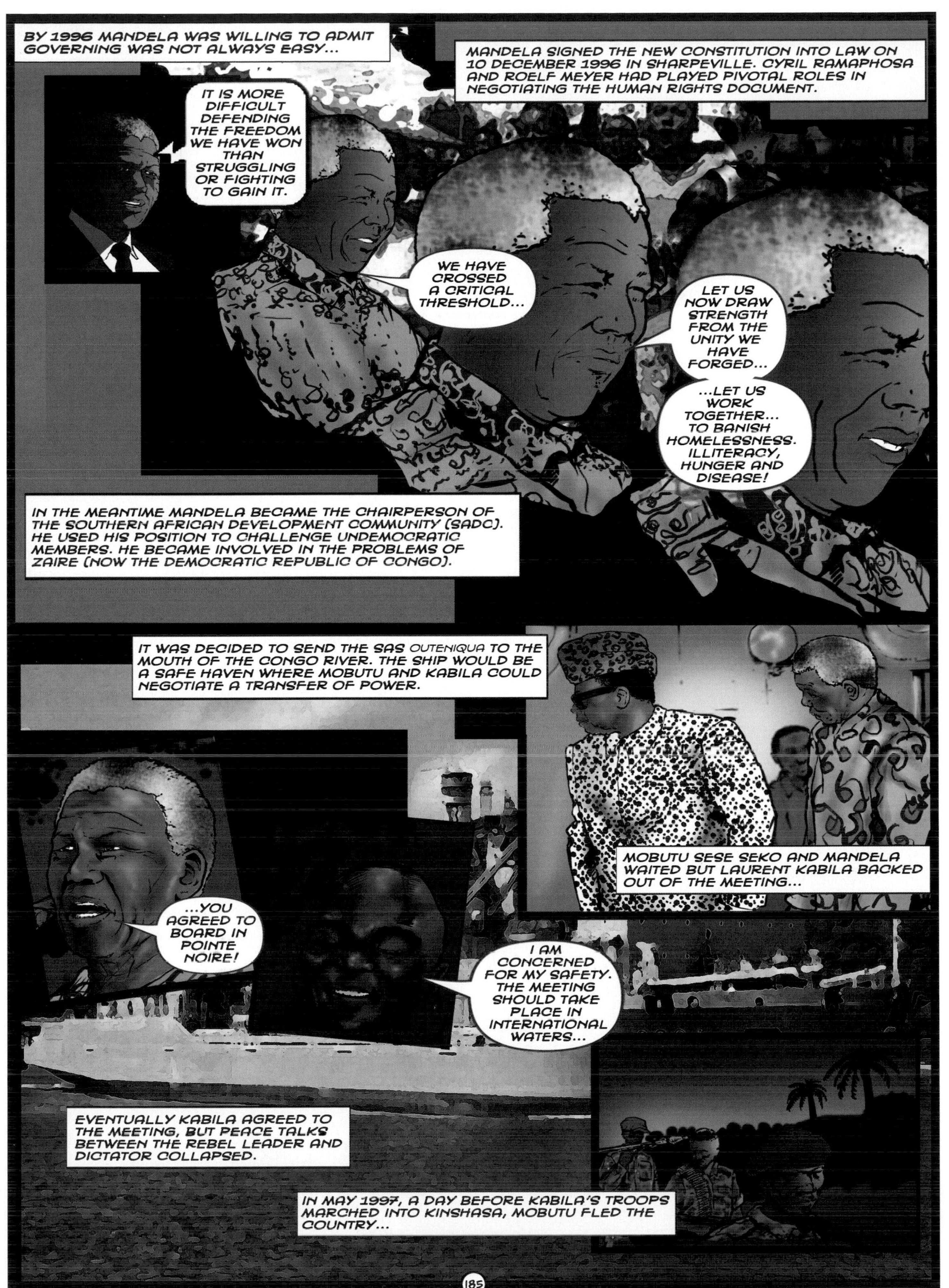
BY 1996 MANDELA WAS WILLING TO ADMIT GOVERNING WAS NOT ALWAYS EASY...
IT IS MORE DIFFICULT DEFENDING THE FREEDOM WE HAVE WON THAN STRUGGLING OR FIGHTING TO GAIN IT.
MANDELA SIGNED THE NEW CONSTITUTION INTO LAW ON 10 DECEMBER 1996 IN SHARPEVILLE. CYRIL RAMAPHOSA AND ROELF MEYER HAD PLAYED PIVOTAL ROLES IN NEGOTIATING THE HUMAN RIGHTS DOCUMENT.
WE HAVE CROSSED A CRITICAL THRESHOLD...
LET US NOW DRAW STRENGTH FROM THE UNITY WE HAVE FORGED...
...LET US WORK TOGETHER... TO BANISH HOMELESSNESS. ILLITERACY, HUNGER AND DISEASE!
IN THE MEANTIME MANDELA BECAME THE CHAIRPERSON OF THE SOUTHERN AFRICAN DEVELOPMENT COMMUNITY (SADC). HE USED HIS POSITION TO CHALLENGE UNDEMOCRATIC MEMBERS. HE BECAME INVOLVED IN THE PROBLEMS OF ZAIRE (NOW THE DEMOCRATIC REPUBLIC OF CONGO).
IT WAS DECIDED TO SEND THE SAS OUTENIQUA TO THE MOUTH OF THE CONGO RIVER. THE SHIP WOULD BE A SAFE HAVEN WHERE MOBUTU AND KABILA COULD NEGOTIATE A TRANSFER OF POWER.
MOBUTU SESE SEKO AND MANDELA WAITED BUT LAURENT KABILA BACKED OUT OF THE MEETING...
...YOU AGREED TO BOARD IN POINTE NOIRE!
I AM CONCERNED FOR MY SAFETY. THE MEETING SHOULD TAKE PLACE IN INTERNATIONAL WATERS...
EVENTUALLY KABILA AGREED TO THE MEETING, BUT PEACE TALKS BETWEEN THE REBEL LEADER AND DICTATOR COLLAPSED.
IN MAY 1997, A DAY BEFORE KABILA'S TROOPS MARCHED INTO KINSHASA, MOBUTU FLED THE COUNTRY...

APARTHEID ERA ATROCITIES WERE STILL HAUNTING THE NATION...
THE NP WANTED A GENERAL AMNESTY FOR ALL PERPETRATORS. MANDELA REFUSED.
THE TRUTH AND RECONCILIATION COMMISSION (TRC) WAS CREATED IN 1995 TO DEAL WITH THE APARTHEID PAST AND PROMOTE RECONCILIATION. PERPETRATORS OF HUMAN RIGHTS VIOLATIONS COULD GET AMNESTY.
ARCHBISHOP DESMOND TUTU WAS CHAIR AND ALEX BORAINE HIS DEPUTY.
THE TRC WAS DEDICATED IN ST GEORGE'S CATHEDRAL IN CAPE TOWN. NOT EVERYONE WAS PLEASED. SOME WANTED VENGEANCE AND SOME WERE FEARFUL.
All South Africans face the challenge of coming to terms with the past in ways which will enable us to face the future as a united nation at peace with itself. To you has been entrusted the particular task of dealing with gross violations of human rights in a manner that ensures that the painful truth is laid bare and that justice is done to the victims within the capacity of our society and within the framework of the constitution and the law. By doing so and by means of amnesty, your goal is to ensure lasting reconciliation.
OVER THE NEXT EIGHT YEARS A RANGE OF HORRORS WERE DESCRIBED. ORDINARY APARTHEID SECURITY PERSONNEL CLAIMED THEY WERE JUST FOLLOWING ORDERS.
I AM TRULY SORRY FOR WHAT I HAVE DONE...
I CAN NEVER HAVE PEACE.
NOT EVERYONE WAS SATISFIED WITH THE OUTCOME. SOME VICTIMS WHO TESTIFIED FELT LET DOWN. THEY DID NOT GET THE REPARATIONS THEY HAD HOPED FOR...
...STRATEGIES NEVER INCLUDED THE AUTHORISATION OF ASSASSINATION, MURDER, TORTURE, RAPE, ASSAULT OR THE LIKE...
FW DE KLERK LATER SUCCESSFULLY APPEALED TO COURT TO SUPPRESS THE TRC'S FINDINGS ON HIM.
PW BOTHA REFUSED TO PARTICIPATE AND DENOUNCED THE TRC AS A CIRCUS. MANDELA EVEN ASKED BOTHA'S CHILDREN TO TRY AND MAKE HIM CHANGE HIS MIND. THE TRC FOUND THAT HE HAD CONTRIBUTED TO A CLIMATE IN WHICH GROSS VIOLATIONS OF HUMAN RIGHTS OCCURRED.
BY THE TIME THE WORK OF THE TRC WAS COMPLETE, IT HAD BECOME CLEAR THAT THE WOUNDS OF THE PAST WOULD TAKE TIME TO HEAL.

MANDELA HAD BEEN BECOMING INCREASINGLY LONELY, BUT...
IS IT TRUE? ARE YOU DATING?
WELL, THERE IS A SPECIAL PERSON...
...BUT, I AM NOT READY TO TALK ABOUT IT.
YEARS AFTER HIS RELEASE MANDELA FELL FOR GRACA MACHEL, THE FORMER FIRST LADY OF MOZAMBIQUE, BUT HE KEPT IT A SECRET...
HER HUSBAND HAD DIED IN A SUSPICIOUS PLANE CRASH IN 1986. AT THE TIME MANDELA WROTE HER A LETTER OF CONDOLENCE FROM PRISON.
I WILL ALWAYS BELONG TO MOZAMBIQUE.
EVENTUALLY MANDELA WON HER OVER AND GRACA STARTED TO SPEND TWO WEEKS A MONTH IN JOHANNESBURG. THEY WERE IN LOVE, AND WERE SNAPPED WALKING IN THE STREETS OF HOUGHTON...
GRACA BECAME HIS OFFICIAL CONSORT AND JOINED HIM ON A TRIP TO SOUTH-EAST ASIA.
ARE YOU GOING TO GET MARRIED SOON?
HE FOBBED OFF JOURNALISTS WITH A STANDARD REPLY:
MY CULTURAL BACKGROUND DOES NOT PERMIT ME TO ANSWER QUESTIONS FROM SOMEONE YOUNGER THAN MY GRANDCHILDREN.
HIS OLD FRIEND, DESMOND TUTU, MADE IT CLEAR THEY SHOULD MARRY. THEY TIED THE KNOT ON MANDELA'S 80TH BIRTHDAY UNDER A CLOAK OF SECRECY.
THE CEREMONY TOOK PLACE AT HIS HOME AND ONLY A FEW FRIENDS AND FAMILY MEMBERS WERE THERE....

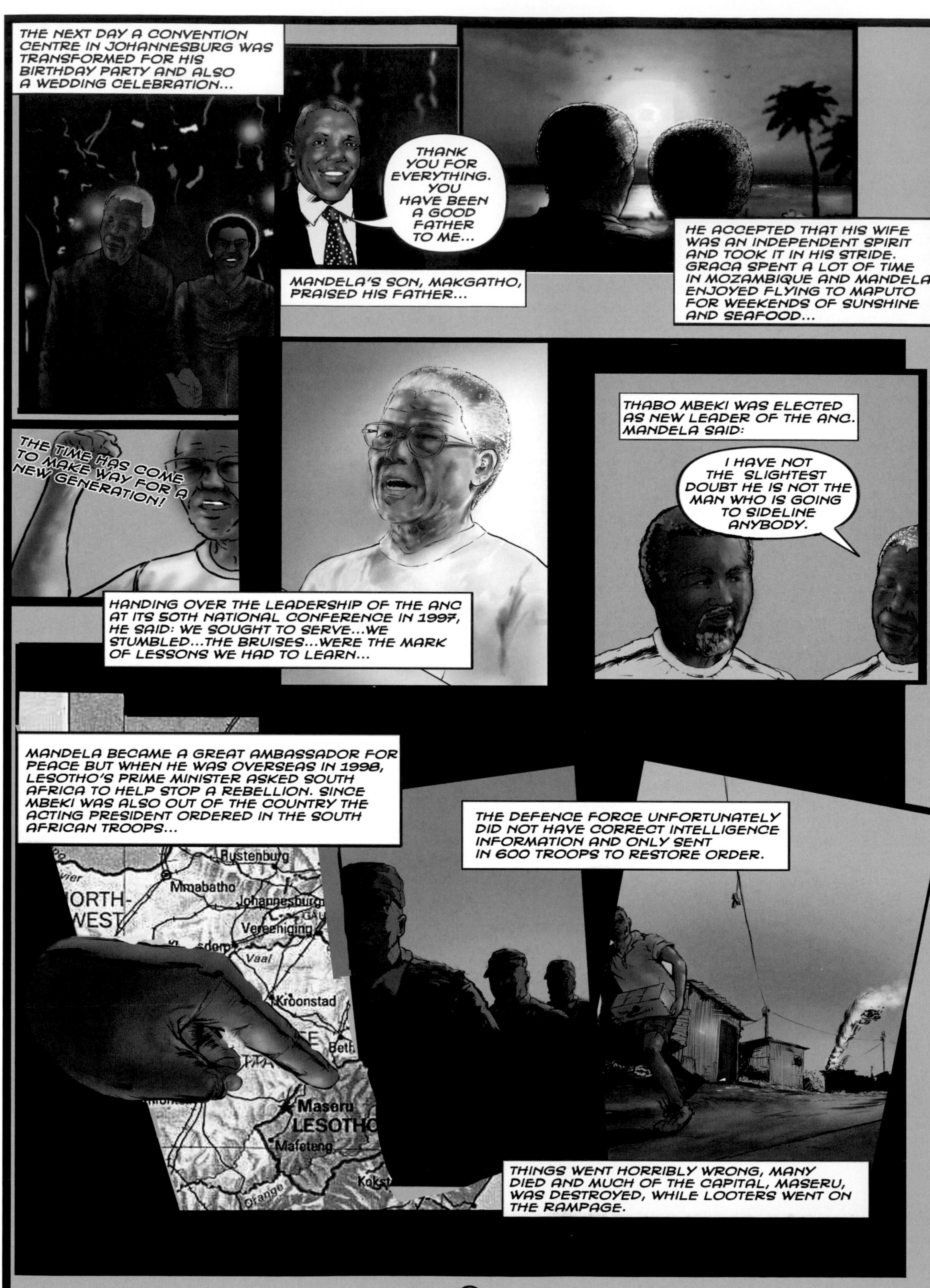
THE NEXT DAY A CONVENTION CENTRE IN JOHANNESBURG WAS TRANSFORMED FOR HIS BIRTHDAY PARTY AND ALSO A WEDDING CELEBRATION...
THANK YOU FOR EVERYTHING. YOU HAVE BEEN A GOOD FATHER TO ME...
MANDELA'S SON, MAKGATHO, PRAISED HIS FATHER...
HE ACCEPTED THAT HIS WIFE WAS AN INDEPENDENT SPIRIT AND TOOK IT IN HIS STRIDE. GRACA SPENT A LOT OF TIME IN MOZAMBIQUE AND MANDELA ENJOYED FLYING TO MAPUTO FOR WEEKENDS OF SUNSHINE AND SEAFOOD...
THE TIME HAS COME TO MAKE WAY FOR A NEW GENERATION!
HANDING OVER THE LEADERSHIP OF THE ANC AT ITS 50TH NATIONAL CONFERENCE IN 1997, HE SAID: WE SOUGHT TO SERVE...WE STUMBLED...THE BRUISES...WERE THE MARK OF LESSONS WE HAD TO LEARN...
THABO MBEKI WAS ELECTED AS NEW LEADER OF THE ANC. MANDELA SAID:
I HAVE NOT THE SLIGHTEST DOUBT HE IS NOT THE MAN WHO IS GOING TO SIDELINE ANYBODY.
MANDELA BECAME A GREAT AMBASSADOR FOR PEACE BUT WHEN HE WAS OVERSEAS IN 1998, LESOTHO'S PRIME MINISTER ASKED SOUTH AFRICA TO HELP STOP A REBELLION. SINCE MBEKI WAS ALSO OUT OF THE COUNTRY THE ACTING PRESIDENT ORDERED IN THE SOUTH AFRICAN TROOPS...
Rustenburg
Mmabatho
NORTH-WEST
Johannesburg
Vereeniging
Vaal
Kroonstad
Beth
Maseru
LESOTHO
Mafeteng
Orange
THE DEFENCE FORCE UNFORTUNATELY DID NOT HAVE CORRECT INTELLIGENCE INFORMATION AND ONLY SENT IN 600 TROOPS TO RESTORE ORDER.
THINGS WENT HORRIBLY WRONG, MANY DIED AND MUCH OF THE CAPITAL, MASERU, WAS DESTROYED, WHILE LOOTERS WENT ON THE RAMPAGE.

SOME OF MANDELA'S FRIENDS WERE CONTROVERSIAL, INCLUDING US PRESIDENT BILL CLINTON WHO WAS AT THE CENTRE OF A SCANDAL IN HIS OWN COUNTRY OVER HIS RELATIONSHIP WITH A WHITE HOUSE INTERN...
AT A JOINT PRESS CONFERENCE WHEN CLINTON WAS ON A STATE VISIT TO SOUTH AFRICA, MANDELA DEFENDED HIS SUPPORT OF LIBYA, CUBA AND THE PALESTINE LIBERATION ORGANISATION.
WE SHOULD NOT ABANDON THOSE WHO HELPED US IN OUR DARKEST HOUR...
THOSE AMERICANS WHO BERATE ME FOR BEING LOYAL TO OUR FRIENDS, LITERALLY THEY CAN GO AND THROW THEMSELVES INTO A POOL...
THE TWO MEN ALSO VISITED MANDELA'S CELL ON ROBBEN ISLAND...
HOW DID YOU MANAGE TO FORGIVE YOUR OPPRESSORS?
THEY TOOK THE BEST YEARS OF MY LIFE...
THEY COULD TAKE EVERYTHING... EXCEPT MY MIND AND HEART...
BUT I WOULD NOT LET THEM... NEITHER SHOULD YOU.
YEARS LATER CLINTON RECALLED HOW MUCH MANDELA'S SUPPORT HELPED HIM THROUGH 'DIFFICULT TIMES'...

MANDELA DID NOT WANT TO STAY ON FOR LONGER THAN ONE TERM AS PRESIDENT. ON 10 FEBRUARY 1999 HE DELIVERED HIS LAST STATE OF THE NATION ADDRESS.
FIVE YEARS AGO, THE SENSE OF COMMON BELONGING, OUR SHARED DESTINY, FOCUSED THE MIND...
WE WERE ABLE TO FIND SOLUTIONS TO PROBLEMS THAT SEEMED DEFIANT OF RESOLUTION...
THIS IS SOUTH AFRICA'S ACHIEVEMENT... OF NATION-BUILDING AND RECONCILIATION.
HE TOOK TIME TO GREET STAFF WHO HAD BEEN WITH HIM FOR FIVE YEARS...
YOUR EXAMPLE HAS CHANGED MY LIFE. THANK YOU TATA.
AT THE END OF MANDELA'S TENURE AS PRESIDENT, THE NELSON MANDELA FOUNDATION WAS ESTABLISHED TO PROMOTE HIS LEGACY.
MANDELA CAMPAIGNED FOR PEACE, CHILDREN'S RIGHTS AND THE FIGHT AGAINST HIV/AIDS.
IN 2002 THE MANDELA RHODES FOUNDATION WAS ANNOUNCED.
THE AIM OF THE FOUNDATION IS TO BUILD EXCEPTIONAL LEADERSHIP CAPACITY IN AFRICA.
MANDELA LAUNCHED THE 46664 CAMPAIGN TO RAISE AWARENESS ABOUT AIDS. THE NAME COMES FROM HIS PRISON NUMBER 466/64 INDICATING HE WAS THE 466TH PRISONER IN 1964.
46664
AIDS TODAY IN AFRICA IS CLAIMING MORE LIVES THAN THE SUM TOTAL OF ALL WARS, FAMINES, FLOODS, AND DISEASES SUCH AS MALARIA...
WE MUST ACT NOW FOR THE SAKE OF THE WORLD...AIDS IS NO LONGER A DISEASE, IT IS A HUMAN RIGHTS ISSUE!
MORE THAN TWO BILLION PEOPLE IN 166 COUNTRIES SAW THE FIRST CONCERT. 46664 CONCERTS WERE STAGED EVERY YEAR AND RAISED MONEY FOR HIV/AIDS PROJECTS IN SOUTH AFRICA AND OTHER AFRICAN COUNTRIES.

IN 2003 MANDELA EXPERIENCED THE DEVASTATING LOSS OF HIS GREAT FRIEND, WALTER SISULU...
FROM THE MOMENT WE FIRST MET HE HAS BEEN MY FRIEND, MY BROTHER, MY KEEPER, MY COMRADE.
...AND TWO YEARS LATER HE SUFFERED THE TRAGIC DEATH OF HIS 54-YEAR-OLD SON MAKGATHO.
MY SON DIED OF AIDS. WE WILL HAVE TO TELL THE WORLD, TO TAKE AWAY THE STIGMA ATTACHED TO THIS DISEASE.
MANDELA'S STAFF HAD TO GUARD AGAINST PEOPLE WHO WANTED TO EXPLOIT HIS NAME FOR THEIR PERSONAL OR COMMERCIAL GAIN.
I MET MANDELA!
DISGRACED POLITICIAN BOASTS OF MANDELA'S SUPPORT
REQUESTS FLOODED IN FROM PEOPLE ASKING HIM TO ENDORSE THEIR PROJECTS.
SOME PEOPLE WOULD USE THEIR MEETINGS WITH MANDELA TO INCREASE THEIR STANDING IN THEIR OWN COUNTRIES OR COMMUNITIES.
MANDELA CONTINUED TO ENJOY RAISING AWARENESS THROUGHOUT THE WORLD ABOUT ISSUES THAT WERE CLOSE TO HIS HEART.

BY 2004 MANDELA FOUND THAT HE WAS STILL HIGHLY IN DEMAND, BUT HE WANTED TO SLOW DOWN. HE FAMOUSLY ANNOUNCED HIS RETIREMENT FROM RETIREMENT...

I AM CONFIDENT THAT NO ONE HERE WILL ACCUSE ME OF SELFISHNESS IF I ASK TO SPEND MORE TIME...WITH FAMILY, FRIENDS AND MYSELF...

IN HIS POST-PRESIDENTIAL YEARS MANDELA RELIED HEAVILY ON HIS EXECUTIVE PERSONAL ASSISTANT AND SPOKESPERSON, ZELDA LA GRANGE. SHE WAS NEVER FAR FROM HIS SIDE.

MY APPEAL THEREFORE IS: DON'T CALL ME, I WILL CALL YOU!

Nelson Mandela
CHILDREN'S FUND
CHANGING THE WAY SOCIETY TREATS ITS CHILDREN AND YOUTH

THE NELSON MANDELA CHILDREN'S FUND FOCUSES ON IMPROVING THE WAY IN WHICH SOCIETY TREATS ITS CHILDREN AND THE YOUTH.

THE MANDELA RHODES FOUNDATION AIMS TO GIVE EXPRESSION TO THE LEGACIES OF LEADERSHIP, EDUCATION, RECONCILIATION AND ENTREPRENEURSHIP.

THE MANDELA RHODES FOUNDATION

HE HANDED OVER THE BULK OF HIS 'LEGACY WORK' TO HIS THREE INDEPENDENT BUT INTERLINKED CHARITABLE ORGANISATIONS. HE WANTED THE FOCUS TO BE ON THEM AND NOT HIM AS AN INDIVIDUAL.

FROM 2004 THE NELSON MANDELA FOUNDATION WAS RESTRUCTURED AROUND ITS CENTRE OF MEMORY AND DIALOGUE, DEDICATED TO COMMEMORATING THE LIFE AND TIMES OF NELSON MANDELA AND CONVENING DIALOGUE AROUND CRITICAL SOCIAL ISSUES.

MANDELA STARTED SPENDING MORE TIME AT HIS HOME IN QUNU...
IN 2007 HE ATTENDED THE INSTALLATION OF HIS GRANDSON, MANDLA, AS CHIEF OF THE MVEZO TRADITIONAL COUNCIL.
HE STILL GAVE MANY HOURS OF HIS TIME TO DOCUMENTING HIS MEMORIES.
NELSON MANDELA'S LEGACY IS IN ALL OUR HANDS...

INDEX

The Nelson Mandela Foundation, through its Nelson Mandela Centre of Memory and Dialogue, contributes to the making of a just society by promoting the vision and work of its Founder and convening dialogue around critical social issues. The Centre was inaugurated by Nelson Mandela on 21 September 2004.

Umlando Wezithombe produces accessible educational comic books. The visual medium is used to cross cultural boundaries and deliver material that addresses a range of literacy levels. Umlando specialises in using the visual medium to address awareness on subjects that include history, HIV/AIDS, healthy living, pandemics, and life skills.

Published by
JONATHAN BALL PUBLISHERS
Johannesburg & Cape Town

ACKNOWLEDGEMENTS

This book began as a series of eight comics distributed free by the Nelson Mandela Foundation in partnership with comic publisher Umlando Wezithombe between 2005 and 2007. The series was a project of the Foundation's Centre of Memory and Dialogue, and was aimed at reaching young South Africans with the story of the life and times of Nelson Mandela, in accessible form. The series drew on a wide range of published work, but also made use of previously unused archival material as well as formal and informal interviews with individuals who appear as characters in the story. We are particularly grateful to Ahmed Kathrada, who acted as special advisor to the series and also assisted with the preparation of this book. His contribution has been immeasurable. The series was made possible financially by a number of generous donors and sponsors – Anglo American, BHP Billiton, the Ford Foundation, GTZ, Independent Newspapers, the Nelson Mandela Legacy Trust (UK), E Oppenheimer and Son, Sasol, and Staedtler.

The Centre of Memory and Dialogue team has relied heavily on the research expertise of Sahm Venter for both the series and this book. Others who have contributed are Anthea Josias, Shadrack Katuu, Boniswa Qabaka and Razia Saleh. Luli Callinicos acted as a consultant for the first five comics in the series.

The Umlando Wezithombe team has been marshalled by Nic Buchanan, and has comprised:
Scriptwriting and research: Santa Buchanan and Andrew Smith
Storyboarding: Santa Buchanan and Pitshou Mampa
Illustrating: Pitshou Mampa, Pascal 'Freehand' Nzoni and Sivuyile Matwa
Inking and colouring: Richie Orphan, Pascal Nzoni, Sivuyile Matwa, Jose 'King' Jungo, Pitshou Mampa and Sean Abbood

The Foundation and Umlando have been supported by an exceptional Jonathan Ball Publishers' team: Francine Blum, Jeremy Boraine and Frances Perryer

Key reference works utilised by our researchers are as follows:
The World that Made Mandela, Beyond the Engeli Mountains, and *Gold and Workers* by Luli Callinicos, *Drum Magazine, Winnie Mandela - A Life* by Anne Marie du Preez Bezdrob, *Walter Sisulu: I Will Go Singing* by George Houser and Herbert Shore, *The Rivonia Story* by Joel Joffe, *Memoirs* by Ahmed Kathrada, *Mandela* by Tom Lodge, *Long Walk to Freedom* by Nelson Mandela, *Higher than Hope* by Fatima Meer, *A Fortunate Life* by Ismail Meer, *Mandela* by Anthony Sampson, *In Our Lifetime* by Elinor Sisulu, *A Step Behind Mandela* by Rory Steyn, and *Portrait of a People* by Eli Weinberg.

Archival holdings of the following institutions were consulted:
Baileys Historical Archives, Brenthurst Library, Historical Papers (University of the Witwatersrand), the National Archives, the Nelson Mandela Centre of Memory and Dialogue, Robben Island Museum and the University of Fort Hare Library.

Inspiration for this project, of course, came primarily from Nelson Mandela himself. This is his story constellated by numerous other stories. In a profound way the constellation is the story of the country, South Africa, for which Tata Nelson Mandela sacrificed so much. More than this, Tata gave his blessing to the project, launched it with a rousing speech, and shared his memories. The book is a gift to him in his ninetieth year.

Verne Harris
Project Manager
Nelson Mandela Foundation

Published in 2008 by
JONATHAN BALL PUBLISHERS (PTY) LTD
P O Box 33977
Jeppestown
2043

ISBN 978 1 86842 302 6

Design and reproduction by Umlando Wezithombe
Printed and bound by Imago Publishing Ltd, UK